AWS Lambda in Action

AWS Lambda
in Action

EVENT-DRIVEN SERVERLESS APPLICATIONS

DANILO POCCIA

MANNING
SHELTER ISLAND

Manning Publications Co. 20 Baldwin Road PO Box 761 Shelter Island, NY 11964	Development editor: Toni Arritola Technical development editor: Brent Stains Project editors: Kevin Sullivan and Janet Vail Copyeditor: Katie Petito Proofreader: Melody Dolab Technical proofreader: Luis Carlos Sanchez Gonzalez Typesetter: Dennis Dalinnik Cover designer: Marija Tudor

ISBN: 9781617293719
Printed in the United States of America
1 2 3 4 5 6 7 8 9 10 – EBM – 21 20 19 18 17 16

brief contents

contents

foreword

At some point in the next few years we're going to see the first billion-dollar startup with a single employee, the founder, and that engineer will be using serverless technology. Serverless takes the permissionless world of IT today to its logical conclusion—developers no longer need to wait for anyone to sign off on a new project. Developers can get started in minutes building apps without worrying about servers, infrastructure, data stores, or configuration tools. From a business perspective, serverless is revolutionary because the developer doesn't need to pay until the point of use. *Unless a customer is using a service, the developer doesn't need to pay for it.* This is the on-demand economy in action.

AWS Lambda in Action is a great introduction to serverless technology in general and AWS Lambda in particular.

I first met the author, Danilo Poccia, an Evangelist at Amazon Web Services, at a briefing for industry analysts at an Amazon event in London. I was immediately pulled in by his down-to-earth approach and his infectious enthusiasm for all things serverless. As a developer Evangelist, Danilo has a wealth of experience explaining serverless technology from the ground up, and it really shows in this book.

AWS Lambda in Action is clear and concise, and the introductions and explanations are extremely well structured. This introduction will suit beginners, as well as those with a grounding in the serverless concepts, such as event-driven programming, with offload for simple tasks and functions. AWS Lambda abstracts away all the configuration and cruft associated with configuring a server environment.

The code samples for *AWS Lambda in Action*, hosted on GitHub in JavaScript and Python, are as well structured as the writing. Poccia takes us through the thought process of building a serverless app from scratch, from authentication services to deployment. He takes us through an explanation of why serverless should be written as single functions for deployment to AWS Lambda. Serverless is event-driven, though, so Poccia also explains how to integrate with third-party services that kick off functions as a service.

Serverless is going to have a huge impact on how we use Amazon Web Services, already the de facto industry standard for cloud, and *AWS Lambda in Action* is an essential starter guide to the next few years of software development.

JAMES GOVERNOR, CO-FOUNDER OF REDMONK

dedication

To my wife Paola, who helped me get through all the effort—and the weekends—behind this book. To my parents, who supported my interest in computing from an early age. To my brother, who gave me guidance for the time we could spend together.

preface

No server is easier to manage than no server.

Werner Vogel, Amazon CTO

In 1996, I started working on client-server architectures, experiencing both the advantages and the complexity of distributed systems. Beginning in the early 2000s, I collaborated on multiple large-scale projects, mainly for telecommunications and media customers. During those years, I often experienced the limits of computing, storage, or networking as a bottleneck that hampered the innovation that companies were trying to put in place.

Then, in the pivotal year of 2006, the idea of using computing resources with a "utility" model—in the same way as we use energy, gas, or water—started to be become a reality. That was the year AWS launched its first services for storage (Amazon S3) and computing (Amazon EC2). I was both intrigued and fascinated.

Since 2012, my focus has been on helping customers implement applications on or migrate applications to the cloud. To learn more about some of the new services and platforms I was experimenting with, I decided to write a shared file system using Amazon S3 as back-end storage. I shared my implementation on GitHub (written in Python) and shortly found an impressive community of users and contributors supporting it.

When AWS Lambda was launched in 2014, I immediately realized that I was positioned at the beginning of something that could change the way we develop and deploy applications. A few months later, during a very rainy weekend, I realized that I could write a complete application without the use of any actual server: I just needed static content (HTML, CSS, and JavaScript files running in a web browser) and the use of Lambda functions to execute my logic in the back end. I found that I could use events to bind a business process. I wrote a "simple" authentication service (an evolution of which you will build in chapters 8 through 10) and shared the result, again, on GitHub (using JavaScript this time). The response was greater than I expected; clearly, I was hitting a nerve in the development community.

The idea of sharing that experience is what triggered this book. I hope the result will help you embrace the new paradigm of serverless computing, develop incredible new applications, and experiment with technology and data. As you do, please share your story with me; there is no greater pleasure for me than helping someone build their own ideas.

acknowledgments

I would like to thank so many people who over the years worked with me, exchanged ideas with me, and shared interesting concepts that made me think and learn from the process. I hate lists of names, so I will not list all of them here. I'm sure it will be easy for those who've helped me to recognize themselves and know they get a big "thank you." A few names truly deserve to be mentioned here: I'm grateful to Toni Arritola, who made my sometimes chaotic thoughts clear in a language most would understand, keeping the right pace through all the chapters; Brent Stains, for his invaluable tips and technical views; and Mike Stephens, who had the original idea that gave birth to this book.

I also need to mention the reviewers who gave generously of their time and whose comments greatly improved this book, including Alan Moffet, Ben Leibert, Cam Crews, Christopher Haupt, Dan Kacenjar, Henning Kristensen, Joan Fuster, Justin Calleja, Michael Frey, Steve Rogers, and Tom Jensen, and also Luis Carlos Sanchez Gonzalez, the technical proofreader.

about this book

This book is split into four parts. Part 1, First steps (chapters 1–3), covers the foundational technology, such as AWS Lambda and Web API with Amazon API Gateway. Part 2, Building event-driven applications (chapters 4–12), is the core of the book and helps you use more functions together, tied by events, to build applications. Part 3, From development to production (chapters 13–15), helps you optimize your DevOps workflow. And Part 4, Using external services (chapters 16–17), describes ways you can integrate Lambda functions with services outside of the AWS platform, giving you some hints about what is possible with AWS Lambda, from improving communication to automating code management.

This book was written to be read in order, from the first chapter to the last.

If you are already knowledgeable about the basics of AWS Lambda, you can skim through Part I and move forward to Part II to build a more complex event-driven application.

Parts III and IV can also be used as a reference that you can return to later for new ideas or to compare what you're doing with what I'm suggesting.

Cloud computing is evolving so fast; for this reason, I focused on fundamental concepts, such as distributed systems and event-driven design. These are, in my opinion, important for anybody developing IT systems in a distributed world.

In this book, my ideal reader is a developer who has no experience with using the cloud and wants to jump ahead into the new frontiers of serverless computing and event-driven applications. If you're already experienced with other AWS services, such as Amazon EC2 and Amazon VPC, this book will give you a new perspective and help you to build applications using services, not servers.

Code conventions

This book provides copious examples that show how you can make use of each of the topics covered. Source code in listings or in text appears in a `fixed-width font like this` to separate it from ordinary text. In addition, class and method names, object properties, and other code-related terms and content in text are presented using `fixed-width font`.

Getting the source code

The source code used in the book is available on the Manning website at www.manning .com/aws-lambda-in-action and on GitHub at https://github.com/danilop/AWS_ Lambda_in_Action.

Author Online

Purchase of *AWS Lambda in Action* includes free access to a private web forum run by Manning Publications where you can make comments about the book, ask technical questions, and receive help from the author and from other users. To access the forum and subscribe to it, point your web browser to www.manning.com/aws-lambda-in-action. This page provides information on how to get on the forum once you are registered, what kind of help is available, and the rules of conduct on the forum. It also provides links to the source code for the examples in the book, errata, and other downloads.

Manning's commitment to our readers is to provide a venue where a meaningful dialog between individual readers and between readers and the authors can take place. It is not a commitment to any specific amount of participation on the part of the authors, whose contribution to the AO remains voluntary (and unpaid). We suggest you try asking the author challenging questions lest his interest stray!

The Author Online forum and the archives of previous discussions will be accessible from the publisher's website as long as the book is in print.

About the author

Danilo Poccia works with startups and companies of all sizes to support innovation. In his role as Technical Evangelist at Amazon Web Services, he uses 20 years of experience to help people bring their ideas to life, focusing on event-driven programming and serverless architectures, and on the technical and business impact of mobile platforms and data analytics.

Danilo's interests include IT, IoT, simulation/modeling, artificial intelligence, machine learning, and photography.

about the cover illustration

The figure on the cover of *AWS Lambda in Action* is captioned "Femme Kamtschadale" (a woman of Kamchatka). The illustration is taken from a collection of dress costumes from various countries by Jacques Grasset de Saint-Sauveur (1757–1810), titled *Costumes de Différents Pays,* published in France in 1797. Each illustration is finely drawn and colored by hand.

The rich variety of Grasset de Saint-Sauveur's collection reminds us vividly of how culturally apart the world's towns and regions were just 200 years ago. Isolated from each other, people spoke different dialects and languages. In the streets or in the countryside, it was easy to identify where they lived and what their trade or station in life was just by their dress.

The way we dress has changed since then, and the diversity by region, so rich at the time, has faded away. It's now hard to tell apart the inhabitants of different continents, let alone different towns, regions, or countries. Perhaps we have traded cultural diversity for a more varied personal life—certainly for a more varied and fast-paced technological life.

At a time when it's hard to tell one computer book from another, Manning celebrates the inventiveness and initiative of the computer business with book covers based on the rich diversity of regional life of two centuries ago, brought back to life by Grasset de Saint-Sauveur's pictures.

Part 1

First steps

Why would you run functions in the cloud? How do you build an event-driven back end for your applications? Is a single back end enough for all the clients you want to support, such as those using web and mobile? And how can you call Lambda functions from a client?

In this first part of the book, you'll learn how to use the foundation services—AWS Lambda and the Amazon API Gateway—that you'll use later to build more complex applications. You'll also see how multiple functions can be used together to build a single application, such as a back end for a web or mobile app. As you'll see, this book is a mix of practice and theory.

Running functions in the cloud

This chapter covers

- Understanding why functions can be the primitives of your application
- Getting an overview of AWS Lambda
- Using functions for the back end of your application
- Building event-driven applications with functions
- Calling functions from a client

In recent years, cloud computing has changed the way we think about and implement IT services, allowing companies of every size to build powerful and scalable applications that could disrupt the industries in which they operated. Think of how Dropbox changed the way we use digital storage and share files with each other, or how Spotify changed the way we buy and listen to music.

Those two companies started small, and needed the capacity to focus their time and resources on bringing their ideas to life quickly. In fact, one of the most important advantages of cloud computing is that it frees developers from spending their time on tasks that don't add real value to their work, such as managing and scaling the infrastructure, patching the operating system (OS), or maintaining the software stack used to run their code. Cloud computing lets them concentrate on the unique and important features they want to build.

You can use cloud computing to provide the *infrastructure* for your application, in the form of virtual servers, storage, network, load balancers, and so on. The infrastructure can be scaled automatically using specific configurations. But with this approach you still need to prepare a whole environment to execute the code you write. You install and prepare an operating system or a virtual environment; you choose and configure a programming framework; and finally, when the overall stack is ready, you can plug in our code. Even if you use a container-based approach in building the environment, with tools such as Docker, you're still in change of managing versioning and updates of the containers you use.

Sometimes you need infrastructure-level access because you want to view or manage low-level resources. But you can also use cloud computing services that abstract from the underlying infrastructure implementation, acting like a *platform* on top of which you deploy your own customizations. For example, you can have services that provide you with a database, and you only need to plug in your data (together with a data model) without having to manage the installation and availability of the database itself. Another example is services where you provide the code of your application, and a standard infrastructure to support the execution of your application is automatically implemented.

If that's true for a development environment, as soon as you get closer to production things become more complex and you may have to take care of the scalability and availability of the solution. And you must never forget to think about security—considering who can do what, and on which resources—during the course of the design and implementation of an application.

With the introduction of AWS Lambda, the abstraction layer is set higher, allowing developers to upload their code grouped in *functions*, and letting those functions be executed by the platform. In this way you don't have to manage the programming framework, the OS, or the availability and scalability. Each function has its own configuration that will help you use standard security features provided by Amazon Web Services (AWS) to define what a function can do and on which resources.

Those functions can be invoked directly or can *subscribe* to events generated by other *resources*. When you subscribe a function to a resource such as a file repository or a database, the function is automatically executed when something happens in that resource, depending on which kinds of events you've subscribed to. For example, when a file has been uploaded or a database item has been modified, an AWS Lambda function can react to those changes and do something with the new file or the updated data. If a picture has been uploaded, a function can create thumbnails to show the pictures on the screens with different resolutions. If a new record is written in an operational database, a function can keep the data warehouse in sync. In this way you can design applications that are driven by events.

Book graphical conventions

This book uses the following graphical conventions to help present information more clearly.

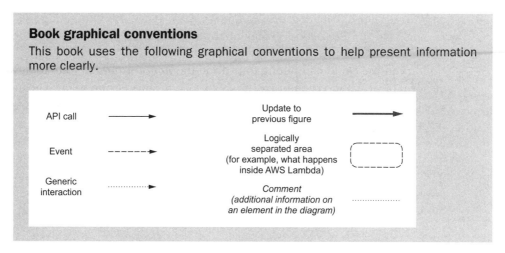

Using multiple functions together, some of them called directly from a user device, such as a smartphone, and other functions subscribed to multiple repositories, such as a file share and a database, you can build a complete event-driven application. You can see a sample flow of a media-sharing application built in this way in figure 1.1. Users use a mobile app to upload pictures and share them with their friends.

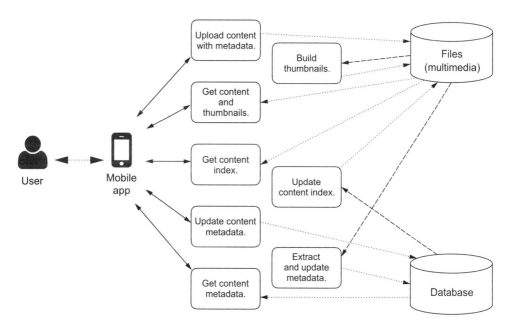

Figure 1.1   An event-driven, media-sharing application built using multiple AWS Lambda functions, some invoked directly by the mobile app. Other functions are subscribed to storage repositories such as a file share or a database.

> **NOTE**   Don't worry if you don't completely understand the flow of the application in figure 1.1. Reading this book, you'll first learn the architectural principles used in the design of event-driven applications, and then you'll implement this media-sharing application using AWS Lambda together with an authentication service to recognize users.

When using third-party software or a service not natively integrated with AWS Lambda, it's still easy to use that component in an event-driven architecture, adding the capacity to generate those events by using one of the AWS software development kits (SDKs), which are available for multiple platforms.

The event-driven approach not only simplifies the development of production environments, but also makes it easier to design and scale the *logic* of the application. For example, let's take a function that's subscribed to the upload of a file in a repository. Every time this function is invoked, it extracts information from the content of the file and writes this in a database table. You can think of this function as a logical connection between the file repository and the database table: every time any component of the application—including the client—uploads a file, the subscribed events are triggered and, in this case, the database is updated.

As you add more features, the logic of any application becomes more and more complex to manage. But in this case you created a *relationship* between the file repository and the database, and this connection works independently from the process that uploads the file. You'll see more advantages of this approach in this book, along with more practical examples.

If you're building a new application for either a small startup or a large enterprise, the simplifications introduced by using functions as the building blocks of your application will allow you to be more efficient in where to spend your time and faster in introducing new features to your users.

1.1   *Introducing AWS Lambda*

AWS Lambda is different from a traditional approach based on physical or virtual servers. You only need to give your logic, grouped in functions, and the service itself takes care of executing the functions, if and when required, by managing the software stack used by the runtime you chose, the availability of the platform, and the scalability of the infrastructure to sustain the throughput of the invocations.

Functions are executed in *containers*. Containers are a server virtualization method where the kernel of the OS implements multiple isolated environments. With AWS Lambda, physical servers still execute the code, but because you don't need to spend time managing them, it's common to define this kind of approach as *serverless*.

> **TIP**   For more details on the execution environment used by Lambda functions, please visit http://docs.aws.amazon.com/lambda/latest/dg/current-supported-versions.html.

When you create a new function with AWS Lambda, you choose a *function name*, create your code, and specify the configuration of the execution environment that will be used to run the function, including the following:

- The maximum *memory size* that can be used by the function
- A *timeout* after which the function is terminated, even if it hasn't completed
- A *role* that describes what the function can do, and on which resources, using AWS Identity and Access Management (IAM)

> **TIP** When you choose the amount of memory you want for your function, you're allocated proportional CPU power. For example, choosing 256 MB of memory allocates approximately twice as much CPU power to your Lambda function as requesting 128 MB of memory and half as much CPU power as choosing 512 MB of memory.

AWS Lambda implements the execution of those functions with an efficient use of the underlying compute resources that allows for an interesting and innovative cost model. With AWS Lambda you pay for

- The number of invocations
- The hundreds of milliseconds of execution time of all invocations, depending on the memory given to the functions

The execution time costs grow linearly with the memory: if you double the memory and keep the execution time the same, you double that part of the cost. To enable you to get hands-on experience, a free tier allows you to use AWS Lambda without any cost. Each month there's no charge for

- The first one million invocations
- The first 400,000 seconds of execution time with 1 GB of memory

If you use less memory, you have more compute time at no cost; for example, with 128 MB of memory (1 GB divided by 8) you can have up to 3.2 million seconds of execution time (400,000 seconds multiplied by 8) per month. To give you a scale of the monthly free tier, 400,000 seconds corresponds to slightly more than 111 hours or 4.6 days, whereas 3.2 million seconds comes close to 889 hours or 37 days.

> **TIP** You'll need an AWS account to follow the examples in this book. If you create a new AWS account, all the examples that I provide fall in the *Free Tier* and you'll have no costs to sustain. Please look here for more information on the AWS Free Tier and how to create a new AWS account: http://aws.amazon .com/free/.

Throughout the book we'll use JavaScript (Node.js, actually) and Python in the examples, but other runtimes are available. For example, you can use Java and other languages running on top of the Java Virtual Machine (JVM), such as Scala or Clojure. For object-oriented languages such as Java, the function you want to expose is a method of an object.

To use platforms that aren't supported by AWS Lambda, such as C or PHP, it's possible to use one of the supported runtimes as a *wrapper* and bring together with the function a static binary or anything that can be executed in the OS container used by the function. For example, a statically linked program written in C can be embedded in the archive used to upload a function.

When you call a function with AWS Lambda, you provide an event and a context in the input:

- The *event* is the way to send input parameters for your function and is expressed using JSON syntax.
- The *context* is used by the service to describe the execution environment and how the event is received and processed.

Functions can be called *synchronously* and return a *result* (figure 1.2). I use the term "synchronous" to indicate this kind of invocation in the book, but in other sources, such as the AWS Lambda API Reference documentation or the AWS command-line interface (CLI), this is described as the `RequestResponse` invocation type.

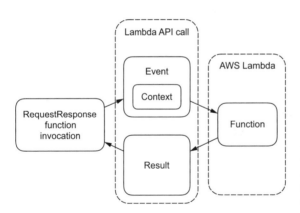

Figure 1.2 **Calling an AWS Lambda function synchronously with the RequestResponse invocation type. Functions receive input as an event and a context and return a result.**

For example, a simple synchronous function computing the sum of two numbers can be implemented in AWS Lambda using the JavaScript runtime as

```
exports.handler = (event, context, callback) => {
    var result = event.value1 + event.value2;
    callback(null, result);
};
```

The same can be done using the Python runtime:

```
def lambda_handler(event, context):
    result = event['value1'] + event['value2']
    return result
```

We'll dive deep into the syntax in the next chapter, but for now let's focus on what the functions are doing. Giving as input to those functions an event with the following JSON payload would give back a result of 30:

```
{
  "value1": 10,
  "value2": 20
}
```

> **NOTE** The values in JSON are given as numbers, without quotation marks; otherwise the + used in both the Node.js and Python functions would change the meaning, becoming a concatenation of two strings.

Functions can also be called *asynchronously*. In this case the call returns immediately and no result is given back, while the function is continuing its work (figure 1.3). I use the term "asynchronous" to indicate this kind of invocation in the book, but in other sources, such as the AWS Lambda API Reference documentation and the AWS CLI, this is described as the Event invocation type.

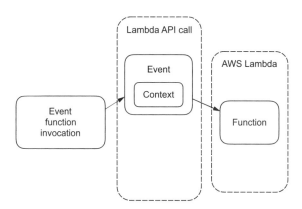

Figure 1.3 Calling an AWS Lambda function asynchronously with the Event invocation type. The invocation returns immediately while the function continues its work.

When a Lambda function terminates, no session information is retained by the AWS Lambda service. This kind of interaction with a server is usually defined as *stateless*. Considering this behavior, calling Lambda functions asynchronously (returning no value) is useful when they are accessing and modifying the status of other resources (such as files in a shared repository, records in a database, and so on) or calling other services (for example, to send an email or to send a push notification to a mobile device), as illustrated in figure 1.4.

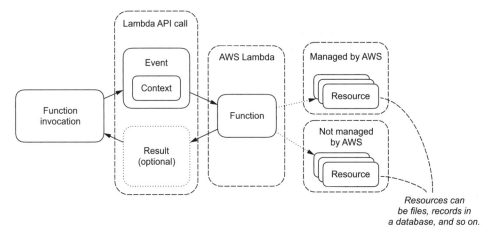

Figure 1.4   Functions can create, update, or delete other resources. Resources can also be other services that can do some actions, such as sending an email.

For example, it's possible to use the logging capabilities of AWS Lambda to implement a simple logging function (that you can call asynchronously) in Node.js:

```
exports.handler = function(event, context) {
    console.log(event.message);
    context.done();
};
```

In Python that's even easier because you can use a normal print to log the output:

```
def lambda_handler(event, context):
    print(event['message'])
    return
```

You can send input to the function as a JSON event to log a message:

```
{
  "message": "This message is being logged!"
}
```

In these two logging examples, we used the integration of AWS Lambda with Amazon CloudWatch Logs. Functions are executed without a default output device (in what is usually called a *headless environment*) and a default logging capability is given for each AWS Lambda runtime to ship the logs to CloudWatch. You can then use all the features provided by CloudWatch Logs, such as choosing the retention period or creating metrics from logged data. We'll give more examples and use cases regarding logging in part 4.

Asynchronous calls are useful when functions are *subscribed* to events generated by other resources, such as Amazon S3, an object store, or Amazon DynamoDB, a fully managed NoSQL database.

When you subscribe a function to events generated by other resources, the function is called asynchronously when the events you selected are generated, passing the events as input to the function (figure 1.5).

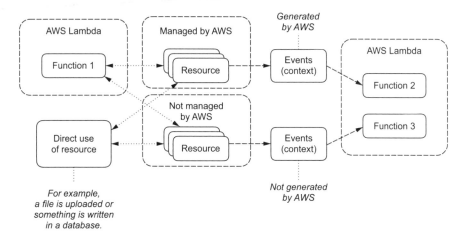

Figure 1.5 Functions can subscribe to events generated by direct use of resources, or by other functions interacting with resources. For resources not managed by AWS, you should find the best way to generate events to subscribe functions to those resources.

For example, if a user of a mobile application uploads a new high-resolution picture to a file store, a function can be triggered with the location of the new file in its input as part of the event. The function could then read the picture, build a small thumbnail to use in an index page, and write that back to the file store.

Now you know how AWS Lambda works at a high level, and that you can expose your code as functions and directly call those functions or subscribe them to events generated by other resources.

In the next section, you'll see how to use those functions in your applications.

1.2 *Functions as your back end*

Imagine you're a mobile developer and you're working on a new application. You can implement features in the mobile app running on the client device of the end user, but you'd probably keep part of the logic and status outside of the mobile app. For example:

- A mobile banking app wouldn't allow an end user to add money to their bank account without a good reason; only logic executed outside of the mobile device, involving the business systems of the bank, can decide if a transfer of money can be done or not.
- An online multiplayer game wouldn't allow a player to go to the next level without validating that the player has completed the current level.

This is a common pattern when developing client/server applications and the same applies to web applications. You need to keep part of the logic outside of the client (be it a web browser or a mobile device) for a few reasons:

- *Sharing*, because the information must be used (directly or indirectly) by multiple users of the application
- *Security*, because the data can be accessed or changed only if specific requirements are satisfied and the client cannot be trusted to check those requirements by itself
- *Access* to computing resources or storage capacity not available on a client device

We refer to this external logic required by a front end application as the *back end* of the application.

To implement this external logic, the normal approach is either to build a web application that can be called by the mobile app or to integrate it into an already existing web application rendering the content for a web browser. But instead of building and deploying a whole back end web application or extending the functionalities of your current back end, you can have your web page or your mobile application call one or more AWS Lambda functions that implement the logic you need. Those functions become your *serverless back end*.

Security is one of the reasons why you implement back end logic for an application, and you must always check the authentication and authorization of end users accessing your back end. AWS Lambda uses the standard security framework provided by AWS to control what a function can do, and on which resources. For example, a function can read from only a specific path of a file share, and write in a certain database table. This framework is based on AWS Identity and Access Management policies and roles. In this way, taking care of the security required to execute the code is simpler and becomes part of the development process itself. You can tailor security permissions specifically for each function, making it much easier to implement a least-privilege approach for each module (function, in this case) of your application.

> **DEFINITION**   By *least privilege*, I mean a security practice in which you always use the least privilege you need to perform an action in your application. For example, if you have a part of your application that's reading the user profiles from a central repository to publish them on a web page, you don't need to have write access to the repository in that specific module; you only need to read the subset of information you need to publish. Every other permission on top of that is in excess of what's required and can amplify the effects of a possible attack—for example, allowing malicious users that discover a security breach in your application to do more harm.

1.3   *A single back end for everything*

We can use AWS Lambda functions to expose the back end logic of our applications. But is that enough, or do we need something different to cover all the possible use cases for a back end application? Do we still need to develop traditional web applications, beyond the functions provided by AWS?

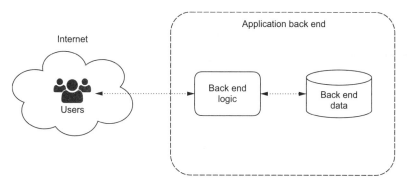

Figure 1.6 How users interact via the internet with the back end of an application. Note that the back end has some logic and some data.

Let's look at the overall flow and interactions of an application that can be used via a web browser or a mobile app (figure 1.6). Users interact with the back end via the internet. The back end has some logic and some data to manage.

The users of your application can use different devices, depending on what you decide to support. Supporting multiple ways to interact with your application, such as a web interface, a mobile app, and public application programming interfaces (APIs) that more advanced users can use to integrate third-party products with your application, is critical to success and is a common practice for new applications.

But if we look at the interfaces used by those different devices to communicate with the back end, we discover that they aren't always the same: a web browser expects more than the others, because both the content required by the user interface (dynamically generated HTML, CSS, JavaScript, multimedia files) and the application back end logic (exposed via APIs) are required (figure 1.7).

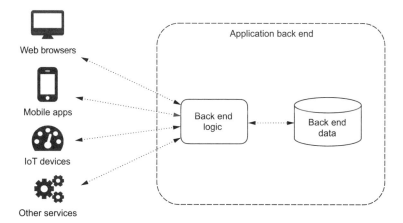

Figure 1.7 Different ways in which users can interact with the back end of an application. Users using a web browser receive different data than other front end clients.

If the mobile app of a specific service is developed after the web browser interface is already implemented, the back end application should be refactored to split API functionalities from web rendering—but that's usually not an easy task, depending on how the original application was developed. This sometimes causes developers to support two different back end platforms: one for web browsers serving web content and one for mobile apps, new devices (for example, wearable, home automation, and Internet of Things devices), and external services consuming their APIs. Even if the two back end platforms are well designed and share most of the functionalities (and hence the code), this wastes the developer's resources, because for each new feature they have to understand the impact on both platforms and run more tests to be sure those features are correctly implemented, while not adding value for their end users.

If we split the back end data between structured content that can go in one or more databases and unstructured content, such as files, we can simplify the overall architecture in a couple of steps:

1 Adding a (secure) web interface to the file repository so that it becomes a standalone resource that clients can directly access
2 Moving part of the logic into the web browser using a JavaScript client application and bringing it on par with the logic of the mobile app

Such a JavaScript client application, from an architectural point of view, behaves in the same way as a mobile app, in terms of functionality implemented, security, and (most importantly for our use case) the interactions with the back end (figure 1.8).

Looking at the back end logic, we now have a *single architecture for all clients* and the same interactions and data flows for all the consuming applications. We can abstract our back end from the actual implementation of the client and design it to serve a

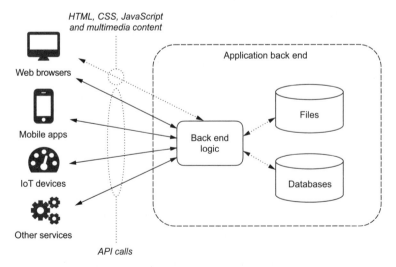

Figure 1.8 Using a JavaScript application running in the browser, back end architecture is simplified by serving only APIs to all clients.

generic *client application* using standard API calls that we define once and for all possible end users.

This is an important step because we've now *decoupled* the front end implementations, which could be different depending on the supported client devices, from the back end architecture (figure 1.9). Also, later you can add a new kind of client application (for example, an application running on wearable devices) without affecting the back end.

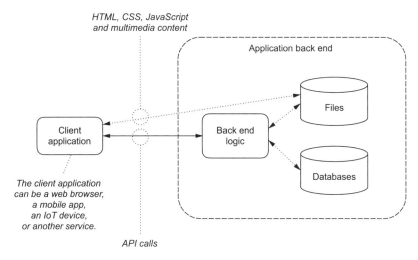

Figure 1.9   Think of your clients as a single client application consuming your APIs, which is possible when you decouple the implementation of the back end from the different user devices that interact with your application.

Looking again at the decoupled architecture, you can see that each of those API calls takes input parameters, does something in the back end, and returns a result. Does that remind you of something? Each API call is a *function exposed by the back end* that you can implement using AWS Lambda. Applying the same approach, all back end APIs can be implemented as functions managed by AWS Lambda.

In this way you have a *single serverless back end*, powered by AWS Lambda, that serves the same APIs to all clients of your application.

1.4   *Event-driven applications*

Up to now, we've used the functions provided by AWS Lambda directly, calling them as back end APIs from the client application. This is what's usually referred to as a *custom event* approach. But you could subscribe a function to receive events from another resource, for example if a file is uploaded to a repository or if a record in a database is updated.

Using subscriptions, you can change the internal behavior of the back end so that it can react not only to direct requests from client applications, but also to changes in the resources that are used by the application. Instead of implementing a centralized workflow to support all the interactions among the resources, each interaction is described by the *relationship between the resources* involved. For example, if a file is added in a repository, a database table is updated with new information extracted from the file.

> **NOTE** This approach simplifies the design and the future evolution of the application, because we're inherently capitalizing on one of the advantages that microservices architectures bring: bottom-up *choreography* among software modules is much easier to manage than top-down *orchestration.*

With this approach, our back end becomes a distributed application, because it's not centrally managed and executed anymore, and we should apply best practices from distributed systems. For example, it's better to avoid synchronous transactions across multiple resources, which are difficult and slow to manage, and design each function to work independently (thanks to event subscriptions) with eventual consistency of data.

> **DEFINITION** By *eventual consistency,* I mean that we shouldn't expect the state of data to always be in sync across all resources used by the back end, but that the data will eventually converge over time to the last updated state.

Applications designed to react to internal and external events without a centralized workflow to coordinate processing on the resources are *event-driven applications.* Let's introduce this concept with a practical example.

Imagine you want to implement a media-sharing application, where the users can upload pictures from their client, a web browser or a mobile app, and share those pictures publicly with everyone or only with their friends.

To do that, you need two repositories:

- A file repository for the multimedia content (pictures)
- A database to handle user profiles (user table), friendships among the users (friendship table), and content metadata (content table).

You need to implement the following basic functionalities:

- Allow users to upload new multimedia content (pictures) with its own metadata. (By metadata, I mean: Is this content public or shared only among friends? Who uploaded the file? Where was the picture taken? At what time? Is there a caption?)
- Allow users to get specific content (pictures) shared by other users, but only if they have permission.
- Get an index of the content a specific user can see (all public content plus what has been shared with that user by their friends).
- Update content metadata. For example, a user can upload pictures only for their friends, and then change their mind and make a picture public for everyone to see.
- Get content metadata to be shown on the client together with the picture thumbnails; for example, adding the owner of the content, a date, a location, and a caption.

Of course, a real application needs more features (and more functions), but for the sake of simplicity we'll consider only the features listed here for now. You'll build a more complex (but still relatively simple) media-sharing application in chapter 8.

Because the content won't change too quickly, it's also effective to compute in advance (precompute) what each user can see in terms of content: end users will probably look at recent content often, and when they do, they want to see the result quickly. Using a precomputed *index* for the most recent content makes the rendering fast for users and makes the application use fewer computing resources in the back end. If users go back to older content outside the scope of the precomputed index, you can still compute that dynamically, but it happens less often and is easier to manage. The precomputed indexes must be updated each time the content (files or metadata) is updated and when the friendships between users change (because picture visibility is based on friendship).

You can see those features, and how they access repositories, implemented using one AWS Lambda function for each feature in figure 1.10.

In this way all interactions from the client application are covered, but you still miss basic back end functionalities here:

- What happens if a user uploads a new piece of content?
- What happens to the index if the user changes the metadata?
- You need to build thumbnails for the pictures to show them as a preview to end users.

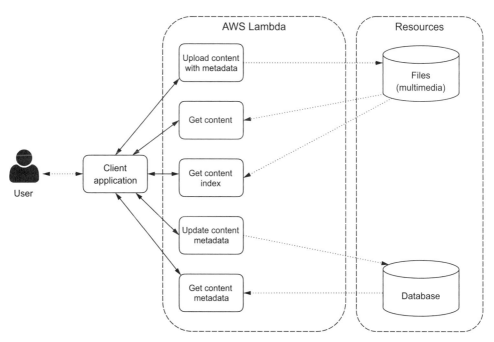

Figure 1.10 Features of a sample media-sharing application implemented as AWS Lambda functions, still missing basic back end functionalities

Those new back end features that you want to introduce are different from the previous ones, because they depend on what's happening in the back end repositories (files and database tables, in this case). You can implement those new features as additional functions that are subscribed to events coming from the repositories. For example:

- If a file (picture) is added or updated, you build the new thumbnail and add it back to the file repository.
- If a file (picture) is added or updated, you extract the new metadata and update the database (in the content table).
- Whenever the database is updated (user, friendship, or content table), you rebuild the dependent precomputed indexes, changing what a user can see.

Implementing those functionalities as AWS Lambda functions and subscribing those functions to the relevant events allows you to have an efficient architecture that drives updates when something relevant happens in the repositories, without enforcing a centralized workflow of activities that are required when data is changed by the end users. You can see a sample architecture implementing those new features as functions subscribed to events in figure 1.11.

Consider in our example the function subscribed to database events: that function is activated when the database is changed directly by end users (explicitly changing something in the metadata) or when an update is made by another function (because a new picture has been uploaded, bringing new metadata with it).

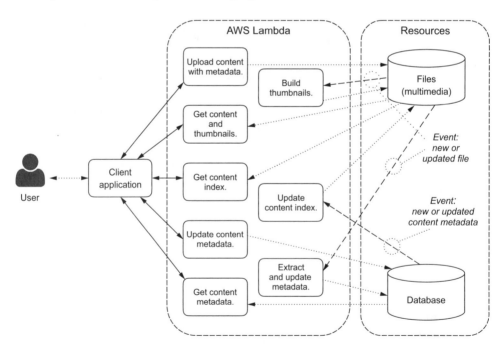

Figure 1.11   Sample media-sharing application with event-driven functions in the back end, subscribed to events from back end resources, such as file shares or databases

You don't need to manage the two use cases separately; they're both managed by the same subscription, a subscription that describes the relationship among the resources and the action you need to do when something changes.

You'll see when implementing this media-sharing application that some of the Lambda functions can be replaced by direct interactions to back end resources. For example, you can upload new or updated content (together with its own metadata) directly in a file share. Or update content metadata by directly writing to a database. The Lambda functions subscribed to those resources will implement the required back end logic.

This is a simplified but working example of a media-sharing application with an event-driven back end. Functions are automatically chained one after the other by the relationships we created by subscribing them to events. For example, if a picture is updated with new metadata (say, a new caption), a first function is invoked by the event generated in the file repository, updating the metadata in the database content table. This triggers a new event that invokes a second function to update the content index for all users who can see that content.

> **NOTE** In a way, the behavior I described is similar to a spreadsheet, where you update one cell and all the dependent cells (sums, average, more complex functions) are recomputed automatically. A spreadsheet is a good example of an event-driven application. This is a first step toward reactive programming, as you'll see later in the book.

Try to think of more features for our sample media-sharing application, such as creating, updating, and deleting a user; changing friendships (adding or removing a friend) and adding the required functions to the previous diagram to cover those aspects; subscribing (when it makes sense) the new functions to back end resources to have the flow of the application driven by events and avoid putting all the workflow logic in the functions themselves.

For example, suppose you have access to a mobile push notification service such as the Amazon Simple Notification Service (SNS). Think about the best way to use that in the back end to notify end users if new or updated content is available for them. What would you need to add, in terms of resources, events, and functions, to figure 1.11?

1.5 *Calling functions from a client*

In the previous discussion we didn't consider how, technically, the client application interacts with the AWS Lambda functions, assuming that a sort of direct invocation is possible.

As mentioned previously, each function can be invoked synchronously or asynchronously, and a specific AWS Lambda API exists to do that: the Invoke API (figure 1.12).

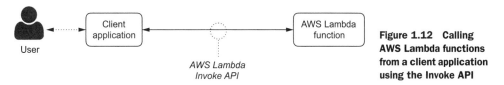

Figure 1.12 Calling AWS Lambda functions from a client application using the Invoke API

To call the Invoke API, AWS applies the standard security checks and requires that the client application has the right permissions to invoke the function. As per all other AWS APIs, you need AWS credentials to authenticate, and based on that authentication, AWS verifies whether those credentials have the right authorization to execute that API call (Invoke) on that specific resource (the function).

> **TIP** We'll discuss the security model used by AWS Lambda in more detail in chapter 4. The most important thing to remember now is to *never put security credentials in a client application,* be that a mobile app or a JavaScript web application. If you put security credentials in something you deliver to end users, such as a mobile app or HTML or JavaScript code, an advanced user can find the credentials and compromise your application. In those cases, you need to use a different approach to authenticate a client application with the back end.

In the case of AWS Lambda, and all other AWS APIs, it's possible to use a specific service to manage authentication and authorization in an easy way: Amazon Cognito.

With Amazon Cognito, the client can authenticate using an external social or custom authentication (such as Facebook or Amazon) and get temporary AWS credentials to invoke the AWS Lambda functions the client is authorized to use (figure 1.13).

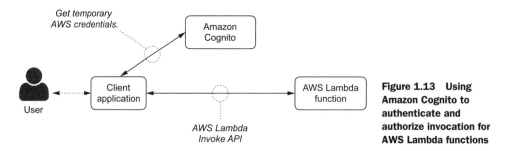

Figure 1.13 Using Amazon Cognito to authenticate and authorize invocation for AWS Lambda functions

> **NOTE** Amazon Cognito provides a simplified interface to other AWS services, such as AWS Identity and Access Management (IAM) and AWS Security Token Service (STS). Figure 1.12 makes the flow easier to visualize, not including all details for the sake of simplicity.

Moving a step forward, it's possible to replace the direct use of the AWS Lambda Invoke API by clients with your own web APIs that you can build by mapping the access to AWS Lambda functions to more generic HTTP URLs and verbs.

For example, let's implement the web API for a bookstore. Users may need to list books, get more information for a specific book, and add, update, or delete a book. Using the Amazon API Gateway, you can map the access to a specific resource (the URL of the bookstore or a specific book) with an HTTP verb (GET, POST, PUT, DELETE, and so on) to the invocation of an AWS Lambda function. See table 1.1 for a sample configuration.

Table 1.1 A sample web API for a bookstore

Resource	+	HTTP verb	→	Method (function)
/books	+	GET	→	GetAllBooksByRange
/books	+	POST	→	CreateNewBook
/books/{id}	+	GET	→	GetBookById
/books/{id}	+	PUT	→	CreateOrUpdateBookById
/books/{id}	+	DELETE	→	DeleteBookById

Let's look at the example in table 1.1 in more detail:

- If you do an HTTP GET on the /books resource, you execute a Lambda function (GetAllBooksByRange) that will return a list of books, depending on a range you can optionally specify.
- If you do an HTTP POST on the same URL, you create a new book (using the CreateNewBook function) and get the ID of the book as the result.
- With an HTTP GET on /books/ID, you execute a function (GetBookById) that will give you a description (a representation, according to the REST architecture style) of the book with that specific ID.
- And so on for the other examples in the table.

NOTE You don't need to have a different Lambda function for every resource and HTTP verb (method) combination. You can send the resource and the method as part of the input parameters of a single function that can then process it to understand if it has been triggered by a GET or a POST. The choice between having more and smaller functions, or fewer and bigger ones, depends on your programming habits.

But the Amazon API Gateway adds more value than that, such as caching results to reduce load on the back end, throttling to avoid overloading the back end in peak moments, managing developer keys, generating the SDKs for the web API you design for multiple platforms, and other features that we'll start to see in chapter 2.

What's important is that by using the Amazon API Gateway we're *decoupling* the client from directly using AWS Lambda, exposing a clean web API that can be consumed by external services that should have no knowledge of AWS. However, even with the web API exposed by the Amazon API Gateway, we can optionally use AWS credentials (and hence Amazon Cognito) to manage authentication and authorization for the clients (figure 1.14).

With the Amazon API Gateway, we can also give public access to some of our web APIs. By *public access* I mean that no credentials are required to access those web APIs. Because one of the possible HTTP verbs that we can use in configuring an API is GET,

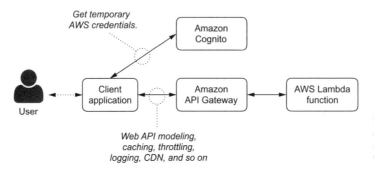

Figure 1.14 Using the Amazon API Gateway to access functions via web APIs

and GET is the default that is used when you type a URL in a web browser, we can use this configuration to create public websites whose URLs are dynamically served by AWS Lambda functions (figure 1.15).

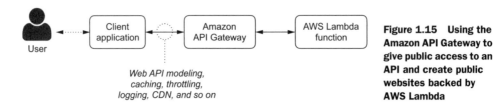

Figure 1.15 Using the Amazon API Gateway to give public access to an API and create public websites backed by AWS Lambda

In fact, the web API exposed publicly via the HTTP GET method can return any content type, including HTML content, such as a web page that can be seen in a browser.

> **TIP** For an example of a joint use of AWS Lambda and the Amazon API Gateway to build dynamic websites, see the Serverless framework at http://www.serverless.com/.

Summary

In this first chapter, I introduced the core topics that will be seen in depth in the rest of the book:

- An overview of AWS Lambda functions.
- Using functions to implement the back end of an application.
- Having a single back end for different clients, such as web browsers and mobile apps.
- An overview of how event-driven applications work.
- Managing authentication and authorization from a client.
- Using Lambda functions from a client, directly or via the Amazon API Gateway.

Now let's put all this theory into practice and build our first functions.

Your first Lambda function

2

This chapter covers

- Creating your first AWS Lambda function
- Understanding function configurations and settings
- Testing functions from the web console
- Using the AWS command-line interface to call functions

In the first chapter you learned how AWS Lambda functions work and how they can be used synchronously (returning a result) or asynchronously (for example, subscribing a function to an event). In the second part of the chapter you learned how a group of functions can be used to build an event-driven application in which the logic is bound to events coming from outside (a client application) or inside (relationships among data).

It's now time to build your first functions and see how they can be used from a client application using the AWS Lambda interface. The AWS Lambda interface is easy to use with the AWS command-line interface (CLI), or one of the AWS software development kits (SDKs) that can run on a server, in a browser, or in a mobile client.

2.1   *Creating a new function*

Any good programming book should start with the "Hello World" example. But with AWS Lambda you don't have standalone applications, but functions that take an input (event) and can optionally provide a result (when called synchronously).

Let's start with a slightly more complex task: a function that's looking into the event for a name to "greet" and returns "Hello <name>!" If no name is provided in the event, then the function should return a more generic "Hello World!"

> **TIP** You need an AWS account to follow the examples in this book. With a new AWS account, the *Free Tier* covers all the examples in this book with no cost to you. For more information on the AWS Free Tier and how to create a new AWS account, please visit http://aws.amazon.com/free/.

To create your first function, open your browser and go to https://console.aws.amazon .com/. Log in with your AWS credentials and select Lambda from the Compute section; choose your preferred AWS region from the menu at the top right (usually the one closest to you to reduce network latency) and then click "Get Started Now" on the welcome page. If this isn't the first function in that region, instead of the welcome page you'll see the list of functions, and you can select "Create a Lambda function" to proceed.

To simplify the creation of a new Lambda function, blueprints are provided to show the integration with other AWS services and other services such as Amazon Alexa, Twilio, and Algorithmia (figure 2.1). Select the "Blank Function" to start from scratch.

You can then choose a *trigger* for the new function (figure 2.2). A trigger is a source of events that will execute the function, providing the event an input. You have multiple options for the trigger; a few of them will be used by the examples you'll build while reading this book.

For example, you can choose the Amazon API Gateway to have a Web API calling a function, or AWS IoT, to build a serverless back end for an Internet of Things (IoT) platform connecting devices with AWS. You'll directly invoke this function and don't need a trigger for now. Select "Next."

You can now create a new AWS Lambda function (figure 2.3). For the name of the function, type "greetingsOnDemand".

> **NOTE** AWS Lambda has no official rule on how to write function names. Sometimes function names are written in all lowercase, with dashes to separate words. In this book, I'll follow the *lowerCamelCase* convention, joining all words together, starting with a lowercase letter and using uppercase for the first letter of every word after the first one.

The description text can be "Returns greetings when you ask for them." Giving a meaningful description can help when building an application with multiple functions or to facilitate reuse of a function (or only its code) for different purposes.

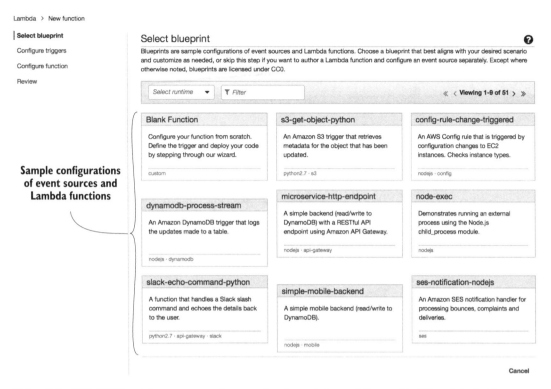

Figure 2.1 With AWS Lambda you can create a new function using one of the provided blueprints, but for your first function you'll start from scratch.

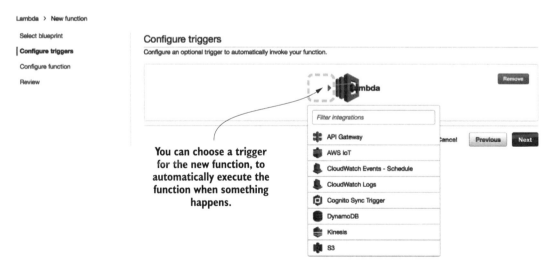

Figure 2.2 You can choose a trigger during the creation of a new function. Triggers invoke a Lambda function when certain events happen.

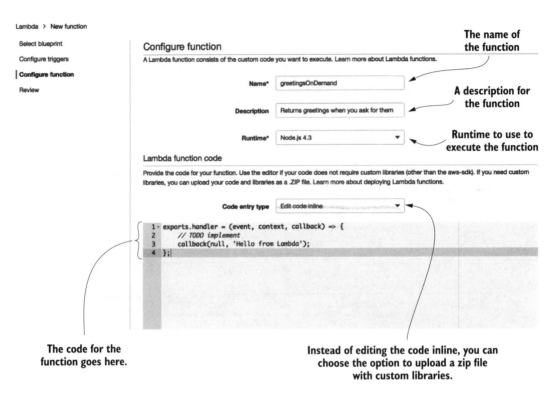

Figure 2.3   Configuring a new AWS Lambda function, starting with a name and a description, the runtime to use, and the code to execute

TIP   Descriptions can also be read through AWS APIs, and having conventions in the content of the description—for example, describing the expected input/output—can help in implementing automated "discovery" for your functions.

Using the AWS Lambda web console, you can provide the code for your function in three different ways:

- Edit code inline, straight from the web browser
- Upload a zip file from your local environment
- Upload a zip file from Amazon S3

You can include custom libraries or modules that your code depends on in the zip file. In part 3 you'll see that uploading functions via Amazon S3 can be an interesting feature for implementing automatic deployments and continuous integration with AWS Lambda.

As the runtime for your function, you can choose Node.js 4.3 or Python 2.7. Examples of both are provided in this chapter; choose the language you prefer for your back end deployment.

> ### Using the Java Runtime
> I'm not providing Java 8 examples throughout the book for the sake of simplicity, because Java code cannot be written inline in the web console and needs to be compiled, packaged, and uploaded. For that, my suggestion is to use the AWS Toolkit for Eclipse, found at https://aws.amazon.com/eclipse.

2.2 Writing the function

Leave the option to "Edit code inline" selected and write the following code in the online editor below it, depending on the runtime you chose. Use the following listing for Node.js or listing 2.2 for Python.

Listing 2.1 Function `greetingsOnDemand` **(Node.js)**

```
console.log('Loading function');                    ◁── Initialization

exports.handler = (event, context, callback) => {   ◁── Function declaration;
    console.log('Received event:',                       the input event is a
        JSON.stringify(event, null, 2));                 JavaScript object.
    console.log('name =', event.name);
    var name = '';
    if ('name' in event) {
        name = event['name'];
    } else {
        name = 'World';
    }
    var greetings = 'Hello ' + name + '!';          Logging to Amazon
    console.log(greetings);                     ◁── CloudWatch Logs
    callback(null, greetings);            ◁── End function and
};                                           return value
```

Listing 2.2 Function `greetingsOnDemand` **(Python)**

```
import json                          Initialization; in Python you need the
                                     "json" module to dump the event.
print('Loading function')

def lambda_handler(event, context):   ◁── Function declaration; the input
    print('Received event: ' +            event is a Python built-in type,
        json.dumps(event, indent=2))      usually a dict.
    if 'name' in event:
        name = event['name']
    else:
        name = 'World'
    greetings = 'Hello ' + name + '!'     Logging to Amazon
    print(greetings)                  ◁── CloudWatch Logs
    return greetings            ◁── End function and
                                    return value
```

The overall organization of the code and the execution flow are similar for both runtimes:

- The code starts with an initialization phase before the function. AWS Lambda can reuse the same "container" for multiple invocations of a function and the initialization isn't executed every time the function is invoked, but only the first time a function is invoked in a container. In the initialization, you should put code that can be executed only once; for example, to open a connection to a database, initialize a cache, or load configuration data required by the function.

- AWS Lambda executes functions in a headless environment without any display. For this reason, all runtimes implement an easy way to write centralized logs to Amazon CloudWatch Logs. Amazon CloudWatch is a monitoring and logging service that can be used to manage metrics, alarms, and logs for your application and the AWS services used by your application. For Node.js, anything written by `console.log()` goes to CloudWatch Logs. For Python, it's anything that you `print`.

- After the initialization, a function takes as input an event and a `context`. Both are in the native format for the runtime; for example, a JavaScript object in Node.js or a dictionary in Python. That function will be the one that's executed for every invocation, and you'll configure it in the next steps.

- The logic of the function is simple: if a "name" key is present in the input `event`, then that name is used to prepare a "greeting"; otherwise, a default "Hello World!" is provided.

- The resulting greeting is then logged and returned by the function.

- In Node.js, you end your function using the `callback` in a way familiar to the standard Node.js programming model. In this case, `callback(null, data)` is used to terminate successfully and return the greeting. If the first parameter of the `callback` is not `null`, you terminate the function with an error; for example, `callback(error)`.

- In Python the `return` of the function terminates successfully, and you can `raise` an exception on failure.

- The input `context` has interesting information on the configuration of the function and how the execution is handled by AWS Lambda. For example, you can check how much time is left before you reach the configured timeout (more details on this in the next section).

2.3   *Specifying other settings*

After you paste the code in the web console, you need to specify which function inside your code should be called by AWS Lambda. You can do that via the Handler field below the code. Because you can upload more than one file in a zip file, the following syntax is used by the handler:

```
<file name without extension>.<function name>
```

For example, the default value for Node.js is `index.handler`, the `handler` (exported) function in the `index.js` file. In Python, the default value is `lambda_function` `.lambda_handler`, for the `lambda_handler` function in the `lambda_function.py` file. When you paste your code in the web console, `index` (for Node.js) and `lambda` `_function` (for Python) are the default file names and the Handler field is already configured to use the default names of the functions you used in the previous code. When using Node.js, remember to export the function used by the Handler.

If you want to use a different function name in the code, you should update the name in the handler (figure 2.4). You can have multiple functions in the code you provide and multiple files if you upload a zip archive, but only the function specified by the Handler is called by AWS Lambda. The other functions can be used internally in the code.

AWS Lambda allows tight control of the security of your environment: everything that's executed by AWS Lambda needs to have the permissions to do what it's supposed to do. This is managed using AWS Identity and Access Management (IAM) roles and policies, which you'll explore in depth in chapter 4. When a function is

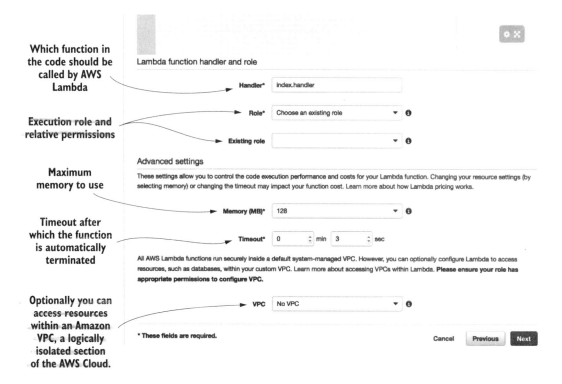

Figure 2.4 After giving the code, you have to choose which function in the code should be called by AWS Lambda, the AWS IAM role that the function will assume to get permissions, how much memory to allocate, and a timeout in seconds. You can optionally specify an Amazon VPC to access resources (for example, a database) inside the VPC.

executed it assumes the role given in the configuration. A "role" can have one or more policies attached. A "policy" describes what you can do in terms of actions, resources, and conditions. Assuming a role allows the function to do what's described in the policies attached to the role.

For this basic example, the function is interacting only with Amazon CloudWatch Logs (for logging)—that's the default behavior and you can use a "basic execution role." You can create a new basic execution role using the Role menu:

1 Choose create a new role.
2 You can use "myBasicExecutionRole" for the role name.
3 Don't select a policy template, leaving the corresponding field empty.

Next time, if you need the same role, you can select the option to use an existing role and select it from the "existing role" menu. It doesn't make sense to have multiple roles with the same configuration, so reuse a role if you can.

> **TIP**   You don't need to select a policy template now because your first function isn't accessing any external resources that would need additional permissions. In the more advanced examples in the book you'll create roles that will enable you to read or write permissions on specific resources. Those roles will not be reused because they're tightly customized for the functions using them.

Now you have to configure two important aspects for a Lambda function:

- *How much memory to use.* This setting also affects the quantity of CPU power and the cost of executing the function, so you should use the least amount of memory (and CPU) you need—in this case, for this simple function, 128 MB is more than enough. If you need a shorter execution time, you can increase memory to have more CPU power.
- *The timeout after which the function is automatically terminated.* This setting is used to avoid mistakes that could start long-running functions, which in turn could introduce a non-planned cost for your application. Three seconds is fine for our simple function. You should use a value here that you're sure is never reached by a normal execution of your function.

You can monitor the usage of memory and the execution time from the logs, as you'll see in the next section on testing a function.

In the final setting, you can specify an Amazon Virtual Private Cloud (VPC), a logically isolated section of the AWS Cloud where you can launch resources in a virtual network that you define, to access those resources from the function you create. For example, a NoSQL database hosted on one or more Amazon EC2 virtual servers or a relational database managed by Amazon RDS can be directly addressed by a Lambda function, via private networking, if the correct VPC is configured here. You can leave the default "No VPC" for now, because we aren't using any resource in a VPC in this example.

You can select Next to review all of the configurations, and then select "Create function." Congrats, you created your first function!

2.4 *Testing the function*

Now that your function has been created, you can test it directly from the web console. Click the Test button in the upper left of the console. You should now prepare a test event (figure 2.5) that will be used for all test invocations in the console. When invoking a Lambda function, events are expressed using a JSON syntax that's translated to native objects or types when the event is received by the actual runtime—for example, a JavaScript object for Node.js or a dictionary in Python.

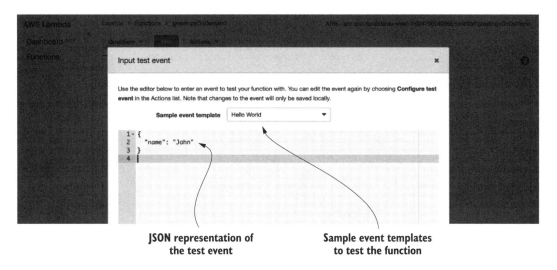

JSON representation of   **Sample event templates**
the test event   **to test the function**

Figure 2.5   Configuring a test event, using a JSON syntax, to quickly test a function from the web console

The drop-down menu has a few sample events that could be received when subscribing to standard resources such as Amazon S3 or Amazon DynamoDB, but this function uses a custom format for the event, so you can't use a standard sample event. Instead, you should edit the proposed event to give the "name" the function needs:

```
{
   "name": "John"
}
```

Feel free to replace "John" with your name.

If you click "Save and test" at the bottom of the window, the function is invoked with the test event you provided. The result of the execution is shown at the bottom of the page (figure 2.6; you need to scroll down to see this) in terms of returned value and logs with a summary of the execution characteristics: actual duration, the billed

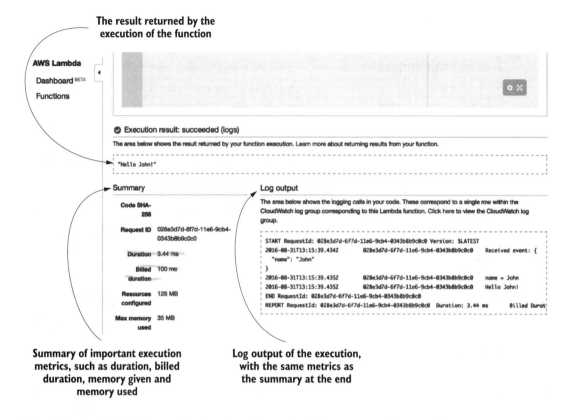

Figure 2.6   Result of a test execution from the web console, with a summary of the execution and the log output

duration (rounded up to 100 ms), and how much memory (out of the 128 MB you gave) was used. All the information is also displayed in the raw log output.

If everything went fine, you should see "Hello John!" (or your name if you changed the sample event) in the execution result. You executed your first function!

> **WARNING** If instead you get an error, please check to be certain that you pasted all the code; the final lines (`callback()` in Node.js and the `return` statement in Python) are very important.

Try executing the function multiple times. You may notice that the first execution is sometimes slower than those that follow, but it shouldn't be an issue in production when multiple invocations are expected.

> **TIP** If your function is rarely executed, AWS can release the execution environment and your next execution may be slower. If you always need a short execution time—for example, to fulfill a Service Level Agreement (SLA) for your customers—you can use a scheduled execution (for example, every five

minutes) with "harmless" parameters that don't change data stored by your function to keep the environment ready.

To test the default behavior when no name is provided, you should change the test event. From the Actions menu, select "Configure test event" and remove the "name" key from the JSON payload, so that event is empty:

```
{}
```

Save and test the empty event, and review the outcome at the bottom of the page: when no "name" is passed in the event, the function logic (check listings 2.1 and 2.2) replaces the name with "World" and you should now have a proper "Hello World!" in the execution results. Congratulations, you executed the mandatory "Hello World" example that any programming book should provide!

2.5 *Executing the function through the Lambda API*

You've tested the function in the web console, but is the function available to be used on demand outside of this web interface? As a matter of fact, any Lambda function can be executed via the AWS Lambda Invoke API call. To do that, you can use the AWS command-line interface.

Installing and configuring the AWS CLI

To install and configure the AWS CLI, you can follow the instructions for Windows, Mac, and Linux on the AWS website at http://aws.amazon.com/cli/.

I suggest that you follow the "Getting Started" link to the documentation and create an AWS IAM user for the CLI. Attach the following (managed) policies to the user so you can follow all the examples in the book:

- AWSLambdaFullAccess
- AmazonAPIGatewayAdministrator
- AmazonCognitoPowerUser

When you configure the CLI with the `aws configure` command, specify the AWS region you're using now as the default. Otherwise, you'll have to add `--region <the region you want to use>` at the end of all AWS CLI commands hereafter.

I also suggest that you enable automatic command completion for the CLI, as described in the documentation.

To test whether the installation and configuration of the AWS CLI worked, you can get a list of the AWS Lambda functions you created (together with configuration info such as memory size, timeout, execution role, and so on) with `aws lambda list-functions`.

By default, the output of the CLI is in JSON format, but you can change that during the initial configuration or by supplying the `--output` option.

To invoke the function you created, use the following syntax from the command line (note that the JSON event is enclosed between single quotation marks):

```
aws lambda invoke --function-name <function name> --payload '<JSON event>'
<local output file>
```

> **WARNING** If you're using a Windows CLI to execute the AWS Lambda invoke commands, you need to replace single quotes with double quotes and escape them by repeating them twice; for example, --payload '<JSON event>' becomes --payload "{"""name""":""John""}"

The output of the function is written to a local file. For example, to greet "John," run the following command from the command line:

```
aws lambda invoke --function-name greetingsOnDemand --payload
'{"name":"John"}' output.txt
```

> **WARNING** If you didn't specify the same region you used for AWS Lambda during the configuration of the AWS CLI, you'll get an error from the previous command unless you add --region <the region you want to use> at the end.

Run the following command from the command line to test the default behavior when no name is provided and receive a "Hello World!":

```
aws lambda invoke --function-name greetingsOnDemand-py --payload '{}'
output.txt
```

You can see the results of the function by looking at the content of the output.txt file after each invocation. The file is created in the same directory where the command is executed. You can specify a different location in the command line if you prefer to use a different directory (for example, /tmp/output.txt or C:/Temp/output.txt).

> **TIP** This file is overwritten each time the CLI is used. You can keep previous results by using a different filename each time.

The AWS CLI has an embedded help system that can give more details on how to invoke a function. To see the help, run the following command from the command line:

```
aws lambda invoke help
```

As discussed in the first chapter, you now call the function directly using the AWS Lambda Invoke API, and the AWS CLI is your client application (figure 2.7).

You used the AWS CLI to invoke and execute Lambda functions, but a similar syntax is available via the AWS SDKs for different programming languages to embed function invocations in a more complex application. Specifically, a simplified syntax to

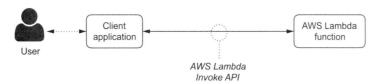

Figure 2.7 Calling AWS Lambda functions from the AWS CLI using the Invoke API

invoke Lambda functions is available in the Mobile SDKs. You'll see how to invoke a function with the JavaScript SDK, and a sample use case from the Mobile SDKs, in chapter 5.

The programming language used by the client application can be different from the one you used to write the function code as they're decoupled and communicate with each other via the AWS Lambda Invoke API. In fact, you can use a different runtime for each function—for example choosing one depending on the syntax, or the available libraries, that can make the development of the function easier.

> **TIP** You saw how to use the AWS CLI with `aws lambda invoke` to invoke a Lambda function. In the same way, using the AWS CLI, you can create or update the configuration or the code of a Lambda function. Try `aws lambda help` to see all available options.

Summary

In this chapter you created your first AWS Lambda function. In particular, you learned

- How the event and the context are used by the function
- All configurations required by AWS Lambda to execute a function
- How to quickly test a function within the web console
- How to invoke a function via the AWS Lambda API, using the AWS CLI

In the next chapter you'll learn how to expose a function via HTTP with a standard web API interface, using the Amazon API Gateway.

EXERCISE

In this chapter you created a function managed by AWS Lambda to greet you on demand. But always saying "Hello" can be boring. What about adding the option to specify a custom greeting as an option to the function? Of course, the default behavior when no custom greeting is provided would continue to say "Hello."

Create a new `customGreetingsOnDemand` function to implement this feature, adding a new `greet` parameter in the input event.

Try passing "Hi" as the value of `greet`. The result should be

```
"Hi John!"
```

Are you managing the edge cases when no greeting or no name is provided?

Solution

Working code for the `customGreetingsOnDemand` function using Node.js is in the next listing; for Python, see the last listing. Your code could be slightly different, for example, depending on how you manage the edge cases where no greeting or no name is provided.

The JSON event that you pass to the function should specify a `greet` and a `name`, but can optionally omit one or both of them:

```
{
  "greet": "Hi",
  "name": "John"
}
```

Function `customGreetingsOnDemand` (Node.js)

```
console.log('Loading function');

exports.handler = (event, context, callback) => {
    console.log('Received event:',
        JSON.stringify(event, null, 2));
    console.log('greet =', event.greet);
    console.log('name =', event.name);
    var greet = '';
    if ('greet' in event) {
        greet = event.greet;
    } else {
        greet = 'Hello';
    };
    var name = '';
    if ('name' in event) {
        name = event.name;
    } else {
        name = 'World';
    }
    var greetings = greet + ' ' + name + '!';
    console.log(greetings);
    callback(null, greetings);
};
```

> The new "greet" parameter is received as part of the event and is managed in a similar way to the "name" before.

> The "greet" is used to compute the result here.

Function `customGreetingsOnDemand` (Python)

```
import json

print('Loading function')

def lambda_handler(event, context):
    print('Received event: ' +
        json.dumps(event, indent=2))
```

```
if 'greet' in event:
    greet = event['greet']
else:
    greet = 'Hello'
if 'name' in event:
    name = event['name']
else:
    name = 'World'
greetings = greet + ' ' + name + '!'
print(greetings)
return greetings
```

The new "greet" parameter is received as part of the event and is managed in a similar way to the "name" before.

The "greet" is used to compute the result here.

Your function as a web API

3

> **This chapter covers**
> - Introducing the Amazon API Gateway
> - Exposing functions as web APIs
> - Customizing the integration between web API and function
> - Testing the web API from the web console, a browser, or the command line
> - Using the API Gateway context in a function

In the previous chapter you built your first AWS Lambda function, learned how to configure the function, edited the code, and quickly tested the function from the web console. You then used the function via the AWS command-line interface (CLI).

In this chapter you'll make your function available over HTTP as a web API using the Amazon API Gateway. You'll learn how to integrate a Lambda function with the API Gateway and test that using the web console, a browser, or a command-line tool. You'll also build a new Lambda function to see how the API Gateway context can be used by a function to have more information about who's calling the web API.

3.1   *Introducing the Amazon API Gateway*

You've learned how to create a single function using AWS Lambda and invoke the function using the Invoke API via the AWS CLI. A similar syntax can be used with any AWS SDK. How can you extend that knowledge to create a web API?

One of the advantages of AWS Lambda is the integration with the Amazon API Gateway to access AWS Lambda functions without using the AWS APIs, CLI, or SDKs: you can use functions via a web API that you design.

Web APIs use a URL to identify an endpoint (for example, https://my.webapi.com) and HTTP verbs (or methods, such as GET, POST, PUT, and DELETE) to interact with the endpoint.

It's possible to build RESTful APIs with the Amazon API Gateway and AWS Lambda, but that's not the focus of this book. Design your web API following the Representational State Transfer (REST) architectural style and use the same techniques described in this book for the actual implementation.

> **TIP**   If you want more information on how to design RESTful APIs, I suggest you look at the original PhD dissertation by Roy Thomas Fielding, "Architectural Styles and the Design of Network-based Software Architectures": https://www.ics.uci.edu/~fielding/pubs/dissertation/top.htm.

With the Amazon API Gateway, you can map web APIs to back end functions that can be implemented using AWS Lambda or an internet-available HTTP invocation (hosted within or outside of AWS), including other AWS APIs or mock implementations. In this book I focus on using Lambda functions for the back end, and I don't include examples for the other implementations.

> **TIP**   If you want to migrate a legacy HTTP-based API to AWS Lambda, you can start using the Amazon API Gateway as a proxy interface to your old implementation and then move one interaction at a time to AWS Lambda, keeping a consistent interface to the clients of the API during the migration.

With the Amazon API Gateway, you build an API that can have different stages. A *stage* defines the path (between the domain and the resources) through which a deployed API is accessible and can be used to specify different environments, such as production, test, and development, or different versions of an API, such as v0, v1, and so on.

Each stage maps the access to URL endpoints, specified as resources, with an HTTP verb (such as GET, POST, PUT, or DELETE) to methods. The methods can be implemented as Lambda functions to provide a serverless back end that's simpler to manage and scale than a traditional web server architecture (figure 3.1). A unique domain is automatically generated for you and you can optionally customize it with a domain you own.

For example, consider a simple bookstore implementation, where you can store information for multiple books, with a web API, as described in table 3.1.

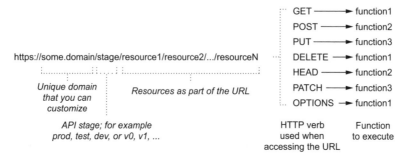

Figure 3.1   How the Amazon API Gateway can map URLs and HTTP verbs to the execution of an AWS Lambda function

Table 3.1   A sample bookstore web API

Resource	HTTP verb	Action
/books	GET	Returns the list of books, within a certain interval specified via parameters or iterators
/books	POST	Creates a new book, specifying the book characteristics (Title, Author, ISBN, and so on) via parameters, and returns the id of the new book
/books/{id}	GET	Returns the information on the book specified by the id
/books/{id}	PUT	Creates or updates the book specified by the id
/books/{id}	DELETE	Deletes the book specified by the id

With the Amazon API Gateway you can map actions to specific methods that can be implemented by AWS Lambda functions (table 3.2).

Table 3.2   A sample bookstore web API implemented as AWS Lambda functions

Resource	HTTP verb	Method (using AWS Lambda functions)
/books	GET	getBooksByRange
/books	POST	createNewBook
/books/{id}	GET	getBookById
/books/{id}	PUT	createOrUpdateBookById
/books/{id}	DELETE	deleteBookById

If you implement the bookstore API with two stages, prod for production and test for testing, you can get the list of books in production with an HTTP GET on https:// some.domain/prod/books and delete the book with id equal to 5 in test with a HTTP DELETE on https://some.domain/test/books/5.

3.2 Creating the API

To start simple, let's build a basic web API to invoke our `greetingsOnDemand` function, using an HTTP GET with query parameters to get the result, as described in table 3.3. The `/greeting` resource is part of a wider API that you'll create in this chapter.

Table 3.3 Greetings on demand via web API

Resource	HTTP verb	Method (using AWS Lambda)
/greeting	GET	greetingsOnDemand

Go to the Application Services section of the Amazon API Gateway web console. Although not a strict requirement, it's a good idea to choose the same region you used previously to create your first lambda function. Select Get Started. If you already have APIs in that region, you can select Create API.

> **WARNING** The first time you use the API Gateway console, you're prompted to create an example API. You can avoid that by selecting the "New API" option, because you're reading this book and already know what to build.

You can now create a generic utility API that you can use and extend with different features over time. Type "My Utilities" as the API name, and leave the default option to not clone them from an existing API selected. Type "A set of small utilities" as the description, and select Create API (figure 3.2).

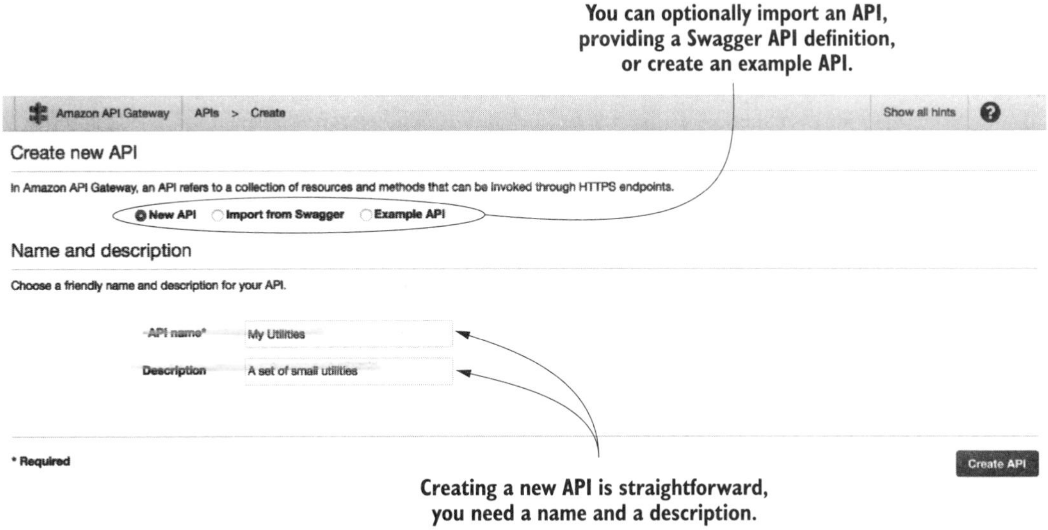

Figure 3.2 Create a new web API that will use the AWS Lambda function you created.

Each API has a custom endpoint (which you can personalize with a domain you own and the relative SSL/TLS certificate). Within that endpoint you can create multiple stages and resources as part of the URL. Resources are specified via a path that's part of the URL and can be nested within each other.

Leave the default resource (/) empty and create one for our /greeting by selecting Create Resource from the Actions menu, and typing "Greeting" as the resource name. This automatically populates the resource path as "greeting" (lowercase). That's fine for this example, and you can proceed by selecting Create Resource (figure 3.3).

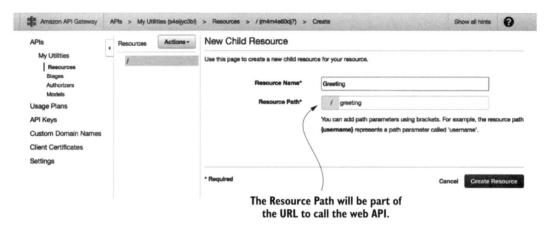

Figure 3.3   Creating a new resource for an API. Resources are specified via a path and can be nested within each other.

The /greeting resource appears on the left of the console, and you can now connect the resource with a method. With /greeting selected, which should be the default after the creation of the resource, choose Create Method from the Actions menu, and choose the HTTP verb GET from the list. Confirm the selection by clicking the check mark to the right of the list.

TIP   To simplify complex configurations, instead of specifying each HTTP verb individually (such as GET, POST, PUT, and so on), you can use the ANY method that will trigger the integration for all kind of requests. The actual method used is passed in input to the function, so that the logic can be different depending on the HTTP verb used.

3.3   *Creating the integration*

You can now choose the integration type. The Amazon API Gateway can be integrated with different kinds of back ends, including legacy web services or mock implementations. To test the integration with AWS Lambda to implement a serverless back end, select Lambda Function.

Choose the region you used to create your first function. The region of the AWS Lambda function can be different from the one you are using the Amazon API Gateway for now, but for the sake of simplicity you should use the same region.

In the Lambda Function field, type the first character of the name of the function you created before (for example, "g" if you used "greetingsOnDemand" as the function name). Type more characters to narrow down the list of matches if you have many functions, then select the function from the list and click Save (figure 3.4). In the dialog box that appears, confirm that you give permission to the API Gateway to invoke the function.

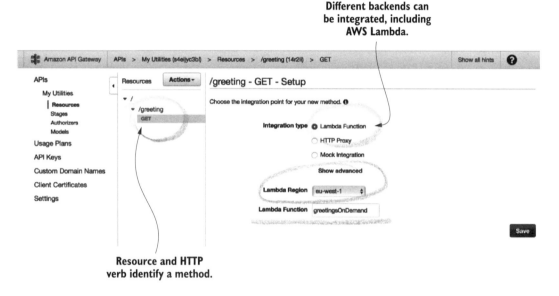

Figure 3.4   Creating a new method on a resource, and choosing the integration type. In this case, you are using a Lambda function to be executed.

You now see on the screen the overall flow of the method execution for an HTTP GET on the /greeting resource (figure 3.5).

Starting from the left, following the execution flow of a request coming from a client, you have in clockwise order:

1   The client invoking the API. At the top there is a Test link to quickly test the integration from the web console.
2   A Method Request section to select the parameters you want to receive as input.

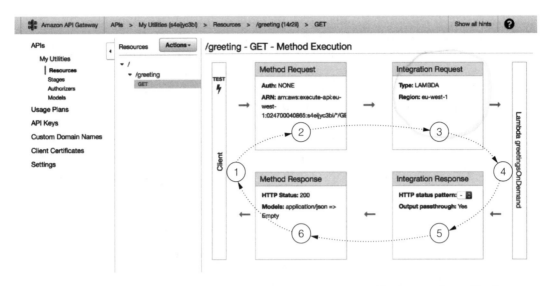

Figure 3.5   The overall method execution flow, from the client to the back-end implementation and back

3 An Integration Request section to map those parameters in the JSON format
   AWS Lambda expects in input.

4 The back-end implementation, in this case using AWS Lambda with the greetingsOnDemand function.

5 An Integration Response section to extract and map the response of the AWS
   Lambda to different HTTP return statuses (for instance, 200 OK) and formats
   ("application/json" is one of them, but probably the most common). Here you
   can also manage errors returned by the function to map them to HTTP error
   codes (for example, should the error returned by the function be mapped to a
   4xx or a 5xx HTTP error?).

6 A Method Response section to customize the HTTP response, including HTTP
   headers.

For our implementation, you need to use a name parameter, so select Method Request
and then expand the URL Query String Parameters section. Add "name" as a query
string. Remember to confirm by clicking the check mark.

Go back by selecting Method Execution at the top. You now need to put the name
parameter in JSON syntax as AWS Lambda expects. Select Integration Request and
expand the Body Mapping Templates section to add a mapping template. Set the
"Request body passthrough" to the recommended option of "When there are no
templates defined." This will let the body (for example, from an HTTP POST) be
passed to the integration (the Lambda function in this case) when no template
exists. It won't be our case, because you're creating one: select "Add mapping template" and write "application/json" as the content type; you need to write it in the

text field even if it's the suggested value. Select the checkmark to the right of the text field to confirm.

In the template area that appears, don't use the drop-down menu to generate a template. The generate template menu is especially useful if you create a *model*. Models, defined by the Amazon API Gateway using JSON Schema,[1] are useful when the same data model is used in more than one method. For example, a model for a book would include title, author, ISBN, and all other fields you want to manage.

> **NOTE** You aren't using a model for this first example, but using models is a good design principle and makes your code cleaner and easier to update, especially if you want to generate a strongly typed SDK from your API.

For now, write the template yourself to be

```
{ "name": "$input.params('name')" }
```

This will build a JSON object with the `name` key equal to the content of the `name` parameter you just configured. The `$input` variable is part of a set that you can use in templates and models too. In particular, `$input.params('someParameter')` returns the value of the input parameter specified in the quotes. A complete reference to the variables used by the Amazon API Gateway is available at http://www.mng.bz/11iJ.

> **TIP** The names of the JSON key and the HTTP parameter could be different, but my suggestion is to use the same name if that makes sense, or use a standard naming convention, such as adding "Param" to the end of the HTTP parameter name (that is, "nameParam" in our case).

Save to confirm. Our integration is done, and you'll test it shortly within the API Gateway console.

3.4 Testing the integration

Go back to Method Execution at the top. Click Test at the top of the client section.

You can now specify a value for the `name` parameter; use "John" or another name, if you prefer. Click the Test button. You should see "Hello John!" (or whatever name you used) in the Response Body (figure 3.6).

Congratulations, you called your Lambda function via HTTP! But you're still in a test environment. And you aren't respecting the web API syntax: you have "application/json" as the Content-Type in the Response Headers section (expand that section in the web console to check), but a string (that is, "Hello John!") as the response body, which isn't a valid JSON output.

---

[1] JSON Schema is a way to describe your JSON data format. For more information, please see http://json-schema.org.

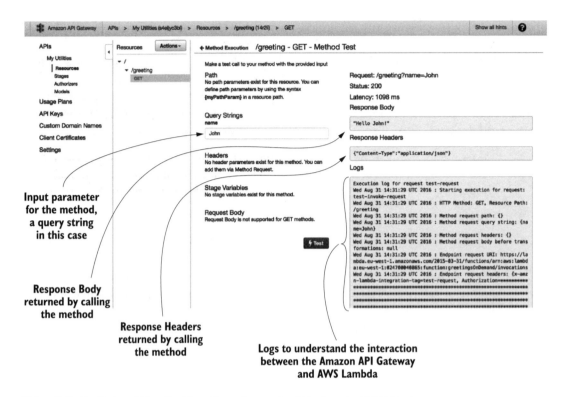

Figure 3.6   Testing an API method from the web console of the Amazon API Gateway

You could change the output of the Lambda function itself, but let's instead use the powerful integrations that the API Gateway provides to manipulate the response from the back end.

> **TIP**   This is a useful exercise because it's often easier to manage this kind of integration in a gateway than it is to change the back end code itself. This is a powerful approach, especially if the back end implementation is managed by a different team or based on a legacy web service implementation that's difficult to change, or if other clients are consuming the back end implementation directly and you don't want to change those interactions.

3.5   *Transforming the response*

Currently you're not doing any transformation on the response, as you can see by expanding the Logs section in the result of the test (figure 3.7).

Let's change that by going back to Method Execution at the top and selecting Integration Response. Expand the only response available (only one is configured by default in the Method Response step), then expand Body Mapping Templates. Select "application/json" and change "Output passthrough" to be a JSON output, using the

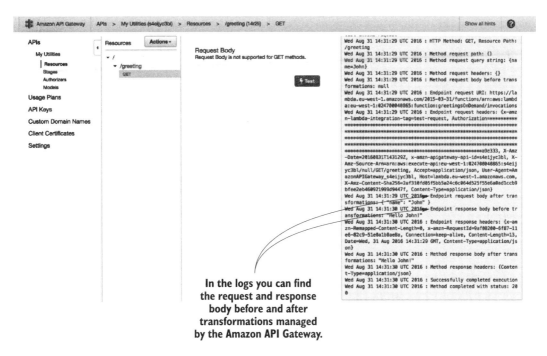

In the logs you can find
the request and response
body before and after
transformations managed
by the Amazon API Gateway.

Figure 3.7   Detailed logs from the Amazon API Gateway show that no transformation was done on the response (body) from the AWS Lambda function.

following mapping template in a way similar to what you did previously for the "Input passthrough" option:

```
{ "greeting": "$input.path('$')" }
```

The $ in the $input.path represents the overall response received by the API Gateway, which is put in as the value of the greeting key.

> **WARNING**   Don't use the "Add integration response" option now. That option is useful if you want to give back different HTTP status codes (for example 201, 302, 404, and so on), depending on patterns in the return value of the Lambda function.

Save and go back to Method Execution again to run another test, using your favorite "name" in the query strings. Click the Test button to actually run a new test and overwrite the result. Now the response body has a fully compliant JSON syntax.

Try it now to test sending an empty name parameter. If no name is provided, you probably expect to get back a default "Hello World!" But that's not the case, and "Hello !" is returned instead, because the name key in the JSON payload that's sent to the Lambda function is always present. It's prepared by our input mapping template to be an empty string in this case.

Again, to get the expected behavior you could modify the Lambda function to handle an empty name the way it handles a missing name key. But you can do that in the API Gateway integration without changing the back end implementation, similar to what you did previously for the response.

To change the default behavior for our REST API, go back to Method Execution and select Integration Request. Change the mapping template to include the name key only if the name parameter isn't empty using an #if ... #end block. To make the template easier to read and avoid repetitions, use #set to set the variable $name to the value of the name input parameter:

```
#set($name = $input.params('name'))
{
#if($name != "")
  "name": "$name"
#end
}
```

Confirm the change by saving. Run a few tests using an empty or not empty name and see if everything works as expected and you get a "Hello World" with an empty name.

> **NOTE**   You may have found the syntax of the input and output mapping templates familiar. To describe a mapping template, the Amazon API Gateway uses the Velocity Template Language (VTL), as described in the Apache Velocity Project: https://velocity.apache.org.

Now that all tests work and the API is ready for release, select Deploy API from the Actions menu to make it available as a public API.

Because this is the first deployment for this API, you need to create a new "stage." Use "prod" as the stage name (this will go in the URL of the web API), "Production" as the stage description, and "First deployment" as the deployment description (figure 3.8).

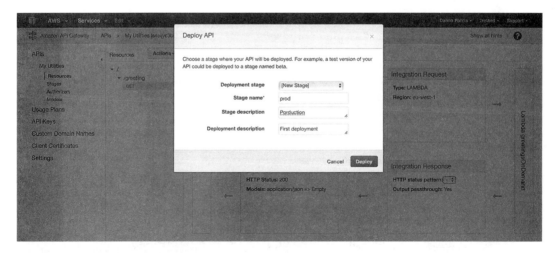

Figure 3.8   First deployment of the new API: you have to create a new stage.

Congratulations, you deployed you first API publicly with the Amazon API Gateway! Using the Amazon API Gateway, you can change other important characteristics of your deployment, such as enabling caching, throttling, and integration with Amazon CloudWatch for metrics and logs (figure 3.9). You also have the option to generate the SDK for multiple platforms and export your API in text format.

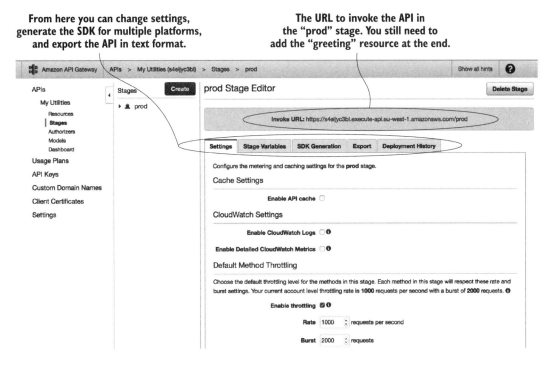

Figure 3.9 Stage configuration for caching, logging, and throttling. The URL to invoke the API in this stage is at the top. You have to add the resource at the end to have a successful invocation.

For now, look at the Deployment History tab (figure 3.10). You can find all the deployments you've done for that API, and you can easily roll back to a previous version if something isn't working with your latest deployment. You can also use the deployment history to push a deployment to a different stage; for example, to release in a production stage a deployment that's been tested and validated in a test stage.

TIP From the SDK Generation panel, you can automatically generate the SDK of your API for the selected stage for multiple platforms: Android, iOS, JavaScript. Try to generate the SDK for JavaScript; you'll automatically download it locally from the browser.

Now you can test the API in a browser. It's relatively simple, because you're using the GET HTTP verb that's the default used by browsers. Return to the Settings panel, and

The deployment
history for your API

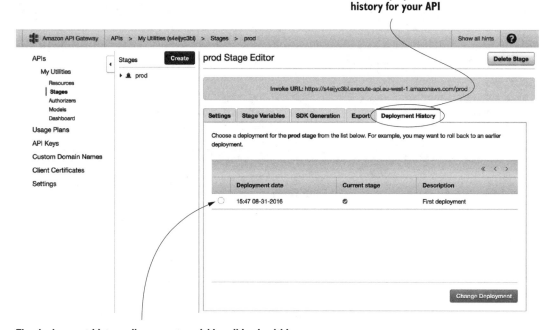

The deployment history allows you to quickly roll back within
a stage to a previous deployment or to repeat the same
deployment in another stage, for example replicating the
state of a "test" stage in production.

Figure 3.10   The deployment history can be used within a stage; for example, to roll back to a previous
deployment, or between different stages, to do the same deployment in another stage.

in the left pane of the window just below Stages, expand the stage name "prod" to see
the configuration of all resources and methods deployed in this stage (figure 3.11).

Choose the HTTP verb GET from the list below the /greeting resource (figure 3.12). You can change method-specific settings, but for now, leave the default
settings inherited from the stage. The Invoke URL has now been updated with the
full URL of the method.

> **WARNING**   If you don't select the GET method, the Invoke URL will link to the
> root of the stage and miss /greeting at the end. If you try to use that URL in
> a browser, you'll get an error, because no method was associated with the root
> resource, / .

Copy the Invoke URL at the top of the page. You can click the Invoke URL link, but that
will change the content of the current browser tab. It's better if you open a new tab in
the browser and paste the invoke URL you copied into the address bar. You should see
"Hello World!" in the response JSON payload because no name was provided.

**Select the small arrow close to "prod"
to see all the resources and the methods
deployed in the stage**

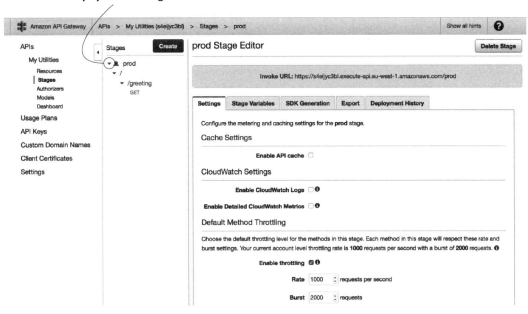

Figure 3.11   Selecting the arrow close to the stage name, you can see all the resources and methods deployed in this stage.

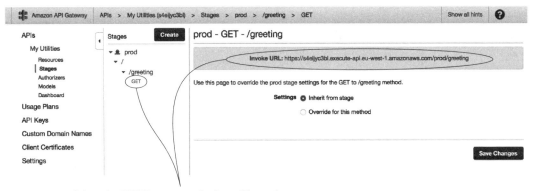

**Select the "GET" to see method-specific settings
(that can be inherited from the stage or customized)
and update the Invoke URL to include "/greeting" at the end.**

Figure 3.12   When you select a method, such as GET, the Invoke URL is updated to link to that method and you can set method-specific settings or inherit the default settings from the stage.

Add "?name=John" at the end of the previous URL to specify a name as a query parameter. Be careful if you want to use different names; certain characters may require URL encoding, so use basic single-word names for now. You should get a "Hello John!" in the response JSON payload.

Depending on the plugins you installed, certain browsers may manage or format JSON content differently. To check, you can test the API from the command line using a tool such as `curl`, an open-source tool for transferring data with URL syntax, which is already installed in most Linux and Mac environments:

```
curl https://<your endpoint>/prod/greetings
curl https://<your endpoint>/prod/greetings?name=John
```

> **TIP** If you don't have `curl` available in your system, you may install it using a package manager (depending on the OS/distribution you are using) or download it (it's available for most OSs, including Windows) from http://curl.haxx.se.

With `curl` you can play with other HTTP verbs, such as `POST` and `DELETE`, which aren't used by this simple API. If you're going to develop a more complex API in the future, `curl` will be a useful tool for testing and prototyping.

> **NOTE** The API will be public and available without authentication, because you didn't select an Authorization in the Method Execution section. For Authentication, you can use AWS credentials (via AWS IAM) or configure a Custom Authorizer for your API. What's interesting about Custom Authorizers is that they're implemented via a specific Lambda function; this function evaluates the input parameters you select and returns a valid AWS IAM policy that gives the required authorization. You'll learn about AWS IAM policies in chapter 4.

3.6   *Using resource paths as parameters*

Our `/greeting` API method uses query parameters to pass the name to greet, with a syntax such as "/greetings?name=John". Let's replace the generic first name you used before with a unique identifier; for example, a "username" such as "JohnDoe123" that could uniquely identify a user in a repository.

We can think of "/user/JohnDoe123" as a unique resource representing a user. Wouldn't it be nice to greet this user with a syntax such as "/user/JohnDoe123/greet"?

> **WARNING** For a web API following a RESTful API design pattern, a URL should identify a unique resource, usually by ID. This isn't the case for a generic "name" as in the previous examples. Better examples in a RESTful context are "/book/{bookId}" or "/user/{username}." We use "/user/{username}/greet" to avoid changing the function and keep things simple, but still make you learn something new. Also consider that as stated before, RESTful API design isn't the focus of this book.

With the API Gateway you can configure a resource path as a variable parameter that can be used by the method execution. Select Resources from the left. Starting from / (which must be selected), create a new "User" resource (leave the default "user" value in the resource path), and with /user selected create a new depending resource using "Username" as the resource name and "{username}" as the resource path. Because the resource path is enclosed by curly brackets, it's interpreted by the API Gateway as a parameter. Note that the resources can have nested resources, and they all join together to form the path of the URL to call to access the web API.

> **TIP** You can use catchall path variables by adding a "+" at the end of the name of the parameters. For example, "/user/{username+}" would intercept any request that starts with "/user/", such as "/user/JohnDoe123/goodbye".

Now, keeping the "Username" resource selected, create a "Greet" resource (leave the default "greet" value in the resource path) and add a GET method to the /greet resource. You should have a configuration similar to figure 3.13.

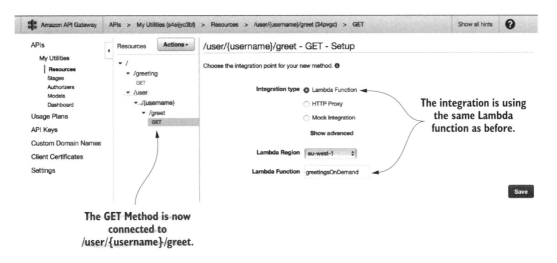

Figure 3.13 Using resource paths as parameters for the greetingsOnDemand function

Now integrate this method with the same Lambda function as before, following almost the same steps as when you created the /greeting method, but with one important change: you have to map the username parameter of the API Gateway to the name key in the event of the function. In the previous method, both parameters were called name, but now they're different. To do that, change the mapping template for the integration request to be

```
#set($name = $input.params('username'))
{
#if($name != "")
  "name": "$name"
```

```
#end
}
```

You can use the same mapping template as before for the integration response because it's only wrapping the result of the Lambda function in JSON syntax.

> **TIP**   If you go to the Method Request section, you can see a new Path section that when expanded already has the `username` parameter configured. You don't need to add resource path parameters to the method request; they're automatically taken from the resources connected to the method.

When testing the method from the web console, you should have an output similar to figure 3.14.

Deploy the updated API in the same stage ("prod") with a meaningful deployment description, such as "Greeting by username added," and test the new method from the command line using `curl`:

```
curl https://<your endpoint>/prod/users/JohnDoe123/greet
```

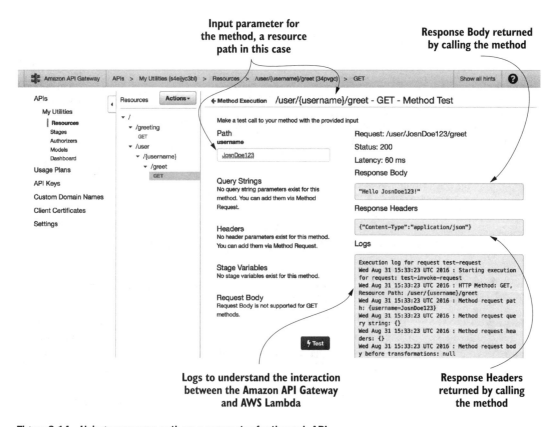

Figure 3.14   Using a resource path as a parameter for the web API

NOTE In a more complex scenario, you could add logic in the Lambda function to handle a `username` in a different way than a `name` in the event. For example, if the input event contains a `username`, the Lambda function could look up the first name of the user in a database and use that to build the output greeting.

3.7 *Using the API Gateway context*

Now let's try to integrate a Lambda function with the context provided by the API Gateway, building a web API that returns the public IP address used to call it. You can call this API "What is my IP?"

How can you get the IP address used to call a web API? In the documentation of the Amazon API Gateway a reference appears of all the variables used by the mapping templates: http://www.mng.bz/11iJ.

There you can find that the `$context.identity.sourceIp` variable contains the IP address of the API caller. That's exactly what you need. To use this variable and implement the "What is my IP?" API, you need to complete two steps:

1. Pass the value of this variable from the Amazon API Gateway to an AWS Lambda function in the back end.
2. Implement a basic Lambda function that gets this value in input and sends back the same value in output as the result.

Let's start with the Lambda function. Create a new function called `whatIsMyIp` with the code in the following listing for Node.js or listing 3.2 for Python.

Listing 3.1 Function `whatIsMyIp` (Node.js)

```
exports.handler = (event, context, callback) => {
  callback(null, event.myip);
};
```

Listing 3.2 Function `whatIsMyIp` (Python)

```
def lambda_handler(event, context):
    return event['myip']
```

Write a meaningful description and use the default values for memory and timeout. The basic execution role is still enough because it has no interactions with other AWS services within the function.

To test the function before the API Gateway integration, in the AWS Lambda console you can use a test event that will simulate what the function will receive from the API Gateway:

```
{
  "myip": "1.1.1.1"
}
```

You should get the IP address (here, "1.1.1.1") as output.

In the Amazon API Gateway console, select the API you created earlier in this chapter ("My Utilities" if you used what I suggested).

Select the root resource, /, and then select Create Resource. Use "My IP" as the resource name, leave the default "/my-ip" as the resource path, and select Create Resource.

With /my-ip selected, choose Create Method and select GET. Remember to confirm via the check mark. Your API should now have two resources, as illustrated in table 3.4.

Table 3.4   Adding "What is my IP?" to the My Utilities API

Resource	HTTP verb	Method (using AWS Lambda)
/greeting	GET	greetingsOnDemand
/user/{username}/greet	GET	greetingsOnDemand
/my-ip	GET	whatIsMyIp

This API call is mapped to a Lambda function, so choose the region and the whatIsMyIp function you created, and confirm access permission for the API Gateway to invoke the function.

Now you need to extract the source IP address from the context of the API Gateway and put that into the JSON payload used to invoke the function. It looks similar to what you already did for the /greeting resource, but this time you don't need to do anything in the method request because the parameter you need (the source IP address) isn't explicit for those invoking the function.

But you do need to configure the integration request to use the value from the context. Select Integration Request and expand the Body Mapping Templates section. You need to build a JSON payload including the source IP as expected by the what-IsMyIp function.

Add a mapping template that gets the source IP address from the context of the API Gateway and puts that into the myip key of the event:

```
{
  "myip": "$context.identity.sourceIp"
}
```

TIP   The $context variable can return useful information about how the web API call has been received by the Amazon API Gateway. For example $context.resourcePath contains the path of the resource and $context.stage the stage used. You can pass those values in the integration to tailor the behavior of a function, depending on the path or the stage used to call it.

Save, go back to Method Execution, and run a test.

You should see in the response body something such as "test-invoke-source-ip," because the test invocation in the web console is populating the context with a "fake" value for the source IP address.

As in the previous use of the API Gateway, you return an "application/json" Content-Type, but the return value isn't JSON.

Fix that in the Integration Response in a way similar to what you did for the /greeting API. The mapping template to use should be something like this:

```
{ "myip": "$input.path('$')" }
```

If you prefer to have a simple answer with just the IP address and no JSON syntax, you can change the Method Response Content-Type to be "text/plain". Or you can support multiple Content-Types, depending on the request.

Now deploy the API in production as you did before, using the same stage ("prod") and a meaningful description (for example, "What is my IP added").

In the Deployment History tab, you can now see the two deployments you made for the production stage, with the latest one selected. You can always roll back to a previous version if needed.

Now test the API in a browser by opening a new tab using the invoke URL. Remember to click the GET method to have "/my-ip" at the end of the URL; otherwise, you'll get an error.

If you prefer, you can use the curl command-line interface:

```
curl https://<your endpoint>/prod/my-ip
```

It should return your public IP. You probably already saw multiple implementations of a similar web API. What's interesting with this approach is that it's completely serverless; availability and scalability are managed by AWS Lambda, and the overall costs are low. You shouldn't incur any costs unless the number of invocations exceeds the free tier—for example, more than 1 million invocations per month.

You've now created two functions using AWS Lambda, greetingOnDemand and whatIsMyIp. You then exposed those functions publicly in a web API that you can use with standard tools, such as web browsers or tools like curl, which have no knowledge of AWS Lambda or of other AWS APIs (figure 3.15).

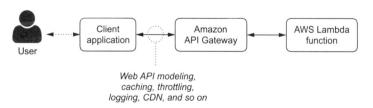

Figure 3.15   Using the Amazon API Gateway to give public access to AWS Lambda functions via a web API

In particular, you used the Amazon API Gateway to enable public access to web APIs created by AWS Lambda functions. The API you implemented returns JSON content, as is common for APIs consumed by other applications.

Built-in Lambda proxy integration template

To simplify the integration of Lambda functions with the Amazon API Gateway, a new default integration has been added as an option. If you configure the Amazon API Gateway as the trigger of your functions in the Lambda console, this integration is automatically selected for you.

This integration template provides a standard way to send to the Lambda function all the parameters used to call the web API (such as query, path parameters, HTTP headers, HTTP method, and so on).

A default syntax to send back HTTP return code, headers, and the body of the response is also put in place. Using this syntax, you only need to work on the Lambda function code and you can lease the configuration in the API Gateway console as it is. The configurations you used in this chapter, using custom mapping templates, are still available.

I suggest you to evaluate this syntax and use it in your new projects, as it can simplify your development workflow.

Summary

In this chapter you exposed your first AWS Lambda function as a web API, learning how to

- Integrate a Lambda function with a method of the API Gateway
- Pass parameters over HTTP to the function in different ways
- Format the result of the function as the response of the web API
- Quickly test the integration of the API Gateway from the web console
- Use the context provided by the API Gateway within a Lambda function

In the next chapter you'll see in more detail how you can use multiple functions together, several of them called directly by the client and others subscribed to specific resources, to build an application that's driven by events.

EXERCISE _____

Looking back at the exercise in the previous chapter, I'd like you to expose the `customGreetingsOnDemand` function as a web API using the Amazon API Gateway, using both of the following syntaxes:

```
https://<your endpoint>/<stage>/say?greet=Hi&name=John
https://<your endpoint>/<stage>/users/{username}/say/{greet}
```

The result with the first syntax, using John as the value of name and Hi as the value of greet, should be

```
{ "greeting": "Hi John!" }
```

With the second syntax, using JohnDoe123 as the value of username and Hi as the value of greet, the URL should be

```
https://<your endpoint>/<stage>/users/JohnDoe123/say/Hi
```

The result should be

```
{ "greeting": "Hi JohnDoe123!" }
```

Are you managing the edge cases when no greet or no name is provided in the URL? If so, are you managing the edge cases in the function or in the web API integration?

Solution

In my solution I manage the edge cases when one or both of the input parameters are missing in the web API integration, keeping the function as simple as possible, as in the solution of the exercise of the previous chapter.

In the API Gateway, two methods should be created, corresponding to the two syntaxes to be supported by the web API:

- One on the resource /say, with GET. Don't forget to add two URL query string parameters in the Method Request section: greet and name.
- One on the resource /user/{username}/say/{greet}, with GET. You need to create the different resources used here to build the path one step at a time: for example, first /user, then, with /user selected, /{username}, and so on. In this case the two parameters, username and greet, are passed as request paths and don't need to be configured in the Method Request section.

Both methods should use the same customGreetingsOnDemand function. This is an interesting pattern: you can create a single Lambda function that, depending on how it's invoked, can be used and integrated with multiple resources of a web API.

Building a valid JSON input for the function with two optional parameters (both greet and name could be missing) is trickier than before, when you had a single parameter. The following listing shows a possible mapping template for the integration request of the first syntax.

customGreetingsOnDemand mapping template (only query parameters)

```
#set($greet = $input.params('greet'))
#set($name = $input.params('name'))
{
#if($greet != "")
  "greet": "$greet"
```

```
#if($name != "")
   ,
   #end
#end
#if($name != "")
   "name": "$name"
#end
}
```

With the second syntax, using the `username` request path parameter, you should replace `'name'` with `'username'` in the second line, as shown in the next listing.

customGreetingsOnDemand mapping template (with path parameters)

```
#set($greet = $input.params('greet'))
#set($name = $input.params('username'))
{
#if($greet != "")
   "greet": "$greet"
   #if($name != "")
   ,
   #end
#end
#if($name != "")
   "name": "$name"
#end
}
```

If you manage the default values for both parameters in the function, checking not only that the parameters are present but also that their values aren't the empty string, then you can simplify the mapping template to build the JSON input for the function:

```
{ "greet": "$input.params('greet')",
  "name": "$input.params('name')" }
```

The integration response should be exactly the same as the one you used before for the `greetingsOnDemand` function.

Choosing the right balance between what to put in a function and what in the integration is a fine art. My general advice is to put everything that's relevant to the business logic in the function (which can be used in different ways, not just via a web API) and use the web API integration to manage and format the I/O of parameters and results.

Part 2

Building event-driven applications

Now that you know the foundations, you can use Lambda function for more interesting purposes. You'll need a deep focus on security and an understanding of how to give functions the permissions they need to do their jobs. You'll then learn how to use external module, libraries, and even binaries with your functions, using them from a web browser or a mobile app.

Diving deeper with Amazon Cognito, you'll build a full authentication service and then a media-sharing application. In the last chapter of this part, you'll look back at what you built to understand the advantages and the impacts of having an event-driven application running on a distributed architecture.

Managing security

4

This chapter covers

- Introducing AWS Identity and Access Management
- Writing policies to allow or deny access to AWS resources
- Using policy variables to make policies more flexible
- Assuming roles to avoid the use of hard-coded AWS credentials
- Using roles with AWS Lambda functions

In the previous chapters, you created your first functions. At first you used those functions directly, using the AWS Lambda interface from the command line. Later, you exposed those functions via a web API provided by the Amazon API Gateway.

This chapter introduces the security framework provided by AWS, mostly based on AWS Identity and Access Management (IAM). You'll learn how to protect your functions and applications implemented using AWS Lambda and (optionally) the Amazon API Gateway. As an example, any interaction with AWS services, such as AWS Lambda and the resources used by your application, must be protected to avoid unauthorized access (figure 4.1). We'll also look back at the functions we created earlier to see how security was managed there.

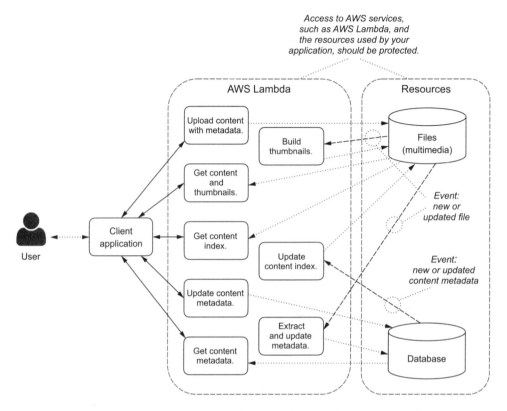

Figure 4.1   You should always protect the use of AWS services and the resources used by your application to avoid unauthorized access. All lines crossing the borders surrounding AWS Lambda and the resources should go through a form of authentication and authorization.

These features are designed to let developers focus on the functionalities they want to build and simplify the realization of an overall secure application. You can use AWS IAM features at no additional cost. Amazon Cognito, which we'll explore in the next chapter, has no charges for authenticating users and generating unique identifiers. This is another reason to use them to secure your AWS resources. The synchronization features of Amazon Cognito do have a charge, but we won't use them in this book.

The first step is to learn how to manage identities within an AWS account.

4.1   *Users, groups, and roles*

To use AWS services, you have to interact with AWS APIs. That can happen directly, via the AWS CLI you used in chapters 1 and 2, via SDKs for your favorite language, or via the web console you used to build the sample functions and the web API in chapters 2 and 3.

In all those interactions, AWS needs to understand who the user making the API call is (this is the *authentication*) and if the user has the necessary permissions to do what's requested in the call (this is the *authorization*).

To provide the necessary authentication, AWS credentials are used to sign API calls. Credentials can be temporary, in which case they have a limited validity in time and must be regenerated (*rotated*, according to the security jargon) every once in a while.

When you create a new AWS account, it only has its own root account credentials that give unrestricted access to all resources within the account, including access to billing information. I recommend you use those root credentials only for the first login and then create users (and roles, as you'll see next in this chapter) with limited permissions for daily use, keeping the root credentials in a safe place for when you need them.

> **TIP** It's good practice to protect root credentials with Multi-Factor Authentication (MFA), using a hardware MFA device or a virtual MFA device running on your smartphone. For more information on MFA, please see https://aws.amazon.com/iam/details/mfa/.

Using AWS Identity and Access Management, you can create *groups* and *users* to reproduce the organization of your company. You can see an example in figure 4.2.

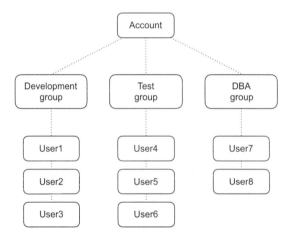

Figure 4.2 **Within an AWS account, you can create groups and users. Users can be added to one or more groups, if that makes sense for your use case.**

> **TIP** Users can be added to more than one group, if that makes sense for your use case. For example, User1 can be part of both the Development and the Test groups.

To create your first groups and users, open your browser and go to https://console .aws.amazon.com. Log in with your AWS credentials and select Identity & Access Management (IAM) from the Security & Identity section.

You'll see the AWS IAM console dashboard (figure 4.3), which provides, among other things, a summary of your IAM resources, the sign-in link for IAM users in your account (which you can customize), and a few tips to improve the security status of your account.

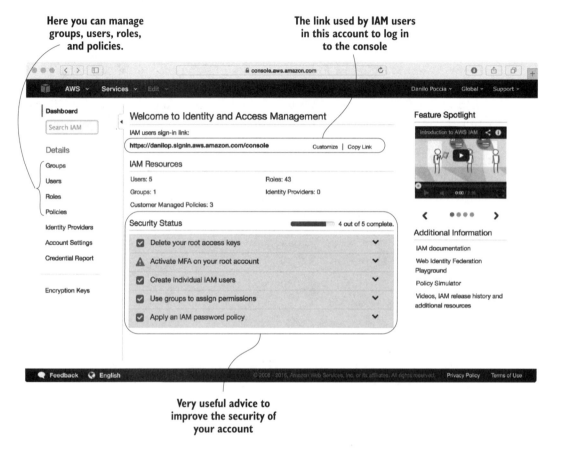

Figure 4.3   The AWS IAM console dashboard, with a summary of your IAM resources, the link that IAM users in your account can use to log in, and the security status of your account

In addition to groups and users, you can create *roles*. The main difference between roles and groups is how they're used:

- Users can be added to groups, inheriting the permissions given to those groups.
- Users, applications, or AWS services can *assume* a role, inheriting the permissions given to the role.

AWS Lambda can use roles: functions can assume a role to get the necessary permissions to do their job. For example, a function can assume a role to get read (or write) permission to a storage service, such as Amazon S3,[1] and then read (or write) data. You can see the relationship between users, groups, and roles within an AWS account in figure 4.4.

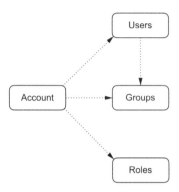

Figure 4.4   This is the relationship between users, groups, and roles within an AWS account. Users can be added to groups, but roles are not linked to a specific user. Roles can be assumed by users, applications, or AWS services.

To make users, groups, and roles useful, you need to attach them to one or more *policies* (figure 4.5). Policies give the actual permissions, describing what those users, groups, or roles are (or are not) allowed to do within the account. By default, nothing is allowed and you need at least one policy. With policies, you give the necessary *authorization* that those users, groups, and roles require.

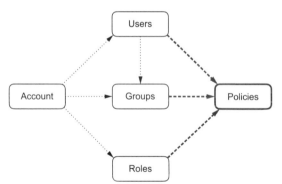

Figure 4.5   Policies can be attached to users, groups, and roles to describe what they are (or are not) allowed to do within the account.

---

[1]   Amazon S3 is an object store with a REST API. Objects are grouped in buckets and the contents of a bucket are uniquely identified by a key.

For *authentication*, you need *security credentials*. Security credentials can be assigned to the root account, but, as discussed, you should use root credentials only to create your first admin user. Users can have permanent credentials, which can be rotated periodically to improve security. Roles don't have credentials assigned to them, but when a user, an application, or an AWS service assumes a role, it gets temporary credentials that will authorize it to do what's described in the policies attached to the role (figure 4.6). Temporary security credentials, when expired, are automatically rotated by the AWS CLI and SDKs. If you obtained temporary security credentials in other ways, you need to rotate them manually.

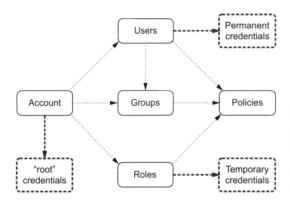

Figure 4.6   How security credentials are used by AWS IAM resources. Users have permanent credentials, which should be periodically rotated for security. Roles, when assumed, give temporary credentials, whose rotation is automatically managed by the AWS CLI and SDKs.

User (and root account) security credentials are composed of

- An access key ID
- A secret access key

The access key ID is added to all AWS API calls. The secret access key is never sent on the wire, but is used to sign the API calls. Usually you don't need to know the details of how AWS API signature works, because the AWS CLI and SDKs will automatically manage that for you.

> **NOTE**   If you want to get more information on how AWS API signature works, AWS currently uses the Signature Version 4 process described in detail at http://docs.aws.amazon.com/general/latest/gr/signature-version-4.html.

Temporary security credentials are generated by the AWS Security Token Service (STS), but usually you don't need to interact directly with it, because AWS services (such as Amazon Cognito) and the CLI and SDKs are designed to manage that on your behalf. Temporary credentials are slightly different from standard security credentials and are composed of

- An access key ID
- A secret access key
- A security (or session) token

Now that you know how an AWS account can use users, groups, and roles to improve the security of its operations, let's see how policies can be implemented to authorize access to AWS resources.

4.2 Understanding policies

At a high level, policies have *effects*, which tell if you're allowing or denying access to perform *actions* on specific *resources* (figure 4.7). In the context of policies, actions are AWS API calls and are expressed by specifying the AWS service and the API call(s) you want to give (or remove) access to. You could use an asterisk (*) to give a service access to all actions, or to all actions that begin with a certain string (for example, Describe*), but that can be risky and I usually recommend the more verbose approach of listing all actions in your policies. Resources depend on the services specified by the actions. For example, for a storage service like Amazon S3, resources are buckets and, optionally, a prefix inside the bucket. For a database service such as Amazon DynamoDB, resources can be tables or indexes.

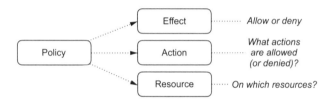

Figure 4.7 High-level summary of how policies work. They have the effect of allowing or denying actions on some resources.

There are three types of policies, each covering a different kind of authorization for AWS resources (figure 4.8):

- *User-based policies* can be attached to users, groups, or roles and describe what a user (or an application or an AWS service) can do.
- *Resource-based policies* can be attached directly to AWS resources and describe who can do what on those resources. For example, S3 bucket policies authorize access to S3 buckets.

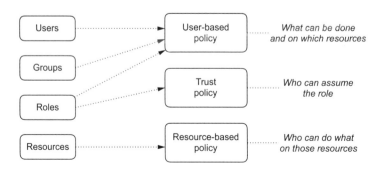

Figure 4.8 How the different types of policies are used by users, groups, roles, and resources

- *Trust policies* describe who can assume a role. Roles used by AWS Lambda have specific trust policies that allow functions to assume those roles. The same applies to roles used by Amazon Cognito, as we'll see in the next chapter.

Policies are written using a JSON syntax. In figure 4.9 you see the different elements that compose a policy. The main elements are *statements*. Statements include the effect (allow or deny), the actions, and the resources, and can optionally include one or more conditions that further limit the scope of the policy. For example, you can limit access to Amazon S3 based on the HTTP referrer used in the API calls. For resource-based and trust policies, the *principal* describes to whom this policy is allowing (or denying) access.

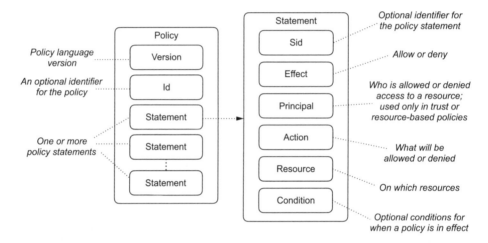

Figure 4.9   The different elements that compose a policy: the main elements are statements, which describe who can do what and on which resources.

Policies can be directly attached to users, groups or roles. To simplify the configuration of policies—for example, when the same policy is used with multiple roles, one that can be assumed by a Lambda function and one by users authenticated via Amazon Cognito—you can use *managed policies*. You can create a managed policy using the Policy link in the left of the AWS IAM console (see figure 4.10). Managed policies can also be versioned.

**You can create managed
policies following this link.**

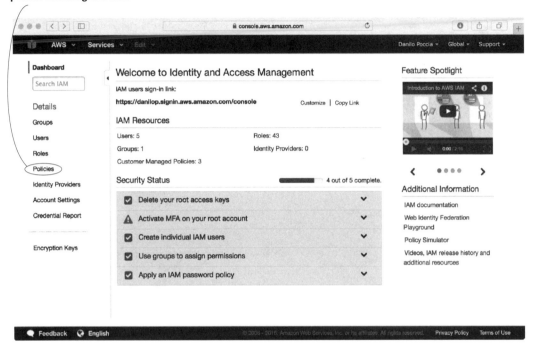

Figure 4.10   **You can create managed policies from the AWS IAM console. Managed policies can be attached to multiple roles, groups, or users and can be versioned.**

4.3   *Policies in practice*

As a first example, I'll use policies that authorize access to Amazon S3 resources. For now, you won't use these policies and don't need to create them, so focus on the syntax. You'll create policies in the next chapter.

> **NOTE**   Amazon S3 buckets have no internal hierarchy, but you can browse objects inside a bucket and specify a delimiter such as / for the keys to list content in a way that resembles accessing a filesystem. For example, you can list objects within a bucket whose keys start with the prefix `folder1/folder2/`. Note that no / is present at the beginning of a prefix. Amazon S3 has additional features that aren't described here. Other features will be introduced as required.

A user-based policy that gives read/write access to an Amazon S3 bucket is shown in the following listing.

Listing 4.1 Policy to give read/write access to an Amazon S3 bucket

Version is used to specify different revisions of the policy language; new versions are introduced when a new feature breaks compatibility with the previous syntax.

```
{
    "Version": "2012-10-17",       ◁——
    "Statement": [
        {
            "Effect": "Allow",     ◁——
            "Action": [
                "s3:ListBucket",
                "s3:GetBucketLocation"
            ],
            "Resource": "arn:aws:s3:::BUCKET"    ◁——
        },
        {
            "Effect": "Allow",
            "Action": [
                "s3:PutObject",
                "s3:GetObject",
                "s3:DeleteObject"
            ],
            "Resource": "arn:aws:s3:::BUCKET/*"   ◁——
        }
    ]
}
```

More than one statement can be included using a JSON list within square brackets.

The effect can be "Allow" or "Deny"; in case of conflicts with multiple statements and/or policies, "Deny" always has precedence over "Allow."

A list of actions from the Amazon S3 API; in this case, you can list objects within a bucket and get the region location of the bucket.

The Amazon S3 bucket is the resource addressed by this statement; you can use a JSON list here if you have multiple resources (buckets).

The second statement in this policy has again the effect to "Allow."

The three allowed actions are to write (PutObject), read (GetObject), and delete (DeleteObject).

For actions in this statement you can limit the effect of the policy to only those objects within a bucket whose keys begin with a certain prefix, but in this case the * after the bucket means all keys.

NOTE   The actions in the previous policy are taken from the AWS API, in this case the Amazon S3 REST API. You can find a detailed description of all possible operations on Amazon S3 at http://docs.aws.amazon.com/AmazonS3/latest/API/APIRest.html.

If you want to use the previous bucket from the web console, you need to give permissions to get the list of all the buckets in your account (shown in the following listing; changes are in **bold**).

Listing 4.2 Adding permissions required by the Amazon S3 web console

```
{
    "Version": "2012-10-17",
    "Statement": [
        {
            "Effect": "Allow",
            "Action": "s3:ListAllMyBuckets",
            "Resource": "arn:aws:s3:::*"
        },
        {
            "Effect": "Allow",
            "Action": [
                "s3:ListBucket",
```

The Amazon S3 web console requires permissions to get the list of all your buckets.

```
          "s3:GetBucketLocation"
        ],
        "Resource": "arn:aws:s3:::BUCKET"
      },
      {
        "Effect": "Allow",
        "Action": [
          "s3:PutObject",
          "s3:GetObject",
          "s3:DeleteObject"
        ],
        "Resource": "arn:aws:s3:::BUCKET/*"
      }
    ]
}
```

To limit read/write access only to a specific prefix inside a bucket, you can

- Add a condition to actions that work on a bucket (such as "ListBucket")
- Include the prefix in the resource for actions that work on objects (such as "PutObject," "GetObject," "DeleteObject")

You can see an example that limits access to a specific prefix in the following listing.

Listing 4.3 Limiting access to a prefix inside an Amazon S3 bucket

```
{
  "Version": "2012-10-17",
  "Statement": [
    {
      "Effect": "Allow",
      "Action": [
        "s3:ListAllMyBuckets",
        "s3:GetBucketLocation"
      ],
      "Resource": "arn:aws:s3:::*"
    },
    {
      "Effect": "Allow",
      "Action": "s3:ListBucket",
      "Resource": "arn:aws:s3:::BUCKET",
      "Condition": {"StringLike": {"s3:prefix": "PREFIX/" }}
    },
    {
      "Effect": "Allow",
      "Action": [
        "s3:PutObject",
        "s3:GetObject",
        "s3:DeleteObject"
      ],
      "Resource": "arn:aws:s3:::BUCKET/PREFIX/*"
    }
  ]
}
```

For actions that work on whole buckets, like "ListBucket," you can add a condition to limit access only for specific prefixes.

For actions that work on single objects, like "PutObject," "GetObject," or "DeleteObject," you can include the prefix in the resources.

TIP If you want to give read-only access, you can remove "PutObject" and "DeleteObject" from the list of allowed actions in the previous policies.

Now, let's see a few examples of policies controlling access to Amazon DynamoDB.

NOTE Amazon DynamoDB is a fully managed NoSQL database. You can scale storage and throughput (in reads or writes per second) of DynamoDB tables via AWS API, CLI, or the web console. Tables don't have a fixed schema, but you need to specify a *primary key*. A primary key can be a single *hash key* or a composite key containing a hash key plus a *range key*. Amazon DynamoDB has more features that are not described here, but which will be introduced as required in the book. If you want to look at those features, you can start with the Amazon DynamoDB Developer Guide found at http://docs.aws.amazon .com/amazondynamodb/latest/developerguide/Introduction.html.

The following listing gives read/write access to items in a specific DynamoDB table.

Listing 4.4 Policy to give read/write access to a DynamoDB table

```
{
  "Version": "2012-10-17",
  "Statement": [
    {
      "Effect": "Allow",
      "Action": [
        "dynamodb:GetItem",
        "dynamodb:BatchGetItem",
        "dynamodb:PutItem",
        "dynamodb:UpdateItem",
        "dynamodb:BatchWriteItem",
        "dynamodb:DeleteItem"
      ],
      "Resource":
        "arn:aws:dynamodb:<region>:<account-id>:table/<table-name>"
    }
  ]
}
```

To read an item from a table

To read one or more items with a single API call

To write an item in a table

To add or update an item

To add or delete one or more items with a single API call

To delete an item

To specify the table, you need to give the AWS region, the AWS account ID, and the table name.

Resources are specified in statements using Amazon Resource Names (ARNs) that are unique. S3 bucket names are unique globally, so you can specify only the bucket name to identify the resource. DynamoDB table names are unique within an AWS account and region, so you need to specify both, together with the table name, to identify the resource in a policy.

Depending on the region you choose to operate in, you can get the region code to build the ARN of the DynamoDB table by looking up the value at http://docs.aws .amazon.com/general/latest/gr/rande.html#ddb_region.

For example, if you used DynamoDB in US East (N. Virginia), the region would be us-east-1. In EU (Ireland), it would be eu-west-1.

You can find the AWS account ID from the web console. Open your browser and go to https://console.aws.amazon.com/, log in with your AWS credentials, and select the drop-down menu with your name on the top right of the web console (figure 4.11).

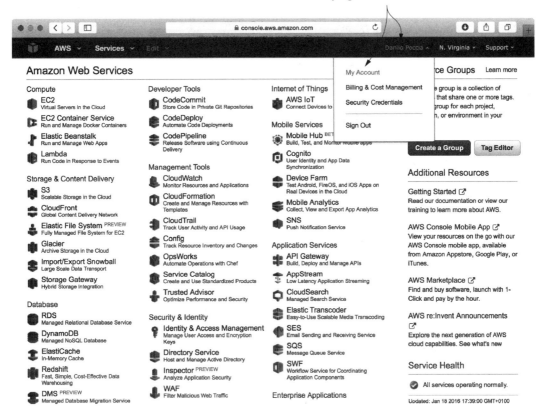

Figure 4.11   You can access account information by selecting the drop-down menu with your name at the top right of the web console.

You'll see a dashboard with your account settings (figure 4.12).

As a result, the ARN used as a resource in a DynamoDB policy is similar to

```
"arn:aws:dynamodb:us-east-1:123412341234:table/my-table"
```

Listing 4.5 adds the option to run queries (but not full table scans, which are I/O expensive) to the previous policy.

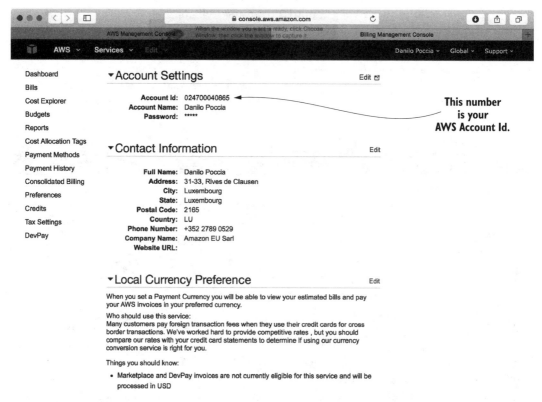

Figure 4.12   In the account page, the account Id is at the top, in the Account Settings section.

Listing 4.5   Adding query permissions to Amazon DynamoDB

```
{
  "Version": "2012-10-17",
  "Statement": [
    {
      "Effect": "Allow",
      "Action": [
        "dynamodb:GetItem",
        "dynamodb:BatchGetItem",          To query a table
        "dynamodb:Query",              ◁┘  on DynamoDB
        "dynamodb:PutItem",
        "dynamodb:UpdateItem",
        "dynamodb:BatchWriteItem",
        "dynamodb:DeleteItem"
      ],
      "Resource":
        "arn:aws:dynamodb:<region>:<account-id>:table/<table-name>"
    }
  ]
}
```

TIP To give read-only access, remove `PutItem`, `UpdateItem`, and `DeleteItem` from the previous policies.

Least privilege

When creating IAM policies, follow the standard security advice of giving the minimum permissions required to perform a task. In doing that, it's more secure to start with a smaller set of permissions and then grant additional ones as necessary, rather than starting with a larger set and then trying to remove the permissions that aren't required.

"Every program and every privileged user of the system should operate using the least amount of privilege necessary to complete the job," Jerome Saltzer, *Communications of the ACM*. The electronic version is located at http://dl.acm.org/citation.cfm?doid=361011.361067.

4.4 Using policy variables

Sometimes you may want to use values in a policy—for example, in a condition—that aren't "fixed" but depend on dynamic parameters, such as who's making the request, or how. You can specify values in a policy that are replaced dynamically every time a request is received by AWS using *policy variables*.

WARNING To use policy variables, you must include the `Version` element and set the version to `2012-10-17`; otherwise, variables such as `${aws:SourceIp}` are treated as literal strings in the policy and aren't replaced by the expected value. Previous versions of the policy language don't support variables.

For example, a few policy variables that can be useful in writing your policies are listed in table 4.1.

Table 4.1 Common policy variables that you can use to enhance your policies

Policy variable	Description and sample usage
`aws:SourceIp`	The IP address of who's making the request to the AWS API; it can be used in an "IpAddress" condition to limit the validity of a policy to a specific IP range: ```"Condition": {` ` "IpAddress" : {` ` "aws:SourceIp" : ["10.1.2.0/24","10.2.3.0/24"]` ` }` `}``` To exclude an IP range from the validity of a policy, you can use the "NotIpAddress" condition: ```"Condition": {` ` "NotIpAddress": {` ` "aws:SourceIp": "192.168.0.0/16"` ` }` `}```

Table 4.1   Common policy variables that you can use to enhance your policies *(continued)*

Policy variable	Description and sample usage
	Be careful that the previous policies work only if the requests are directly made by a user, but wouldn't work if the requests come through another AWS service, such as AWS CloudFormation.
`aws:CurrentTime`	The current time of the request; it can be used to give or block access before or after a specific date and time. A condition valid only during the month of January 2016 would be ```\n"Condition": {\n "DateGreaterThan":\n {"aws:CurrentTime": "2016-01-01T00:00:00Z"},\n "DateLessThan":\n {"aws:CurrentTime": "2016-02-01T00:00:00Z"}\n}\n```
`aws:SecureTransport`	A Boolean value that tells if the API request is using a secure transport such as HTTPS. This is particularly useful to force S3 access via "https://..." URLs. For example, if you host the static assets of a website on S3, you can use an S3 bucket policy (a particular case of resource-based policies) to give public access to reads only in HTTPS using the following statement (that can be included in a wider policy): ```\n"Statement": [{\n "Effect": "Allow",\n "Principal": "*",\n "Action": "s3:GetObject",\n "Resource": "arn:aws:s3:::your-bucket/*",\n "Condition": {\n "Bool": {\n "aws:SecureTransport": "true"\n }\n }\n}]\n```
`aws:MultiFactor-AuthPresent`	A Boolean value that tells if the request was made using Multi-Factor Authentication (MFA) using a hardware or virtual MFA device. A sample condition (that you can include in a statement as part of a policy) would be ```\n"Condition": {\n "Bool": {\n "aws:MultiFactorAuthPresent": "true"\n }\n}\n```
`aws:Referer`	The HTTP referrer (as described by the relevant HTTP header) in the request. Using this policy variable in a condition, S3 bucket policies (a particular case of resource-based policies) can limit access only to requests that originate from specific webpages. For example, if you put the static assets of a website (such as images, CSS, or JavaScript files) on S3, you can give access to everyone to read

Table 4.1 Common policy variables that you can use to enhance your policies *(continued)*

Policy variable	Description and sample usage

	the objects and use this policy variable to avoid other websites linking to your assets. A sample statement that you can include in a policy would be
	
	 ```"Statement": [{```
	``` "Effect": "Allow",```
	``` "Principal": "*",```
	``` "Action": "s3:GetObject",```
	``` "Resource": "arn:aws:s3:::your-bucket/*",```
	``` "Condition": {```
	``` "StringLike": {"aws:Referer": [```
	``` "http://www.your-website.com/*",```
	``` http://your-website.com/*```
	```] }```
	``` }```
	```}]```

NOTE You can get a list of all available policy variables at http://docs.aws .amazon.com/IAM/latest/UserGuide/reference_policies_variables.html#policy- vars-infotouse.

Other interesting use cases use policy variables for users authenticated by Amazon Cognito, which you'll see in the next chapter, after you get a better understanding of roles.

4.5 Assuming roles

Roles can be assumed by users, applications, or AWS services to get specific permissions on AWS resources without hard-coding AWS credentials in your application. For example, AWS services like Amazon EC2 (which provides virtual servers on the AWS Cloud) or AWS Lambda (which we're exploring in this book) can assume an IAM role. In those cases, assuming a role means that you get temporary security credentials to allow the code running in an EC2 instance or in a Lambda function to perform actions on other AWS resources, such as reading from an S3 bucket or writing in a DynamoDB table.

Code using AWS SDKs in an EC2 instance or in a Lambda function will use those credentials automatically to get the necessary authorizations: the AWS SDK gets and rotates the temporary credentials for the corresponding role without any intervention on your part. Using roles, you don't need to put AWS credentials explicitly in your code or in a file distributed with your application, avoiding the risk that those credentials might leak outside of your control or that those credentials are released publicly by mistake—for example, when committing your code to a public code repository on GitHub or Bitbucket.

Roles have two policies attached to them:

- A user-based policy describing the permissions that the role gives.
- A trust policy describing who can assume the role; for example, a user in the same AWS account or in a different account, or an AWS service. This is sometimes called the *trust relationship* of the role.

For example, in chapter 2, when you created your first AWS Lambda function "greetingsOnDemand," you created a "Lambda basic execution" role and assigned that role to the function. Let's look now at that role in more detail.

You can get more information from the AWS IAM console by selecting Role on the left, as described in figure 4.13. I suggest you always look for the roles that are created by the AWS console to better understand what's allowed and what's not.

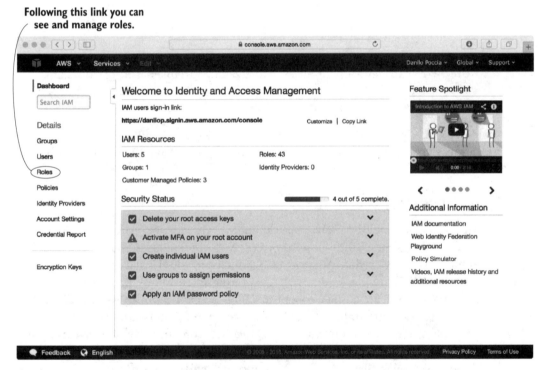

Figure 4.13   You can see and edit current roles and create new roles from the web console. Always check the roles that are created on your behalf by the AWS console to understand what they allow.

There you can search for the role using the text form on the top of the window:

- The user-based policy describes permissions; for that function, you needed to write to CloudWatch Logs (listing 4.6).
- The trust policy describes who can assume the role; in this case, the AWS Lambda service (listing 4.7).

Listing 4.6 Lambda basic execution role permissions

```
{
  "Version": "2012-10-17",
  "Statement": [
    {
      "Effect": "Allow",              ◁──┐
      "Action": [
        "logs:CreateLogGroup",
        "logs:CreateLogStream",
        "logs:PutLogEvents"
      ],
      "Resource": "arn:aws:logs:*:*:*"  ◁──┐
    }
  ]
}
```

This statement in the user-based policy allows access to actions and resources.

The actions are the ones required to write to Amazon CloudWatch Logs.

The resource is using the asterisks ("*:*:*") to give access to anything managed by Amazon CloudWatch Logs.

Listing 4.7 Lambda basic execution role trust relationships

```
{
  "Version": "2012-10-17",
  "Statement": [
    {
      "Sid": "",
      "Effect": "Allow",              ◁──┐
      "Principal": {
        "Service": "lambda.amazonaws.com"  ◁──
      },
      "Action": "sts:AssumeRole"      ◁──┐
    }
  ]
}
```

This statement in the trust policy allows access to the role.

The access is given to the principal, the AWS Lambda service in this case.

The action is the AssumeRole API of AWS Security Token Service (STS), used by AWS Lambda to assume the role.

You can look at how the role is used by AWS Lambda to have a better understanding of all the moving parts. The greetingsOnDemand function is executed by AWS Lambda, a service that has a trust relationship with the "Lambda basic execution" role and can assume that role for the execution of the function. As a result, the function has access to CloudWatch Logs and can log relevant information there, using "console.log()" in the Node.js runtime and "print" in the Python runtime. For example, if you modify the user-based policy in listing 4.6 by removing the "logs:PutLogEvents" action, the function won't log anymore.

If you need to access other AWS services—for example, to read from Amazon S3 or write to Amazon DynamoDB—you can add statements to the policy giving permissions to the role using the syntax you learned earlier in this chapter. You'll build finely tailored policies later in this book when creating a sample event-driven serverless application.

Summary

In this chapter you saw how AWS security works and how you can secure your application with AWS Lambda. In particular, you learned about

- Using AWS Identity and Access Management (IAM) to create users, groups, and roles
- Authenticating via AWS temporary credentials
- Writing policies to authorize access to AWS resources
- Using policy variables to have dynamically replaced values in your policies
- Authorizing Lambda functions via roles

In the next chapter you'll learn how to use functions from a device, such as a mobile device or a JavaScript web page running in a web browser, and how to subscribe functions to events in the AWS Cloud.

EXERCISE

Write a user-based policy to give read-only access to a bucket called *my-bucket* only for content under the prefix *my-prefix/*.

Solution

Starting from listing 4.3, you should remove writing actions such as `PutObject` and `DeleteObject`:

```
{
  "Version": "2012-10-17",
  "Statement": [
    {
      "Effect": "Allow",
      "Action": [
        "s3:ListAllMyBuckets",
        "s3:GetBucketLocation"
      ],
      "Resource": "arn:aws:s3:::*"
    },
    {
      "Effect": "Allow",
      "Action": "s3:ListBucket",
      "Resource": "arn:aws:s3:::my-bucket",
      "Condition": {"StringLike": {"s3:prefix": "my-prefix/" }}
    },
    {
      "Effect": "Allow",
      "Action": [ "s3:GetObject ],
      "Resource": "arn:aws:s3::: my-bucket/my-prefix/*"
    }
  ]
}
```

Using standalone functions

This chapter covers

- Importing custom libraries in your function
- Subscribing functions to events coming from other AWS services
- Creating back-end resources such as S3 buckets and DynamoDB tables
- Using binaries with your function
- Implementing a serverless face detection function
- Scheduling functions for recurring execution

In the previous chapters, you learned how to manage security within the AWS platform. Many concepts were introduced using AWS IAM, such as roles and policies, that you can use with Lambda functions to give them the necessary authorization to access other resources.

In this chapter you'll use that knowledge to create standalone functions that can be scheduled for periodic execution or triggered by events coming from other AWS services such as Amazon S3. This is the first step toward building an event-driven application using multiple functions together.

5.1   *Packaging libraries and modules with your function*

At this point, the functions you've created are basic and don't include any modules other than what's already included in AWS Lambda—for example, the AWS SDKs for Node.js and Python. But sometimes you need to include more powerful libraries that can help you implement sophisticated functionalities.

For modules managed by standard package managers, such as npm for Node.js or pip for Python, you can use those tools to install the module locally in your development environment in a folder where you have the source of the function. That's the default behavior for npm. For pip, you have to use the -t option to specify the local directory (for example, "-t ."). Then you need to create a zip archive that includes your function (in the root folder) and all dependencies. This archive is your *deployment package,* which you can upload directly to AWS Lambda (if smaller than 10 MB) or via Amazon S3.

> **WARNING**   During the installation, certain Node.js and Python modules use a compiler (for example, for C/C++) to build native binaries that are required or more efficient to use than a cross-platform implementation distributed with the module. To use those modules, see section 5.3 on using binaries with your function.

For example, to include the popular async[1] module in your Node.js function, you can run the following command in the same directory as your function source code:

```
npm install async
```

> **NOTE**   To download and install Node.js, including npm, in your development environment, follow the information provided at https://nodejs.org/.

> **TIP**   In Node.js, you can also create a package.json file to describe your function and the module dependencies. In that case, npm install will retrieve all the required modules from the package.json file. For more information, see https://docs.npmjs.com/getting-started/using-a-package.json.

In Python, if you want to include the requests[2] library (which is common if you need to interact via HTTP with external endpoints), you can run this command in the same directory as your function source code:

```
pip install requests -t .
```

> **NOTE**   To install pip in your development environment, follow the installation instructions at https://pip.pypa.io/en/stable/installing/.

---

[1]   For more information on the "async" Node.js module, see https://github.com/caolan/async.

[2]   For more information on the "requests" library, see http://docs.python-requests.org.

WARNING The `pip install requests -t` command may fail on Mac OS X. When that occurs, use the Virtualenv option described next to prepare your Python deployment package.

Optionally, you can replace the "." in the previous command with the full path of the directory you're using for your function.

TIP Python has another option to create a deployment package that I usually suggest, especially if there's more than one module: using Virtualenv,[3] a tool to create isolated Python environments. In this case, you need to include the content of the `site-packages` folder with your function.

Creating the deployment package

A common mistake when creating a deployment package is to create a zip archive from the parent directory where your function code is saved. Your function must be in the root folder of the archive. What I usually suggest is to zip from inside the folder where the function source code is.

For example, if your function uses the Node.js runtime and the `async` module, you can have a folder structure such as

```
MyFunction/
    index.js
    node_modules/
        async/
            ...
```

In this case, from within the `MyFunction` directory, you can create the zip archive of version 1.2 of your function in a Linux/Unix environment with

```
zip -9 -r ../MyFunction-v1.2.zip *
```

The same approach applies to Windows and graphical front ends to the zip utility.

Let's look at an example of how to package custom modules with a Lambda function, using a common use case: reacting to new or updated content on Amazon S3.

5.2   *Subscribing functions to events*

In event-driven applications, you want back end logic to be executed in reaction to changes in data. An example of that is when users upload high-resolution pictures to share with other users. To show the pictures at different resolutions, you need to build thumbnails. Those pictures probably have metadata, such as the photographer or a description, that you want to store in a database.

In a traditional application, you need to implement a front end component to manage the upload and then process the picture and the data according to a workflow that you define (figure 5.1).

---

[3] For more information on Virtualenv, see https://virtualenv.readthedocs.org/.

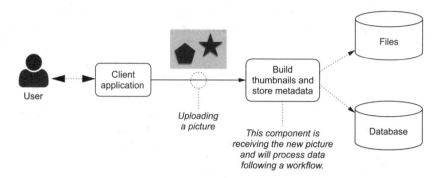

Figure 5.1 To manage a workflow triggered by the upload of picture, you usually need to implement a front end tier and put your logic there.

But with AWS Lambda you can use features of Amazon S3 to store metadata with objects and subscribe a function to process information in the metadata when an object is created or updated (figure 5.2). The client application uploads straight to the S3 bucket, and you don't need to manage the upload, only react to the new content.

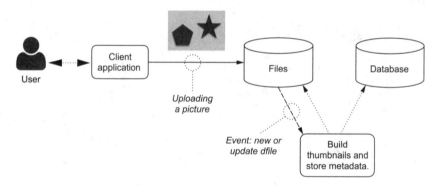

Figure 5.2 With AWS Lambda you can upload straight from your client application to Amazon S3 and then trigger a function when there is new or updated content.

5.2.1 Creating the back-end resources

Let's create an S3 bucket to use for this example. Bucket names are globally unique and you need to decide which name to use. For example, if you have a short single-word nickname, you can pick up a name such as "<your-nickname>-pictures."

To create a bucket, you can use the AWS CLI. Be sure you configured the AWS CLI to use the same region you're using for AWS Lambda. You can create a bucket with the following command:

```
aws s3 mb s3://bucket-name
```

Otherwise, in the AWS console, choose S3 from the Storage & Content Delivery section, select Create Bucket, and then insert the bucket name and the region you want to use. You can then select Create.

> **WARNING** Use the same region for the S3 bucket that you're using for the Lambda functions. Otherwise you can't configure the bucket as an event source for the function. If you're using US East for AWS Lambda, use US Standard for Amazon S3.

To store metadata for the picture, use Amazon DynamoDB. You need to create a table for this function. In the AWS console, choose DynamoDB from the Database section and then Create table. Use "images" as Table name and "name" as the Primary key Partition key (figure 5.3). Then click Create. It takes time for the new table to be available, usually a few seconds. In the Overview tab of the table, write down the Amazon Resource Name (ARN). You'll need the table ARN to give access to the resource with AWS IAM.

The idea now is to create a Lambda function subscribed to this bucket that will be run every time an object with the `images/` prefix is created or updated in the S3 bucket.

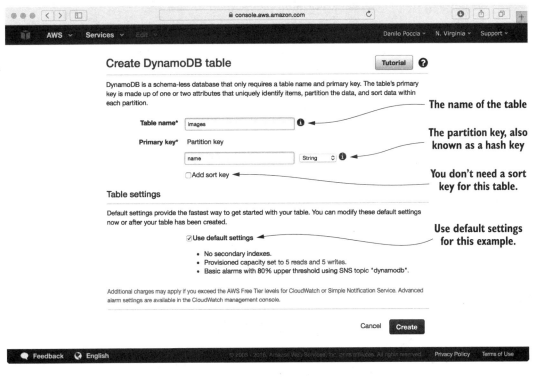

Figure 5.3 To create a DynamoDB table for the picture metadata, you need a name for the table and a partition key for the primary key.

To make the example more interesting, the S3 object metadata can optionally contain the following values:

- width, the maximum width of the thumbnail in pixels
- height, the maximum height of the thumbnail in pixels
- author, the author of the picture
- title, the title of the picture
- description, a description of the picture

Based on the metadata (and the default values if they're not provided) the function will

1 Create a thumbnail of the picture and store it in the same bucket, adding the thumbs/ prefix at the beginning of the object key.

2 Extract the metadata and store the information on the picture, including the link to the thumbnail, in the DynamoDB table you created.

5.2.2 Packaging the function

The code for the createThumbnailAndStoreInDB function in Node.js is in listing 5.1. This function uses external modules, such as async, gm, and util, that aren't included by default in the AWS Lambda execution environment. You need to install them locally and then create a deployment package.

> NOTE This function uses ImageMagick, a software suite to create, edit, compose, or convert images that's available in the AWS Lambda execution environment for Node.js. Because ImageMagick isn't provided in the Python execution environment, a similar example in Python would be more complex and isn't provided at this point. For more and updated information on the Lambda execution environments and the available libraries with each runtime, see http://docs.aws.amazon.com/lambda/latest/dg/current-supported-versions.html.

Listing 5.1　createThumbnailAndStoreInDB **(Node.js)**

Import the async module to simplify the flow in the function.

Import the AWS SDK; it's preinstalled in the Lambda execution environment.

Import the gm module, a wrapper on top of ImageMagik, preinstalled in the Lambda execution environment.

The default size of the thumbnail

The DynamoDB table to store metadata in

Service interface objects for Amazon S3 and Amazon DynamoDB

```
var async = require('async');
var AWS = require('aws-sdk');
var gm = require('gm')
            .subClass({ imageMagick: true }); // Enable ImageMagick
    integration.
var util = require('util');

var DEFAULT_MAX_WIDTH  = 200;
var DEFAULT_MAX_HEIGHT = 200;
var DDB_TABLE = 'images';

var s3 = new AWS.S3();
var dynamodb = new AWS.DynamoDB();
```

```
function getImageType(key, callback) {
  var typeMatch = key.match(/\.([^.]*)$/);
  if (!typeMatch) {
      callback("Could not determine the image type for key: ${key}");
      return;
  }
  var imageType = typeMatch[1];
  if (imageType != "jpg" && imageType != "png") {
      callback('Unsupported image type: ${imageType}');
      return;
  }
  return imageType;
}

exports.handler = (event, context, callback) => {
  console.log("Reading options from event:\n",
    util.inspect(event, {depth: 5}));
  var srcBucket = event.Records[0].s3.bucket.name;
  var srcKey    = event.Records[0].s3.object.key;
  var dstBucket = srcBucket;
  var dstKey    = "thumbs/" + srcKey);

    var imageType = getImageType(srcKey, callback);

  async.waterfall([
    function downloadImage(next) {
      s3.getObject({
        Bucket: srcBucket,
        Key: srcKey
      },
      next);
    },
    function tranformImage(response, next) {
      gm(response.Body).size(function(err, size) {

        var metadata = response.Metadata;
        console.log("Metadata:\n", util.inspect(metadata, {depth: 5}));

        var max_width;
        if ('width' in metadata) {
          max_width = metadata.width;
        } else {
          max_width = DEFAULT_MAX_WIDTH;
        }
        var max_height;
        if ('height' in metadata) {
          max_height = metadata.height;
        } else {
          max_height = DEFAULT_MAX_HEIGHT;
        }

        var scalingFactor = Math.min(
          max_width / size.width,
          max_height / size.height
        );
```

Get the source bucket and the key of the S3 object that triggered this event.

Compute the output bucket and key of the thumbnail S3 object.

Use async waterfall to execute multiple functions in sequence.

Download the source image from S3 into a buffer.

Function to transform the source image and create the thumbnail

Get custom size for the thumbnail from the S3 object custom metadata (if present).

```
        var width  = scalingFactor * size.width;
        var height = scalingFactor * size.height;

        this.resize(width, height)
          .toBuffer(imageType, function(err, buffer) {
            if (err) {
              next(err);
            } else {
              next(null, response.ContentType, metadata, buffer);
            }
          });
      });
    },
    function uploadThumbnail(contentType, metadata, data, next) {
      // Stream the transformed image to a different S3 bucket.
      s3.putObject({
          Bucket: dstBucket,
          Key: dstKey,
          Body: data,
          ContentType: contentType,
          Metadata: metadata
      }, function(err, buffer) {
        if (err) {
          next(err);
        } else {
          next(null, metadata);
        }
      });
    },
    function storeMetadata(metadata, next) {
      // adds metadata do DynamoDB
      var params = {
        TableName: DDB_TABLE,
        Item: {
          name: { S: srcKey },
          thumbnail: { S: dstKey },
          timestamp: { S: (new Date().toJSON()).toString() },
        }
      };
      if ('author' in metadata) {
        params.Item.author = { S: metadata.author };
      }
      if ('title' in metadata) {
        params.Item.title = { S: metadata.title };
      }
      if ('description' in metadata) {
        params.Item.description = { S: metadata.description };
      }
      dynamodb.putItem(params, next);
    }], function (err) {
      if (err) {
        console.error(err);
      } else {
        console.log(
          'Successfully resized ' + srcBucket + '/' + srcKey +
```

This is where the actual resize for the thumbnail happens.

Function to upload the thumbnail to S3

This is how to upload an object to S3 using the JavaScript SDK.

Function to store metadata in Amazon DynamoDB

Preparing parameters for the DynamoDB call

Adding more data (author, title, description) if present in S3 custom metadata

Put item in the DynamoDB table.

```
            ' and uploaded to ' + dstBucket + '/' + dstKey
        );
    }
    callback();
}
);
};
```

Successfully
terminates the
function

When creating a deployment package, the function in listing 5.1 will be one of the files included, and you need to choose a name for the file. I suggest you use index.js, because it's the default value used by the AWS Lambda configuration, but you can use a different one if you want.

First, create an index.js file with the content of the createThumbnailAnd-StoreInDB function (listing 5.1). Then, from within the same directory containing the index.js file, use npm, the Node.js package manager, to install the required modules locally:

```
npm install async gm util
```

This creates a node_modules folder in the directory that contains a local installation of the modules, where you executed the npm command. The deployment package you need to create is a ZIP file that contains the function and all dependencies. From within the directory containing the index.js file and the node_modules folder, create the deployment package by running the following command:

```
zip -9 -r ../createThumbnailAndStoreInDB-v1.0.zip *
```

> **TIP** It's always a good practice to include versioning in the file name of your deployment package. For example, when you have multiple versions of a function, having different file names reduces the risk of uploading the wrong one.

5.2.3 Configuring permissions

You're almost ready to create the function. You still need an AWS IAM role that will allow access to the resources required by this function:

- Read from the S3 bucket with the images/ prefix.
- Write in the S3 bucket with the thumbs/ prefix.
- Put an item on the DynamoDB table you created.

For this role, you'll create a managed policy and then attach the policy to the role. From the AWS IAM console, select Policies on the left and then Create Policy. Choose Create Your Own Policy (figure 5.4) to write the policy in the online editor.

> **TIP** You can use the Policy Generator to have support in writing policies with the correct syntax. You can try to build the same policy in listing 5.2 using the Policy Generator to get used to it and see the benefits the Policy Generator provides.

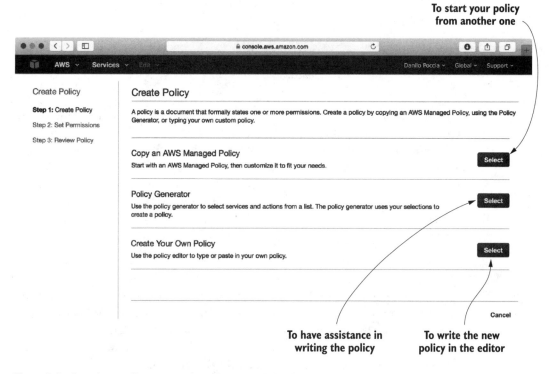

Figure 5.4   Creating a policy, you can start from an existing policy, use the Policy Generator to have assistance, or write down the policy document using the online editor.

Use CreateThumbnailAndStoreInDB as the Policy Name and write a meaningful description; for example, "To read the source image, write the thumbnail and store the metadata in the DB." In the policy Document, use the code from the following listing. Remember to replace the S3 bucket name and the DynamoDB table ARN with the ones you're using, and then select Create Policy.

Listing 5.2   Policy_CreateThumbnailAndStoreInDB

```
{
    "Version": "2012-10-17",
    "Statement": [
        {
            "Effect": "Allow",
            "Action": [
                "s3:GetObject"
            ],
            "Resource": [
                "arn:aws:s3:::<BUCKET-NAME>/images/*"
            ]
        },
```

Allow read access to the S3 bucket for objects with the image/ prefix.

```
{
    "Effect": "Allow",
    "Action": [
        "s3:PutObject"
    ],
    "Resource": [
        "arn:aws:s3:::<BUCKET-NAME>/thumbs/*"
    ]
},
{
    "Effect": "Allow",
    "Action": [
        "dynamodb:PutItem"
    ],
    "Resource": [
        "<DYNAMODB-TABLE-ARN>"
    ]
}
]
}
```

Allow write access to the S3 bucket for objects with the thumbs/ prefix.

Allow write access (put item) to the DynamoDB table.

Now, still in the AWS IAM console, choose Roles on the left and Create New Role. Use lambda_createThumbnailAndStoreInDB as the Role Name and then select Next Step. You can now specify the type of role you want to use. This will configure the trust policy for you. In the list of AWS Service Roles, click the button for AWS Lambda (figure 5.5).

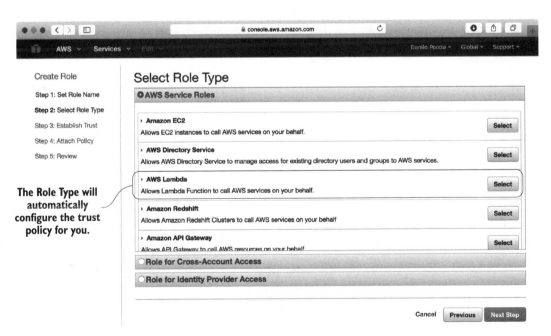

The Role Type will automatically configure the trust policy for you.

Figure 5.5 The Role Type preconfigures the trust relationships for the policy.

You need to attach two policies to the role, selecting the checkbox for each of them. You can use the filter text box to make it easier to look up the policies you need:

- The CreateThumbnailAndStoreInDB policy you created, to have access to Amazon S3 and Amazon DynamoDB.
- The AWSLambdaBasicExecutionRole policy, managed by AWS, to have access to Amazon CloudWatch Logs.

Select Next Step, verify that both policies are in the summary review, and then click Create Role.

> **WARNING**   If you forget the CreateThumbnailAndStoreInDB policy when creating the role, the function will fail with errors in the logs. But if you forget the AWSLambdaBasicExecutionRole policy, the function can't *write* logs.

5.2.4   *Creating the function*

Now that you've completed all necessary requirements, you can create the function. In the AWS Lambda console, choose Create a Lambda function and skip the blueprints.

You can now configure Amazon S3 as the trigger for this function. Click the ellipse representing the source of the events, and choose Amazon S3 from the list. In the dialog that appears (figure 5.6), select S3 as Event source type and the Bucket you created. As Event type, choose Object Created (All). In the prefix, type images/ to trigger the function only for objects uploaded with a key that starts with images/. Leave the

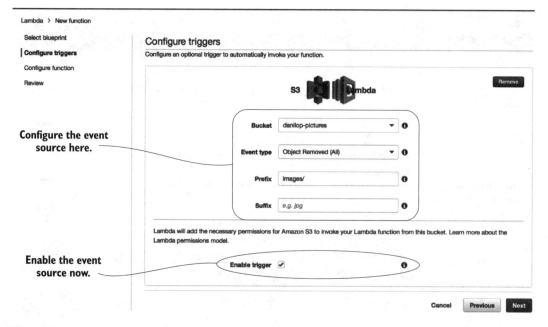

Figure 5.6   When configuring the event source, you have multiple parameters, depending on the service that's generating the source. For Amazon S3, you can customize the type of event and filter by prefix and suffix.

suffix empty; for example, you could use this field to receive events only for files that have a .jpg or .png extension, but my suggestion is to not specify a suffix right now. Choose to enable the event source and click Next.

> **TIP** If you want to invoke different Lambda functions depending on the file extension of the object uploaded to Amazon S3, you can use the suffix in the event sources to specify which file extension should trigger that function.

Use `createThumbnailAndStoreInDB` as the function name, and write a meaningful description; for example, "Creates a thumbnail and stores the metadata in the DB." Use Node.js as Runtime.

You can't write the function code inline this time because you have to bring several dependencies with you, as we discussed in the previous section. Choose to Upload a zip file and use the Upload button to look up the zip archive you previously created in the file dialog.

Leave index.handler as Handler (or update it with a different file name if you didn't use index.js as the file name for the function). For Role, select from the menu the one you created: lambda_createThumbnailAndStoreInDB.

For memory, 128 MB is enough unless you use large high-resolution pictures (you can check how much memory is used in the logs of the function). For the timeout, in this function you're calling multiple services one after the other, so even if 3 seconds will be more than enough, use 10 seconds and be conservative. The timeout is useful to avoid possible errors that create long-running functions, but shouldn't be too close to the expected execution time. You don't need a VPC here, so leave the default "No VPC" option selected and click Next. Check the review and if everything is okay, select Create function.

Creating Lambda functions from the CLI

If you want, you can create the Lambda function using the AWS CLI:

```
aws lambda create-function \
    --function-name createThumbnailAndStoreInDB \
    --runtime nodejs \
    --role <ROLE-ARN> \
    --handler index.handler \
    --zip-file fileb://<DEPLOYMENT PACKAGE>.zip \
    --timeout 10 \
    --region <REGION>
```

You can get the Role ARN selecting the lambda_createThumbnailAndStoreInDB role in the AWS IAM console. You need to specify a region only if you're not using the one you chose when configuring the AWS CLI. The ZIP archive is a binary file, so you need the `fileb://` URL. If you use `fileb:///` (with three slashes) the file path is absolute; with two slashes (`file://`) the path is relative to where you're executing the command.

> **(continued)**
> Similar syntaxes exist in the AWS CLI to update the configuration or the code of a function. Those commands are useful for automating the update of a function. For more information on how to update a function from the CLI, use the embedded help:
>
> ```
> aws lambda update-function-code help
> aws lambda update-function-configuration help
> ```

You can see a recap of the previous configuration in the Triggers panel of the function (figure 5.7). You can come back to this panel any time you want to check or update the triggers for this function.

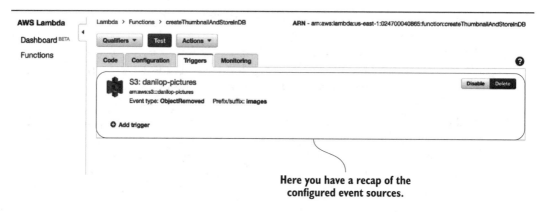

Figure 5.7   In the Lambda console, for every function, the event sources tab gives a summary of the configured sources.

> **TIP** To subscribe a Lambda function to an event in a resource managed by AWS, you can use the AWS Lambda console or the AWS console of the service managing the resource. For this example, I used the AWS Lambda console. You may want to check how to do the same configuration from the Amazon S3 console: the Properties section of the bucket has an Events section where you can choose to send the events to a Lambda function or to other destinations, such as an SNS topic or an SQS queue. For more information on Amazon SNS and Amazon SQS, go to https://aws.amazon.com/sns/ and https://aws.amazon.com/sqs/.

5.2.5   Testing the function

To test the function, you can upload a picture to Amazon S3 using the AWS CLI:

```
aws s3 cp <YOUR-PICTURE-FILE> s3://<BUCKET-NAME>/images/
```

To verify that the function is correctly invoked, check the Monitoring tab in the AWS Lambda console. In the S3 console, you can verify that the thumbnail is generated and that the `thumbs/` prefix is added at the beginning. Double-clicking the object in the web console will show the thumbnail. If you prefer, you can use the AWS CLI to list the thumbnails:

```
aws s3 ls --recursive s3://<BUCKET-NAME>/thumbs/
```

On the DynamoDB console you can verify in the Items tab that an item has been added with the `name`, `thumbnail`, and `timestamp` attributes.

To add custom metadata, using `author`, `title` and `description`, and a different size (`height`, `width`) for the thumbnail, the syntax to run at the AWS CLI is

```
aws s3 cp <YOUR-PICTURE-FILE> s3://<BUCKET-NAME>/images/ \
--metadata '{"author": "John Doe", "title": "Mona Lisa", "description": "Nice
    portrait!", "width": "100", "height": "100" }'
```

> **NOTE** In the AWS CLI command, the payload for the metadata is embedded in single quotes to avoid the OS shell removing the double quotes required by the JSON syntax.

Feel free to replace title and description with something related to the actual picture you're using. The size of the thumbnail will now be smaller than before (the default height and width are 200 pixels), and the new metadata will be stored in the DynamoDB table (figure 5.8).

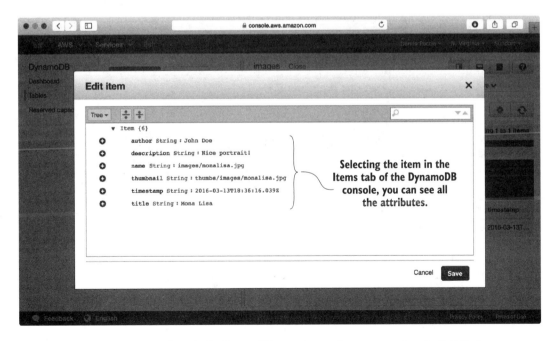

Figure 5.8   When you select an item in the DynamoDB console, you have an overview of all attributes.

TIP If something isn't working as expected, select the Monitoring tab in the AWS Lambda console and use the link to View logs in CloudWatch to understand what's happening. If no logs are displayed, either the event source configuration was wrong and the function isn't executed, or the function is missing the permissions to write logs to Amazon CloudWatch.

5.3   *Using binaries with your function*

Sometimes including an external module in a Lambda function can be more complex than what you've done because it includes binaries or dependencies that are installed by default in a shared folder of the operating system. An example is `/usr/lib` or `/usr/local/lib` in a Linux/Unix environment or shared DLLs in Windows.

In those cases, you need to create a local static build that you can easily include and ship with your deployment package. This build must use an environment that's similar to what AWS Lambda uses to execute your functions. For that, I suggest you use an Amazon Linux EC2 instance, which you can create temporarily when you need to create the package. You can shut down or terminate the instance as soon as you don't need it.

TIP For a detailed description of the Lambda execution environment and the available libraries depending on the runtime, see http://docs.aws.amazon.com/lambda/latest/dg/current-supported-versions.html.

For example, imagine you want to create a web application that can detect faces in the pictures that your users upload with your application. This is a feature similar to what's implemented by social networking services such as Facebook.

You don't need to implement a face detection algorithm from scratch because you can use the powerful tools that have been prepared by experts in the field. In the case of face recognition, you can use OpenCV.

OpenCV—Open Source Computer Vision

OpenCV is a powerful computer vision library originally developed by Intel and now available as open source. It has interfaces for multiple programming languages; for example, you can use JavaScript and Python bindings with a Lambda function.

For more information on OpenCV, see http://opencv.org.

OpenCV installs by default in a shared folder of your operating system. To avoid that, you need to look at the configuration tool used by the project (cmake for OpenCV) to find options that enable a static build.

5.3.1 Preparing the environment

To make it easy to experiment with OpenCV and AWS Lambda, I put an example deployment package, which includes those binaries and the Lambda functions in Node.js and Python here:

- For Node.js, download
  https://eventdrivenapps.com/downloads/faceDetection-js.zip.
- For Python, download
  https://eventdrivenapps.com/downloads/faceDetection-py.zip.

Preparing OpenCV for AWS Lambda use

This procedure can be complex and time-consuming. Certain commands are related to the specific version of OpenCV I used, and you may need to adjust those commands for newer environments. If you're more interested in the results than the technicalities, start your development from the sample deployment packages that I shared.

Starting from a new Amazon Linux instance and an empty folder for the user, these are the commands to build a local static environment for OpenCV:

```
sudo yum -y update
sudo yum -y install gcc48 libgcc48 gcc-c++ cmake
wget https://nodejs.org/download/release/v0.10.36/node-v0.10.36.tar.gz
tar xzvf node-v0.10.36.tar.gz
cd node-v0.10.36 && ./configure && make
sudo make install
node -v
cd ..
wget https://github.com/Itseez/opencv/archive/2.4.12.zip
mv 2.4.12.zip opencv-2.4.12.zip
mkdir opencv_build
mkdir opencv_test
cd opencv_build
unzip ../opencv-2.4.12.zip
cmake -D CMAKE_BUILD_TYPE=RELEASE -D BUILD_SHARED_LIBS=NO -D
    BUILD_NEW_PYTHON_SUPPORT=ON -D CMAKE_INSTALL_PREFIX=~/opencv
    opencv-2.4.12/
make && make install
```

I found a bug where the linker was not finding a few libraries in the next `npm install` command. I had to manually edit several library names in the file ~/opencv/lib/pkg-config/opencv.pc, adding lib at the beginning of `jasper`, `tiff`, `png`, and `jpeg` so that in the Libs section the options for those libraries are

```
-llibjasper -llibtiff -llibpng -llibjpeg
```

This command prepared the environment for the Node.js runtime in the ~/opencv_test folder:

```
PKG_CONFIG_PATH=~/opencv/lib/pkgconfig/ npm install --prefix=~/
opencv_test opencv
```

> **(continued)**
>
> Now you can copy `./opencv_build/lib/cv2.so` in the root folder of the function and import the `cv2` module in the Python source code. To use the Python runtime, you also need the `numpy` module installed locally (or via Virtualenv):
>
> ```
> pip install numpy -t.
> ```

5.3.2 Implementing the function

Using the deployment package, including the OpenCV binaries, you can now create a Lambda function that detects faces in an input image. Before implementing the function, let's design the expected input and output behavior.

The input event for the function gives the URL of the input image:

```
{
  "imageURL": "http(s)://…"
}
```

The function saves an output image, where faces are marked with white rectangles on Amazon S3. The result returned by the function is a JSON structure with the number of faces detected and the URL of the output image with the faces marked:

```
{
  "faces": 3
  "outputURL": "https://… "
}
```

In this function, you need to specify the S3 bucket you want to use to store the output images and the output domain to use to access those pictures. The output domain is the domain used by the bucket , `<bucket>.s3.amazonaws.com`.

> **TIP** You can have a different output domain if you use a Content Delivery Network (CDN) such as Amazon CloudFront to distribute the content of the bucket. I'm not covering this specific configuration in the book, but you should consider using a CDN to optimize the performance and costs of your application if you expect to download large amounts of data (for example, on the order of TBs) from Amazon S3.

Let's create an S3 bucket to use for this function. You need to decide which name to use for the bucket (remember, bucket names are globally unique). For example, if you have a short nickname, you can pick up a name like "<nickname>-faces".

To create a bucket, you can use the AWS CLI; just be sure you configured the AWS CLI to use the same region you're using for AWS Lambda. You can create a bucket with the following command:

```
aws s3 mb s3://bucket-name
```

Otherwise, you can open the AWS console, choose S3 from the Storage & Content Delivery section, select Create Bucket, and then insert the bucket name and the region you want to use. You can then select Create.

You need to give public access to objects stored in this bucket. From the S3 console, select the bucket and then the Properties tab, look for Permissions, and then select Edit bucket policy. Use the bucket policy in the following listing to give public read access to all objects.

Listing 5.3   Policy_Public_S3_Bucket

```
{
    "Version": "2012-10-17",
    "Statement": [
        {
            "Sid": "",
            "Effect": "Allow",
            "Principal": "*",
            "Action": "s3:GetObject",
            "Resource": "arn:aws:s3:::<BUCKET-NAME>/*"
        }
    ]
}
```

A bucket policy is a type of resource-based policy and you need a principal to specify who is allowed (or denied) access. In this statement, "*" means anyone, which gives public read access.

The source code in Node.js and Python for the face detection function is in listings 5.4 and 5.5, respectively. Remember to replace the bucket and the output domain with your choice. For the output domain, you can use `<bucket>.s3.amazonaws.com`.

TIP   To optimize content distribution in production, you may want to configure a CDN such as Amazon CloudFront in front of the S3 bucket, but I don't cover it in this book.

Listing 5.4   faceDetection (Node.js)

```
var cv = require('opencv');
var util = require('util');
var request = require('request').defaults({ encoding: null });
var uuid = require('node-uuid');
var AWS = require('aws-sdk');

var s3 = new AWS.S3();

var dstBucket = '<S3-BUCKET-TO-STORE-OUTPUT-IMAGES>';
var dstPrefix = 'tmp/';
var outputDomain = '<OUTPUT-DOMAIN>';

function getFormattedDate() {
  var now = new Date().toISOString(); // YYYY-MM-DDTHH:mm:ss.sssZ
  var formattedNow = now.substr(0,4) + now.substr(5,2) + now.substr(8,2)
    + now.substr(11,2) + now.substr(14,2) + now.substr(17,2);
  return formattedNow;
}
```

Import the "opencv" module created in the first part of this chapter.

```
exports.handler = (event, context, callback) => {
  console.log("Reading options from event:\n", util.inspect(event, {depth:
5}));
  var imageUrl = event.imageUrl;
  request.get(imageUrl, function (err, res, body) {          Download the
    if (err) {                                                input image.
      console.log(err);
      callback(err);
    }
    cv.readImage(body, function(err, im) {            Convert the input
      if (err) {                                     image in the OpenCV
        console.log(err);                            image format.
        callback(err);
      }
      if (im.width() < 1 || im.height() < 1) callback('Image has no size');
      im.detectObject("node_modules/opencv/data/
      haarcascade_frontalface_alt.xml",
      {}, function(err, faces) {                     Looping on the detected
        if (err) callback(err);                      faces to draw rectangles
        for (var i = 0; i < faces.length; i++){      around them
          var face = faces[i];
          im.rectangle([face.x, face.y], [face.width, face.height], [255,
255, 255], 2);
        }
        if (faces.length > 0) {
          var dstKey = dstPrefix + getFormattedDate() + '-' + uuid.v4() +
'.jpg';
          var contentType = 'image/jpeg';
          s3.putObject({                             Uploading the image
            Bucket: dstBucket,                       with the detected
            Key: dstKey,                             faces to Amazon S3
            Body: im.toBuffer(),
            ContentType: contentType
          }, function(err, data) {
            if (err) console.log(err);
            if (err) callback(err);
            console.log(data);
            outputUrl = 'https://' + outputDomain + '/' + dstKey;
            var result = {
              faces: faces.length,                   Preparing the result object
              outputUrl: outputUrl                   with the number of faces
            };                                        and the output URL
            callback(null, result);
          });
        } else {                             If no faces have been found,
          var result = {                     return the input URL as output,
            faces: 0,                         and no upload is required.
            outputUrl: imageUrl
          };
          callback(null, result);            Return the result for a
        }                                     synchronous (RequestResponse)
      });                                     invocation.
    });
  });
}
```

Fail if the input image has no width or height.

Detect faces using one of the templates included in OpenCV.

Listing 5.5 `faceDetection` (Python)

```python
from __future__ import print_function

import numpy
import cv2
import json
import urllib2
import uuid
import datetime
import boto3

print('Loading function')

dstBucket = '<S3-BUCKET-TO-STORE-OUTPUT-IMAGES>'
dstPrefix = 'tmp/'
outputDomain = '<OUTPUT-DOMAIN>'

cascPath = 'share/OpenCV/haarcascades/haarcascade_frontalface_alt.xml'

s3 = boto3.resource('s3')
faceCascade = cv2.CascadeClassifier(cascPath)

def lambda_handler(event, context):
    print('Received event: ' + json.dumps(event, indent=2))
    imageUrl = event['imageUrl']

    imageFile = urllib2.urlopen(imageUrl)

    imageBytes = numpy.asarray(bytearray(imageFile.read()),
     dtype=numpy.uint8)
    image = cv2.imdecode(imageBytes, cv2.CV_LOAD_IMAGE_UNCHANGED)

    gray = cv2.cvtColor(image, cv2.COLOR_BGR2GRAY)
    faces = faceCascade.detectMultiScale(
        gray,
        scaleFactor=1.1,
        minNeighbors=5,
        minSize=(30, 30),
        flags = cv2.cv.CV_HAAR_SCALE_IMAGE
    )
    if len(faces) > 0:
        for (x, y, w, h) in faces:
            cv2.rectangle(image, (x, y), (x+w, y+h), (255, 255, 255), 2)

        r, outputImage = cv2.imencode('.jpg', image)
        if False==r:
            raise Exception('Error encoding image')

        dstKey = dstPrefix +
datetime.datetime.now().strftime('%Y%m%d%H%M%S') + '-' + str(uuid.uuid4())
+ '.jpg'

        s3.Bucket(dstBucket).put_object(Key=dstKey,
            Body=outputImage.tostring(),
            ContentType='image/jpeg'
        )
```

Import the "opencv" module created in the first part of this chapter.

Download the input image.

Convert the input image in the OpenCV image format.

Detect faces using one of the templates included in OpenCV.

Looping on the detected faces to draw rectangles around them

Uploading the image with the detected faces to Amazon S3

```
                     outputUrl = 'https://' + outputDomain + '/' + dstKey
```

Preparing the
result object   ⌐▷
with the
number of
faces and the
output URL

```
                     result = { 'faces': len(faces), 'outputUrl': outputUrl }

                 else:

                     result = { 'faces': 0, 'outputUrl': imageUrl }  ◁
```
    If no faces have been
    found, return the input
    URL as output, and no
    upload is required.

```
                 return result  ◁
```
    Return the result for a
    synchronous (RequestResponse)
    invocation.

You can now choose which runtime to use and create the `faceDetection` function from the AWS Lambda console in a similar way to what you did previously for the `greetingsOnDemand` function. This time, you may need more memory (depending on the size of the image) and a longer timeout, because this function is more computationally intensive and therefore much slower than previous functions.

As we discussed in chapter 4, with AWS Lambda, increasing memory also increases computational power to the container where the functions are executed. That reduces the overall execution time; 1 GB of memory and 10 seconds of timeout are good settings for this function. Usually, for most invocations, the execution time is still less than one second.

5.3.3   *Testing the function*

Now you can call the function directly from the AWS CLI by running the following command:

```
aws lambda invoke --function-name facialDetect --payload
'{"imageUrl":"http://somedomain/somepic.jpg"}' output.txt
```

In the output.txt file, you'll find the number of faces and the link to the picture stored on Amazon S3, with the faces marked:

```
{
  "faces": 3
  "outputURL": "https://bucket.s3.amazonaws.com/tmp/<date + unique
UUID>.jpg"
}
```

Open the "outputURL" in a browser to check the result. Using JavaScript (you'll learn about that in the next chapter) you can render the result of the `FaceDetection` function as in figure 5.9.

> **NOTE**   Using a similar syntax via one of the AWS SDKs, you can use this function as a back-end call of your client application. Multiple examples of calling a Lambda function from a client are in the next chapter.

There are 6 faces in the picture.

This is the original image.

Here faces are marked with white rectangles.

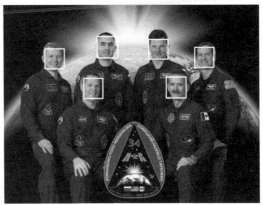

Figure 5.9 Sample output of the `FaceDetection` function, rendered in a browser using JavaScript

TIP You can configure a lifecycle rule in the properties of the S3 bucket to automatically delete all content starting with the tmp/ prefix after one (or more) days. In this way, all the pictures generated by the faceDetection function remain available for the specified time and are then deleted. Note that S3 isn't a file system and when configuring the lifecycle rule, you don't need a "/" at the beginning of the tmp/ prefix, only at the end.

5.4 *Scheduling function execution*

You learned how to subscribe a function to events coming from another AWS service, such as Amazon S3. One particular use of subscription is given by Amazon CloudWatch Events, where you can tie the execution of a Lambda function with a rule that can be triggered by generic events coming from the AWS platform, such as the transition of state of a virtual server managed by Amazon EC2, or a schedule that you define.

Using a recurring schedule opens new use cases for Lambda functions. For example, you can execute a function daily to get the number of new users that joined your application and have that information mailed to you via Amazon Simple Email Service (SES). A Lambda function has a broad range of housekeeping tasks that it can execute every week, every day, or every hour.

In the face-detection example in the previous section, the function creates a new picture every time the face detection is applied to an image, marking the faces in that image. The new picture is saved in Amazon S3 with a temporary prefix of tmp/, which can be used to configure a lifecycle rule to remove all files with that prefix older than one day. Imagine you want to remove these temporary pictures more often, for example every hour. You can use a Lambda function to do that.

NOTE   If you consider the costs for such a function (24 hours by 30 days gives 720 invocations monthly) whose execution time is probably less than a second, you're barely scratching the surface of what's provided by the AWS Free Tier.

Listing 5.6 is a sample function, `purgeBucketByPrefix`, that looks for all objects older than some duration (configurable in seconds) and deletes them. The function uses parallelism in the AWS API calls to reduce the overall execution time.

NOTE   The `purgeBucketByPrefix` function uses Node.js to execute multiple asynchronous calls to AWS in parallel and reduce the execution time of the function. Implementing the same level of parallelism in Python requires the use of additional modules—for example, the `multiprocessing` or `threading` modules—so a related code listing for Python isn't provided in this book.

Listing 5.6   `purgeBucketByPrefix` (Node.js)

```
var AWS = require('aws-sdk');
var util = require('util');

var s3 = new AWS.S3();

var dstBucket = '<BUCKET-NAME>';      ◁──    The S3 bucket to purge
var dstPrefix = 'tmp/';               ◁──    The prefix to purge
var maxElapsedInSeconds = 3600;       ◁──    The elapsed time after which
                                             objects must be deleted

var dstPrefixLength = dstPrefix.length;
                                             To check if all parallel
                                             requests have completed
function checkIfFinished(state, callback) {  ◁── and the function can finish
    if (state.processed == state.found && !state.searching) {
        callback(null, state.deleted + " objects deleted");
    }
}                                            Internal function to manage
                                             multiple (recursive) list
function getObjectKeys(marker, state, callback) {  ◁── objects calls
    var params = {
        Bucket: dstBucket,
        Prefix: dstPrefix
    };                                       If a marker is passed, use it
    if (marker !== null) {                   in the next list objects call
        params.Marker = marker;             ◁── to continue listing.
    }
    console.log(params);                     Amazon S3 list
    s3.listObjects(params, function(err, data) {  ◁── object call
        if (err) {
            console.log(err, err.stack); // an error occurred
            callback(err);
        } else {
            state.found += data.Contents.length;
            if (data.IsTruncated) {
                getObjectKeys(data.NextMarker, state, callback);
            } else {
                state.searching = false;
            }
```

If there are too many objects to return (truncated), use the marker to do another list objects.

```
                    if (data.Contents.length === 0) {
                        checkIfFinished(state, callback);
                    }
                    data.Contents.forEach(function(item) {          Get the file date from the
                        var fileName = item.Key;                    file name and avoid a call
                        var fileDate = new Date(          ◁─────     to Amazon S3 for each file.
                            fileName.substr(dstPrefixLength,4),
                            fileName.substr(dstPrefixLength + 4,2) - 1,
                            fileName.substr(dstPrefixLength + 6,2),
                            fileName.substr(dstPrefixLength + 8,2),
                            fileName.substr(dstPrefixLength + 10,2),
                            fileName.substr(dstPrefixLength + 12,2)      Compute the
                        );                                               elapsed time
                        var elapsedInSeconds = (now - fileDate) / 1000;  ◁─ for the file.
                        if (elapsedInSeconds > maxElapsedInSeconds) {
                            var params = {
                                Bucket: dstBucket,
                                Key: fileName                            Amazon
                            };                                           S3 delete
                            s3.deleteObject(params, function(err, data) {  ◁── object call
                                if (err) {
                                    console.log(err, err.stack);
                                    console.fail(err);
                                } else {
                                    console.log('Deleted ' + fileName);
                                    state.deleted++;
                                }
                                state.processed++;
                                checkIfFinished(state, callback);
                            });
                        } else {
                            state.processed++;
                            checkIfFinished(state, callback);
                        }
                    });
                }
            });
    }

    exports.handler = (event, context, callback) => {
        console.log("Reading options from event:\n", util.inspect(event,
    {depth: 5}));

        now = new Date();                                    ◁─┐ Get current time
        console.log('Now is ' + now.toISOString());

        var state = {                    ◁─┐ Prepare a state object to be
            found: 0,                        used by the checkIfFinished
            processed: 0,                    function.
            deleted: 0,
            searching: true
        };
                                                     Start listing objects; can have
        getObjectKeys(null, state, callback);   ◁─   recursive calls if there are too
    };                                               many objects to return
```

If the elapsed time is greater than the threshold, proceed to delete the object from Amazon S3.

To execute the function in listing 5.6, you need an IAM role to allow listing and deleting from the S3 bucket objects with the /tmp prefix. Also, remember to give the function basic Lambda execution permissions to write logs. You can attach the policy in the following listing to the role, together with the AWSLambdaBasicExecutionRole managed policy.

Listing 5.7 Policy

```
{
    "Version": "2012-10-17",
    "Statement": [
        {
            "Effect": "Allow",
            "Action": [
                "s3:ListBucket"
            ],
            "Resource": [
                "arn:aws:s3:::<BUCKET-NAME>"
            ],
            "Condition": {
                "StringLike": { "s3:prefix": [ "tmp/*" ] }
            }
        },
        {
            "Effect": "Allow",
            "Action": [
                "s3:DeleteObject"
            ],
            "Resource": [
                "arn:aws:s3:::<BUCKET-NAME>/tmp/*"
            ]
        }
    ]
}
```

Use a Condition to limit access to the list bucket (objects) call by prefix.

Use a Resource to limit access to the delete object call by prefix.

After you create the purgeBucketByPrefix function from the Lambda console, you can schedule a recurring execution from the Event sources tab. Select Add event source, choose "CloudWatch Events–Schedule" from the menu, and give your required recurrence in the Schedule expression.

For example, you can use rate(1 hour) to execute this function once per hour. Or you can use a more flexible Cron[4] syntax such as cron(0 17 ? * MON-FRI *). Give the rule a name and a description so that you can easily reuse the same rule for more than one function. Enable the event source and click Submit to start the scheduled execution you configured. The temporary content of the S3 bucket will be purged every hour.

---

[4] Cron is a time-based job scheduler usually present in Unix operating systems.

Summary

In this chapter, you learned how to use standalone AWS Lambda functions in common use cases, such as the following:

- Building a deployment package to bring together libraries, modules, and binaries with your function
- Using functions to react to events from AWS resources, such as Amazon S3
- Using functions for scheduled activities

In the next chapter you'll learn how to manage identities for users coming from outside of AWS and provide them with the necessary authentication and authorization to access Lambda functions and other AWS resources, such as S3 buckets or DynamoDB tables.

EXERCISE

To test what you've learned in this chapter, try to answer these multiple-choice questions:

1. When a new object is uploaded to Amazon S3, you want to trigger different Lambda functions depending on the extension of the file. For example, one function is triggered by .pdf files and another function by .png files. How can you implement that with AWS Lambda?

   a Create all the functions you need and then, for each function, in the event source configuration, put the extension you want to use as a trigger in the prefix option.

   b Create all the functions you need and then, for each function, in the event source configuration, put the extension you want to use as a trigger in the suffix option.

   c Create a single function containing multiple subroutines. A main function will call the corresponding subroutine, depending on the value of the extension in the S3 object key as part of the event.

   d Create a single function containing multiple subroutines. A main function will call the corresponding subroutine depending on the value of the extension in the S3 object key as part of the context.

2. When a new document is uploaded to Amazon S3, you want to process those files with different service levels depending on the prefix used by the object. For example, files with the premium/ prefix should be processed faster than files with the basic/ prefix. How can you implement that with AWS Lambda?

   a Create one function, and then in the event source tab configure more memory (and hence more CPU) with the premium/ prefix and less memory with the basic/ prefix.

   b Create one function, and then in the event source tab configure a smaller timeout with the premium/ prefix and a bigger timeout with the basic/ prefix.

c Create two functions with the same code, but configure one function to have more memory (and hence more CPU) than the other. Subscribe the function using less memory to the basic/ prefix and the function using more memory to the premium/ prefix.

d Create two functions with the same code, but configure one function to have a shorter timeout than the other. Subscribe the function using the smaller timeout to the basic/ prefix and the function using the bigger timeout to the premium/ prefix.

3 You want to schedule a Lambda function for execution every 30 minutes from Monday to Friday. What's the syntax you have to use in the event source?

a rate(30 minutes)

b cron(0/30 * ? * MON-FRI *)

c rate(5 days)

d cron(30 * ? * MON-FRI *)

Solution

1 b or c; b is a better solution than c because you have multiple smaller functions to manage, instead of a single larger function, and you don't need to manage part of the configuration in the code of the function.

2 c

3 b

Managing identities

This chapter covers

- Introducing the identity features provided by Amazon Cognito
- Using external authentications already integrated with Amazon Cognito
- Integrating your own custom authentication
- Managing authenticated and unauthenticated identities in your application

In the previous chapter you learned how to use Lambda functions in different use cases, configuring the required permissions for those functions to act on other AWS resources such as S3 buckets or DynamoDB tables. But it's still not clear how to manage authentication for external users interacting with AWS resources and Lambda functions via a client application (figure 6.1).

Amazon Cognito has been designed specifically to make it simple for external users and applications to assume a role on AWS and get temporary security credentials. Amazon Cognito makes it easy to follow AWS security best practices, such as not hard-coding AWS credentials whenever possible, especially where you

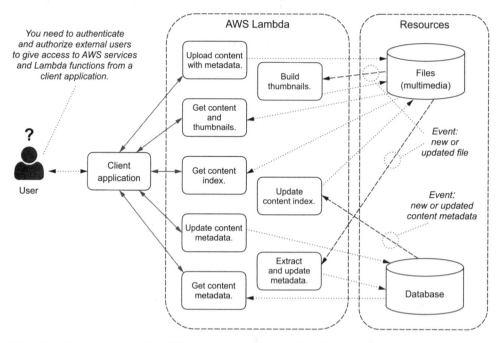

Figure 6.1   External users using AWS resources, such as Lambda functions from a client application, need to be authenticated and authorized. But for security reasons you can't embed AWS credentials in the client application.

can't control access to those credentials, such as in a mobile app or JavaScript code downloaded from a web browser.

6.1   *Introducing Amazon Cognito Identity*

In chapter 1, we mentioned that Amazon Cognito could be used to provide AWS credentials to the client, so that the client application could directly invoke AWS Lambda functions (figure 6.2).

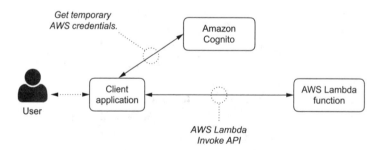

Figure 6.2   Using Amazon Cognito to authenticate and authorize invocation for AWS Lambda functions

The same approach can be used to protect access to the web API exposed by Amazon API Gateway (figure 6.3). To do that, in the API Gateway web console you can choose the AWS IAM authorization type in the Authorization Settings of the Method Request.

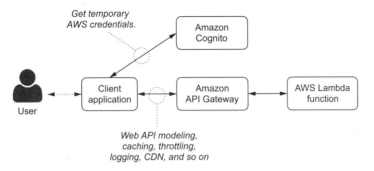

Figure 6.3   Using the Amazon API Gateway to access functions via web APIs

> **NOTE**   The Amazon API Gateway also supports custom authorizations using a Lambda function as a *custom authorizer*, so you can implement the authentication strategy you need; for example, OAuth.

Cognito provides more than AWS credentials. It's designed to trust an external authentication: a standard one, such as Facebook or Twitter, or a custom authentication that you can easily integrate. Based on the external authentication, Cognito gives a unique Identity ID that follows users across any device they use. For unauthenticated users, Cognito gives a guest Identity ID that will stick with the device they're using (such as a smartphone, tablet, or a web browser). In this way, Cognito supports two kinds of identities, unauthenticated and authenticated, each with a different IAM role that can be assumed using the returned (temporary) credentials. Usually you'd give less powerful permissions to the unauthenticated role; for example, unauthenticated users can only read from the AWS resources used by the app, while authenticated users have a more powerful role that allows them to write on those resources.

> **NOTE**   To assume a role and get temporary credentials, Amazon Cognito provides an easy-to-use interface that uses the functionalities of the AWS Security Token Service (STS) in the background.

Because a single AWS account can manage multiple applications, Cognito allows you to create different *pools* of identities that have no dependencies with each other. You can specify which pool to use using a unique *identity pool ID* provided by Cognito. Each identity pool has an authenticated role. Optionally, you can enable unauthenticated users for the identity pool. In that case, you have an unauthenticated role as well. Those features are at the basis of Amazon Cognito Identity.

NOTE   Amazon Cognito also provides the option to synchronize data (in the form of a key/value store) locally on all devices used by the same identity. That part of the service is Amazon Cognito Sync, which you won't use in this book and isn't free of charge as the Federated Identities feature.

Now let's see in detail how the interaction works between the client, Amazon Cognito, the external (or custom) authentication service, and other AWS services. Starting with *unauthenticated* users (which you can optionally enable for an identity pool), the usage flow is as follows (also depicted in figure 6.4):

1   The user is using a client application, such as a mobile device or a JavaScript application running in a browser.
2   The client application sends the identity pool ID to Amazon Cognito to get an Identity ID.
3   If the identity pool is configured to allow unauthenticated users, the client application receives a guest Identity ID for the unauthenticated user that will be stored locally on the device (smartphone, tablet, web browser) and will be reused in future connections by the same client application. The client application can also get temporary AWS credentials to assume the unauthenticated role of this identity pool.
4   The client application can directly use other AWS services authenticating with the temporary AWS credentials it has received from Amazon Cognito, which allow access to the actions and the resources specified in the policies attached to the unauthenticated role of the identity pool.

For example, you can give unauthenticated users limited read-only access to AWS resources used by your application. You can also give access only to those AWS Lambda functions that aren't making important changes. As a result, unauthenticated users can only visualize what authenticated users are doing.

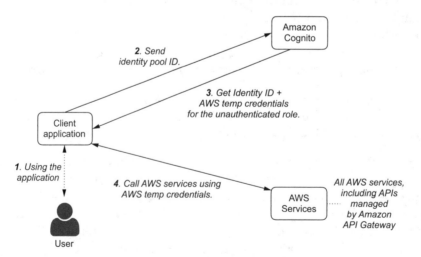

Figure 6.4   Cognito Identity usage flow for unauthenticated users

The only information required by the client application at the beginning of this flow is the identity pool ID; no AWS credentials are embedded in the application or transferred over a nonsecure channel.

6.2 *External identity providers*

To have authenticated users, you need a place to authenticate to. A common way for client applications running on mobile devices or in a web browser is to use an external authentication, such as Facebook or Twitter. This removes the burden of managing the authentication from the developers and simplifies the user experience since users can use an account they might already have.

At the time of writing this book, Amazon Cognito supports the following external identity providers:

- Amazon
- Facebook
- Twitter
- Digits
- Google
- Any OpenID Connect–compatible provider, such as Salesforce

Cognito trusts the authentication from the external provider using the authentication token received by the client to validate the authentication.

For *authenticated* users, the following usage flow is also shown in figure 6.5:

1. The user uses a client application, such as a mobile device or a JavaScript application running in a browser.
2. The client application authenticates with the external identity provider, usually using the provider SDK, sending the identity provider credentials (not related to AWS in any way).
3. If authentication is successful, the client application receives an authentication token from the identity provider.
4. The client application sends the identity pool ID and the authentication token to Amazon Cognito to get an Identity ID.
5. Amazon Cognito checks the validity of the authentication token with the identity provider.
6. If the authentication token is valid, the client application receives a unique Identity ID for the authenticated user that will follow across any device (smartphone, tablet, web browser) where the same authentication is used. The client application can also get temporary AWS credentials to assume the authenticated role of this identity pool.
7. The client application can directly use other AWS services authenticating with the temporary AWS credentials it has received from Amazon Cognito, which allow access to the actions and the resources specified in the policies attached to the authenticated role of the identity pool.

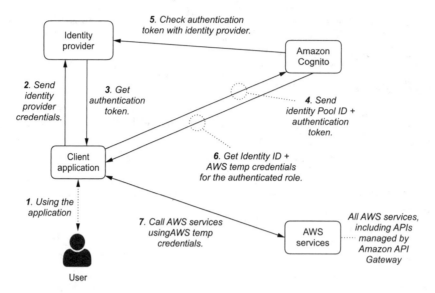

igure 6.5   Cognito Identity usage flow for authenticated users using external lentity providers

For example, you can give authenticated users write access to AWS resources used by your application, directly or via AWS Lambda functions, so that they can upload files or change data on a database.

The only information required by the client application is still the identity pool ID; no AWS credentials are embedded in the application or transferred over a nonsecure channel. The authentication with the identity provider is managed by the tools and the SDKs maintained by the provider.

6.3   *Integrating custom authentications*

Apart from the external identity providers directly supported, Amazon Cognito can use any custom authentication service. For successful authentication, the service has to do a back-end call to Amazon Cognito to ask for an authentication token, which is returned to the client together with the result of the authentication.

This particular case of an authenticated user is referred to in the AWS documentation as *developer authenticated identities*. Except for the back-end call to request the authentication token, the usage flow is the same as for the external identity providers (figure 6.6):

1 The user uses a client application, such as a mobile device or a JavaScript application running in a browser.

2 The client application authenticates with the custom identity provider, usually using the provider SDK, sending the identity provider credentials (not related to AWS in any way).

3 If authentication is successful, the custom authentication service does a back-end call to Amazon Cognito to get a token for the developer identity (the actual API call is `GetOpenIdTokenForDeveloperIdentity`).

4 The client application receives the authentication token returned by Cognito from the custom authentication service.

5 The client application sends the identity pool ID and the authentication token to Amazon Cognito to get an Identity ID.

6 If the authentication token (originally generated by Cognito) is valid, the client application receives a unique Identity ID for the authenticated user that will follow across any device (smartphone, tablet, web browser) where the same authentication is used. The client application can also get temporary AWS credentials to assume the authenticated role used by this identity pool.

7 The client application can directly use other AWS services, authenticating with the temporary AWS credentials it has received from Amazon Cognito, which allow access to the actions and the resources specified in the policies attached to the authenticated role of the identity pool.

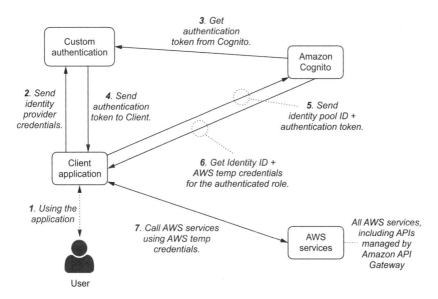

Figure 6.6   Cognito Identity usage flow for authenticated users using custom authentication

Users authenticated via custom authentication have the same capabilities as users authenticated via external identity providers directly supported by Cognito.

6.4   *Having authenticated and unauthenticated users*

There are two possible usage patterns for an identity pool managed by Amazon Cognito:

- Have only authenticated users
- Have both unauthenticated and authenticated users

Depending on how you use AWS services within your application, users can interact with the application in different ways:

- No authentication is necessary for the purpose of the application, but you can still use Cognito and get an Identity ID for the users to get usage analytics and understand how they use the application (for example, using Amazon Mobile Analytics or streaming data to Amazon Kinesis).
- Authentication is optional; unauthenticated users have access to a limited subset of features and are naturally brought to authenticate to gain access to more advanced functionalities.
- Authentication is mandatory and is the first step when a user is starting to use your application.

Usually, the second approach (optional authentication) provides the better user experience, because users can immediately start using some features, understand what they can do, and—if they like it—authenticate to do more.

Forced authentication isn't the best way for a user to experience a new application. It can slow adoption unless your application is clearly targeting a private environment, such as an enterprise application where nobody should have access unless they are an employee of the company.

Having no authentication limits the ability to customize the user experience and to follow the same user across different devices.

6.5   *Using policy variables with Amazon Cognito*

Using Amazon Cognito for authentication has another interesting advantage: specific policy variables that you can use to build more advanced policies, as listed in table 6.1.

Table 6.1   Amazon Cognito—specific policy variables to enhance your policies

Policy variable	Description and sample usage
`cognito-identity.amazonaws.com:aud`	The identity pool ID.
`cognito-identity.amazonaws.com:sub`	The user Identity ID.
`cognito-identity.amazonaws.com:amr`	The Authenticated Methods Reference contains login information about the user. For unauthenticated users, the variable contains only "unauthenticated." For authenticated users, the variable contains the value "authenticated" and the name of the login provider used in the call (for example, "graph.facebook.com," "accounts.google.com," or "www.amazon.com").

Imagine you want to use a bucket B with a prefix P. Using those policy variables you can write policies that provide:

- Access to private folders on Amazon S3 (listing 6.1), where only a specific user can either read or write. This is useful for holding private data.
- Access to public folders on Amazon S3 (listing 6.2), where a specific user can write only in their own folder, but all folders can be read by all users. This is useful for holding shared data.

Listing 6.1 Policy to give access to private folders on Amazon S3

```
{
  "Version": "2012-10-17",
  "Statement": [
    {
      "Action": ["s3:ListBucket"],
      "Effect": "Allow",
      "Resource": ["arn:aws:s3:::B"],
      "Condition":
      {"StringLike":
        {"s3:prefix": ["P/${cognito-identity.amazonaws.com:sub}/*"]}
      }
    },
    {
      "Action": [
        "s3:GetObject",
        "s3:PutObject"
      ],
      "Effect": "Allow",
      "Resource":
        ["arn:aws:s3:::B/P/${cognito-identity.amazonaws.com:sub}/*"]
    }
  ]
}
```

For all read/write actions, the object key must contain a "folder" equal to the user Identity ID provided by Amazon Cognito.

Listing 6.2 Policy to give access to public folders on Amazon S3

```
{
  "Version": "2012-10-17",
  "Statement": [
    {
      "Action": ["s3:ListBucket"],
      "Effect": "Allow",
      "Resource": ["arn:aws:s3:::B"],
      "Condition":
      {"StringLike":
        {"s3:prefix": ["P/*"]}
      }
    },
    {
      "Action": ["s3:GetObject"],
      "Effect": "Allow",
```

For read actions, only the initial prefix is required.

```
      "Resource":
        ["arn:aws:s3:::B/P/*"]
    },
    {
      "Action": ["s3:PutObject"],
      "Effect": "Allow",
      "Resource":
        ["arn:aws:s3:::B/P/${cognito-identity.amazonaws.com:sub}/*"]
    }
  ]
}
```

◄── **For read actions, only the initial prefix is required.**

◄── **For write actions, the object key must contain a folder equal to the user Identity ID provided by Amazon Cognito.**

Also, Amazon Cognito policy variables can be used to provide

- Private access to Amazon DynamoDB (listing 6.3), where a user can only read or write items in a table if their own Identity ID is in the hash key
- Shared access to Amazon DynamoDB (listing 6.4), where a user can only write items if their own Identity ID is in the hash key, but users can read all records in the table

Listing 6.3   Policy to give private access to DynamoDB

```
{
  "Version": "2012-10-17",
  "Statement": [
    {
      "Effect": "Allow",
      "Action": [
        "dynamodb:GetItem",
        "dynamodb:BatchGetItem",
        "dynamodb:Query",
        "dynamodb:PutItem",
        "dynamodb:UpdateItem",
        "dynamodb:DeleteItem",
        "dynamodb:BatchWriteItem"
      ],
      "Resource": [
        "arn:aws:dynamodb:<region>:<account-id>:table/<table-name>"
      ],
      "Condition": {
        "ForAllValues:StringEquals": {
          "dynamodb:LeadingKeys":
            ["${cognito-identity.amazonaws.com:sub}"]
        }
      }
    }
  ]
}
```

◄── **For all read/write actions, the condition requires that the Leading Keys (the hash key) is equal to the user Identity ID provided by Amazon Cognito.**

Listing 6.4 Policy to give shared access to DynamoDB

```
{
  "Version": "2012-10-17",
  "Statement": [
    {
      "Effect": "Allow",
      "Action": [
        "dynamodb:GetItem",
        "dynamodb:BatchGetItem",
        "dynamodb:Query"
      ],
      "Resource": [
        "arn:aws:dynamodb:<region>:<account-id>:table/<table-name>"
      ]
    },
    {
      "Effect": "Allow",
      "Action": [
        "dynamodb:PutItem",
        "dynamodb:UpdateItem",
        "dynamodb:DeleteItem",
        "dynamodb:BatchWriteItem"
      ],
      "Resource": [
        "arn:aws:dynamodb:us-east-1:123456789012:table/MyTable"
      ],
      "Condition": {
        "ForAllValues:StringEquals": {
          "dynamodb:LeadingKeys":
            ["${cognito-identity.amazonaws.com:sub}"]
        }
      }
    }
  ]
}
```

For read actions, there is no condition and all items are available to all users.

For write actions, the condition requires that the Leading Keys (the hash key) is equal to the user Identity ID provided by Amazon Cognito.

Using the previous policies for Amazon S3 and Amazon DynamoDB, you can give secure access to a file store and a database straight from the client application, without other components in between. To add custom logic to those interactions, you can subscribe a Lambda function to changes in the file store or the database. For example, you can subscribe a function to Amazon S3 and check the validity of any file that's uploaded. If you're expecting users to upload pictures, then you can check that the uploaded files are pictures with the format and size you need.

Even if the previous policies could be used for an unauthenticated role, for unauthenticated users, the Identity ID is bound to a single device and can change if the app is removed and downloaded again or the cache of the web browser is cleared. I suggest using those policies only for an authenticated role.

To use the authenticated and unauthenticated roles, you also need a trust relationship to allow Amazon Cognito to let external users or applications assume the role.

The trust policies you use must distinguish between authenticated and unauthenticated users; otherwise, unauthenticated users could assume the authenticated roles.

When you create a new identity pool from the Amazon Cognito web console, the roles (there can be one or two, depending on whether you enable unauthenticated access to the pool) are automatically created with the right trust relationships to the specific identity pool and a small set of permissions to allow access to Amazon Cognito Synch and Amazon Mobile Analytics from the client. You then can add permissions as you need them, following the "least privilege" approach described previously. Let's look at examples of trust policies:

- The unauthenticated role (listing 6.5)
- The authenticated role (listing 6.6)

The `<identity-pool-id>` is automatically populated by the Cognito web console with the specific value for the pool you create.

Listing 6.5 Amazon Cognito trust policy for the unauthenticated role

```
{
  "Version": "2012-10-17",
  "Statement": [
    {
      "Sid": "",
      "Effect": "Allow",
      "Principal": {
        "Federated": "cognito-identity.amazonaws.com"
      },
      "Action": "sts:AssumeRoleWithWebIdentity",
      "Condition": {
        "StringEquals": {
          "cognito-identity.amazonaws.com:aud": "<identity-pool-id>"
        },
        "ForAnyValue:StringLike": {
          "cognito-identity.amazonaws.com:amr": "unauthenticated"
        }
      }
    }
  ]
}
```

The first condition requires that the user is in the right identity pool ID.

The second condition requires that the used isn't authenticated.

Listing 6.6 Amazon Cognito trust policy for the authenticated role

```
{
  "Version": "2012-10-17",
  "Statement": [
    {
      "Sid": "",
      "Effect": "Allow",
      "Principal": {
        "Federated": "cognito-identity.amazonaws.com"
      },
```

```
      "Action": "sts:AssumeRoleWithWebIdentity",
      "Condition": {
        "StringEquals": {
          "cognito-identity.amazonaws.com:aud": "<identity-pool-id>"
        },
        "ForAnyValue:StringLike": {
          "cognito-identity.amazonaws.com:amr": "authenticated"
        }
      }
    }
  ]
}
```

The first condition requires that the user be in the right identity pool ID.

The second condition requires that the user be authenticated.

Summary

In this chapter you saw how AWS security works and how you can secure your application with AWS Lambda and Amazon Cognito. In particular, you learned about

- Using roles with Amazon Cognito
- Authenticating external users and applications using Amazon Cognito
- Using external identity providers or integrating your own custom authentication
- Using authenticated and unauthenticated users in your application
- Configuring advanced policies to give access to Amazon S3 and Amazon DynamoDB

In the next chapter you'll learn how to use functions from a device, such as a mobile device or a JavaScript web page running in a web browser, and how to subscribe functions to events in the AWS Cloud.

EXERCISE

Write a policy to give external users authenticating via Amazon Cognito access to an Amazon S3 bucket called myapp with public folders under the prefix pub/ and private folders under the prefix priv/. Add to the same policy DynamoDB private access to a `private-table` and shared access to a `shared-table`.

Solution

Using the option to include multiple statements in a single policy, you can merge the policies in listings 6.1, 6.2, 6.3, and 6.4. You could possibly use the policy syntax to group together similar statements into one, but keeping them separated as in the original policies improves the readability and maintainability of the resulting policy.

Composed policy to provide public and private folders on Amazon S3

```
{
  "Version": "2012-10-17",
  "Statement": [
    {
      "Action": ["s3:ListBucket"],
      "Effect": "Allow",
```

```
    "Resource": ["arn:aws:s3:::myapp"],
    "Condition":
     {"StringLike":
       {"s3:prefix": ["priv/${cognito-identity.amazonaws.com:sub}/*"]}
     }
},
{
    "Action": [
      "s3:GetObject",
      "s3:PutObject"
    ],
    "Effect": "Allow",
    "Resource":
      ["arn:aws:s3:::myapp/priv/${cognito-identity.amazonaws.com:sub}/*"]
},
{
    "Action": ["s3:ListBucket"],
    "Effect": "Allow",
    "Resource": ["arn:aws:s3:::myapp"],
    "Condition":
     {"StringLike":
       {"s3:prefix": ["pub/*"]}
     }
},
{
    "Action": ["s3:GetObject"],
    "Effect": "Allow",
    "Resource":
      ["arn:aws:s3:::myapp/pub/*"]
},
{
    "Action": ["s3:PutObject"],
    "Effect": "Allow",
    "Resource":
      ["arn:aws:s3:::myapp/pub/${cognito-identity.amazonaws.com:sub}/*"]
},
{
    "Effect": "Allow",
    "Action": [
      "dynamodb:GetItem",
      "dynamodb:BatchGetItem",
      "dynamodb:Query",
      "dynamodb:PutItem",
      "dynamodb:UpdateItem",
      "dynamodb:DeleteItem",
      "dynamodb:BatchWriteItem"
    ],
    "Resource": [
      "arn:aws:dynamodb:<region>:<account-id>:table/private-table"
    ],
    "Condition": {
      "ForAllValues:StringEquals": {
        "dynamodb:LeadingKeys":
          ["${cognito-identity.amazonaws.com:sub}"]
      }
```

```
        }
      },
      {
        "Effect": "Allow",
        "Action": [
          "dynamodb:GetItem",
          "dynamodb:BatchGetItem",
          "dynamodb:Query"
        ],
        "Resource": [
          "arn:aws:dynamodb:<region>:<account-id>:table/shared-table"
        ]
      },
      {
        "Effect": "Allow",
        "Action": [
          "dynamodb:PutItem",
          "dynamodb:UpdateItem",
          "dynamodb:DeleteItem",
          "dynamodb:BatchWriteItem"
        ],
        "Resource": [
          "arn:aws:dynamodb:us-east-1:123456789012:table/shared-table"
        ],
        "Condition": {
          "ForAllValues:StringEquals": {
            "dynamodb:LeadingKeys":
              ["${cognito-identity.amazonaws.com:sub}"]
          }
        }
      }
    ]
}
```

The trust policy for this role would be the same as in listing 6.6; no change is required except the update of the identity pool ID.

Calling functions
from a client

This chapter covers

- Using a Lambda function from within a web page via JavaScript
- Invoking a Lambda function from a native mobile app
- Serving a dynamic website with AWS Lambda and Amazon API Gateway

---

In the previous chapter, you learned how to use standalone functions for common tasks, subscribing the functions to events or scheduling a recurring execution. You also learned how to use modules and libraries with Lambda functions. In this chapter, you'll build on that knowledge to call Lambda functions from clients outside of AWS.

7.1 Calling functions from JavaScript

When we created our first function in chapter 2, we tested the function from the web console and invoked the function using the AWS CLI. But you can use any AWS SDK to call Lambda functions. When you build a web application, one interesting use case is to call Lambda functions as your back end, directly from the JavaScript code running in the browser of your users.

126

There are two primary ways you can call a Lambda function from a web browser:

- Invoke the Lambda function directly, using the AWS Lambda API.
- Call the function through a web API that you modeled via the Amazon API Gateway.

In this section, we'll focus on the first case, as described in figure 7.1, where the client application is JavaScript code running in a web browser.

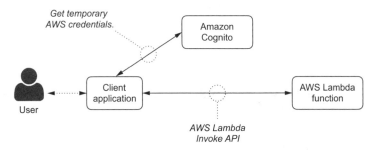

Figure 7.1   Calling a Lambda function directly from a client application, such as JavaScript code running in a web browser, requires AWS credentials that can be provided by Amazon Cognito.

Let's build a web interface for the greetingsOnDemand function you built in chapter 2 so that users can go to a web page in a browser, give their name, and receive a nice greeting!

> **NOTE**   An alternative approach, not using Amazon Cognito, is to use the AWS Security Token Service (STS) directly via the AssumeRoleWithWebIdentity or AssumeRoleWithSAML actions. This approach isn't described in this book and provides fewer features. My advice is to always use Amazon Cognito instead. For example, compared with Amazon Cognito, you don't get a unique Identity ID that follows your users across any device. For more information on using AWS STS directly, see http://docs.aws.amazon.com/IAM/latest/User-Guide/id_credentials_temp_sample-apps.html.

7.1.1   Creating the identity pool

First, we need a Cognito identity pool to give temporary AWS credentials to our users. To create your first identity pool, open your browser and go to https://console.aws.amazon.com/. Perform the following steps to create the identity pool:

1 Log in with your AWS credentials and select Cognito from the Mobile Services section.
2 Choose the closest AWS region from the menu at the top right that has Amazon Cognito available and then select "Manage Federated Identities."

3 If the region you use for Amazon Cognito is different from the one you used for AWS Lambda, you need to create the `greetingsOnDemand` function again in the new region.

4 If this isn't the first identity pool in that region, instead of the welcome page you'll see an overview of the identity pools already created and can select "Create new identity pool" to proceed.

5 Use "greetings" as the identity pool name. Because you want anyone visiting the web page to call the Lambda function, you don't need any form of authentication, and you have to enable access to unauthenticated identities (figure 7.2).

6 Select "Create pool."

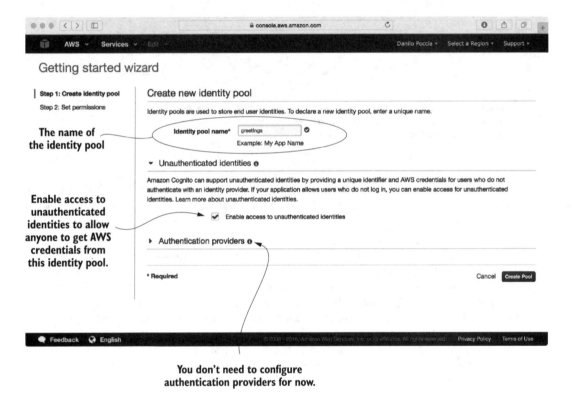

Figure 7.2   Creating a new Amazon Cognito identity pool for giving access to unauthenticated identities

The wizard from the web console creates two IAM roles (figure 7.3), one for authenticated identities (required by all identity pools) and one for unauthenticated identities (because you enabled them). You can use those roles to give access to the resources that the identities need to use. In this example, the users need to invoke a Lambda function.

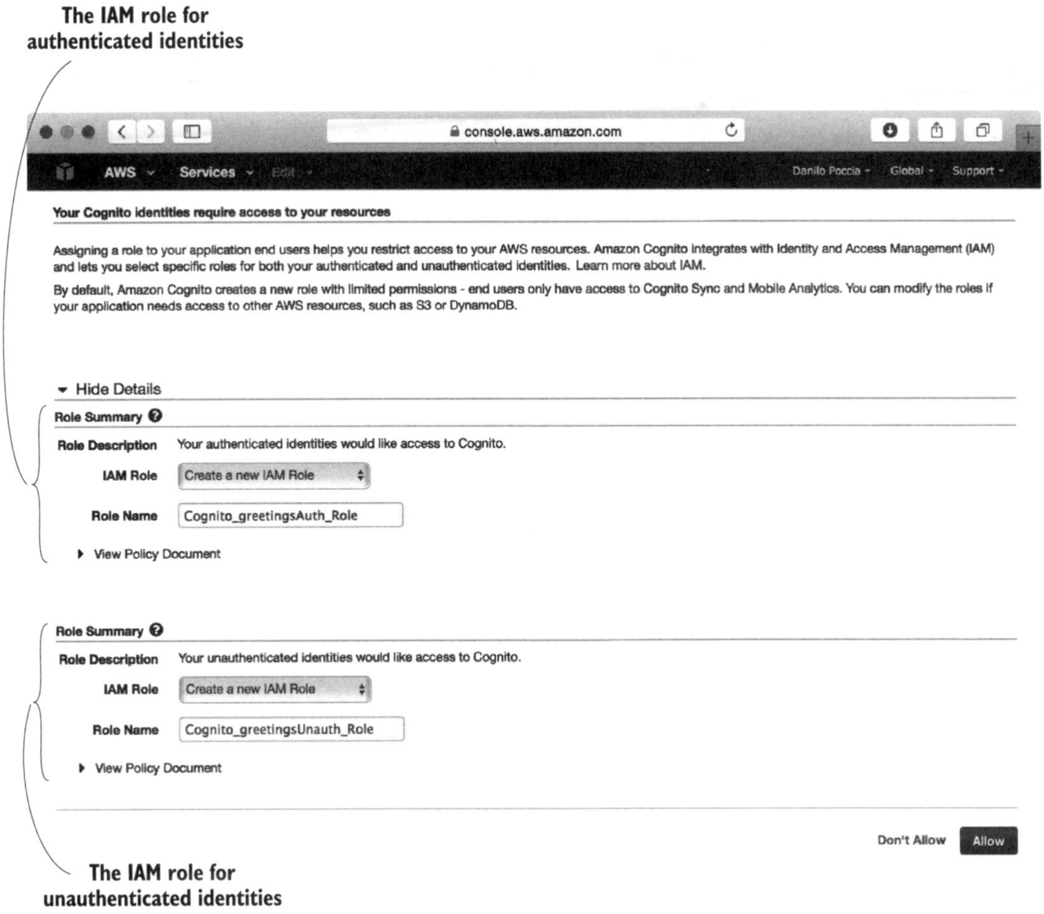

The IAM role for authenticated identities

The IAM role for unauthenticated identities

Figure 7.3 The AWS web console will guide you in creating the necessary roles for the Cognito identity pool. You must always have a role for authenticated identities. Because you enabled access to unauthenticated identities, you'll have two roles here.

You can expand the view on the policy document to understand what those roles will initially enable the identities to do (figure 7.4). The initial policy documents can be considered as almost "empty roles" because they allow only the following features:

- The put event, using Amazon Mobile Analytics (a service to understand usage and revenue for mobile and web apps, which we're not using in this book).
- The use of Amazon Cognito Sync (the part of Amazon Cognito that enables cross-device synching of application-related user data. We're not using these features in this book; we're focusing on Amazon Cognito Identity here).

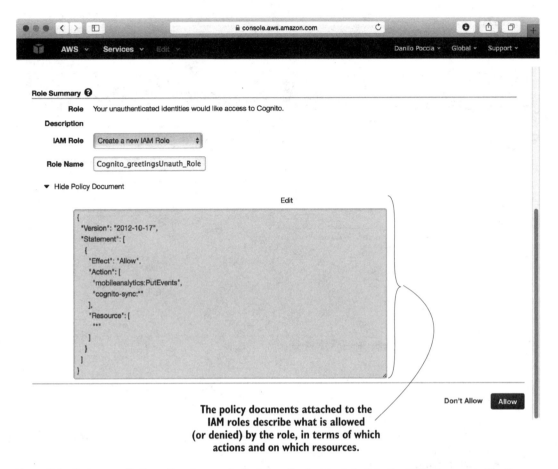

The policy documents attached to the
IAM roles describe what is allowed
(or denied) by the role, in terms of which
actions and on which resources.

Figure 7.4   You can verify the policy documents that are attached by default to the IAM roles created by the web console. You can then add more actions and resources to those roles, depending on your application.

These two IAM roles will also be automatically configured with the necessary trust policy to be used by this Cognito identity pool.

Typically, you'd add more capabilities in terms of actions and resources, depending on the use case of your application. In our case, we'll need to add to the unauthenticated role (Cognito_greetingsUnauth_Role, if you didn't change the default name) permissions to invoke the greetingsOnDemand Lambda function. You'll do that later using the AWS IAM console.

Select Allow to create those roles. You'll land on a page that helps you use Amazon Cognito (figure 7.5). You can select the platform you want to use—JavaScript, in this case—and see links to download the SDK and read the documentation. Beneath that

You can choose a platform and get
specific information on how to start
using the identity pool with sample
code and how to link to documentation.

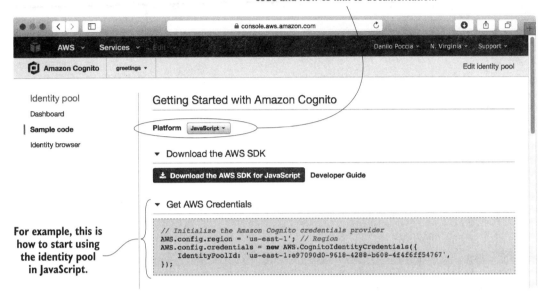

Figure 7.5 After you create the Cognito identity pool, you can see useful information and sample code for different platforms. You can choose JavaScript, iOS, Android, and more from the drop-down menu.

is sample code. Look at the code in the section "Get AWS Credentials," because you'll need it to specify the right AWS region and the Cognito identity pool ID in your code. You can go back to the Sample Code section of the Cognito console to get the code.

You don't need to download the AWS JavaScript SDK to use it in a browser because you can include it in the HTML page with a link to a standard URL. For example:

```
<script src="https://sdk.amazonaws.com/js/aws-sdk-2.2.32.min.js"></script>
```

7.1.2 *Giving permissions to the Lambda function*

To enable access to the Lambda function by identities not authenticated in your identity pool, go to the AWS console and select Identity & Access Management from the Security & Identity section. Select Roles on the left, and filter the results using "greetings," the name of the identity pool that was used by the web console as part of the names of the roles (figure 7.6).

Next, select the role for the unauthenticated identities (Cognito_greetingsUnauth _Role if you didn't change the default name) to get specific information about that

**Use this filter to
quickly find the roles you need.**

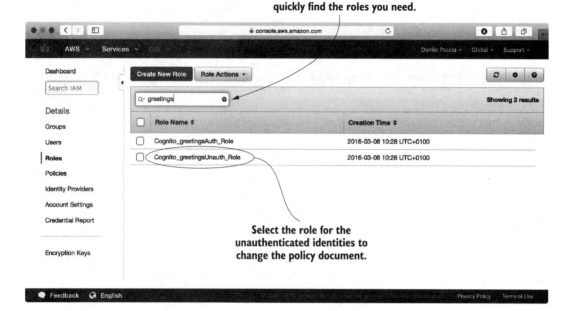

**Select the role for the
unauthenticated identities to
change the policy document.**

Figure 7.6   Use the filter in the AWS IAM console to quickly find the roles you need. Select a role to view (or edit) permissions and trust relationships.

role (figure 7.7). If you changed the name of the role and you don't remember it, go into the Cognito console, select the identity pool, and then select the option to "Edit identity pool." The two roles (authenticated and unauthenticated) are beneath the identity pool ID.

> **NOTE** When you select a role in the AWS IAM console, you can check permissions and trust relationships. From the Access Advisor tab, you can verify when the role was used recently and for which services. In the Permissions tab, you can attach a managed policy, which you can version and reuse multiple times; for example, in different roles or groups.

For now, in the Inline Policies section, select Edit Policy to edit the document created automatically by the console.

> **TIP** When I use multiple AWS services via the web console, I usually have multiple tabs open in my browser (at least one for each service I'm using) so that I can quickly switch from one to the other. For example, I have one tab for AWS Lambda, where I edit or configure the function; one tab for AWS IAM with the role of the function; one tab for Amazon Cognito to view or edit the identity pool; another one or two tabs with the AWS IAM roles used by the Cognito identity pool, and so on.

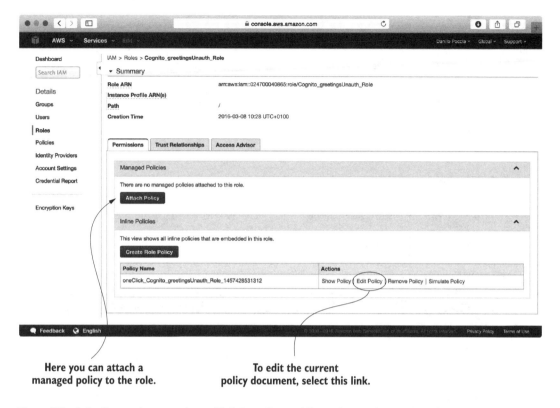

Here you can attach a managed policy to the role.

To edit the current policy document, select this link.

Figure 7.7 Selecting a role, you get specific information and the option to change the policy documents attached to the role. You can attach a managed policy (that can be versioned and reused multiple times) or edit the default inline policy created by the web console.

Update the policy document to add the invoke action on the `greetingsOnDemand` function using the code in the following listing. Replace the Lambda function ARN with the one for your function.

Listing 7.1 Policy_Cognito_greetingsOnDemand

```
{
  "Version": "2012-10-17",
  "Statement": [
    {
      "Effect": "Allow",
      "Action": [
        "mobileanalytics:PutEvents",
        "cognito-sync:*"
      ],
      "Resource": [
        "*"
      ]
    },
```

This statement is the default created by Amazon Cognito, giving access to Amazon Mobile Analytics and Amazon Cognito, Sync.

```
  {
    "Effect": "Allow",
    "Action": [
      "lambda:InvokeFunction"
    ],
    "Resource": [
      "arn:aws:lambda:<REGION>:<ACCOUNT>:function:greetingsOnDemand"
    ]
  }
    ]
}
```

This statement gives invocation access to a specific AWS Lambda function.

To use the correct Lambda function ARN, you can replace only the AWS region and your account number. If you don't remember it, the full ARN appears in the AWS Lambda console when you select a function, as shown in figure 7.8. My advice is to

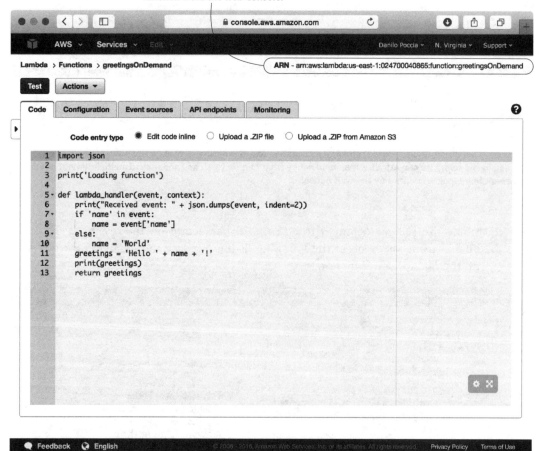

Figure 7.8   The function ARN, which you need to identify a function as a resource in a policy, is on the top right in the AWS Lambda console.

open the Lambda console in another tab of your browser, and cut and paste the full ARN from there.

To check the syntax of the policy, you can use the Validate Policy button (figure 7.9). If everything is okay, select Apply Policy to confirm your changes.

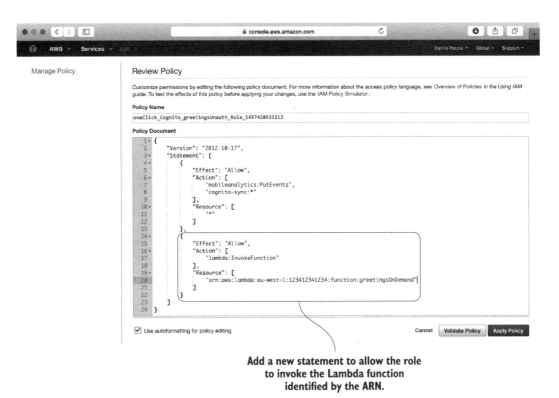

Add a new statement to allow the role
to invoke the Lambda function
identified by the ARN.

Figure 7.9   When editing a policy document in the AWS IAM Console, you can verify the syntax via the Validate Policy button before applying your changes.

7.1.3   Creating the web page

Now everything is set on the permissions and you can prepare am HTML web page for your users. For manageability, it's better to put all the JavaScript client-side logic in a separate file that's executed by the web page as a script on loading. Create two files (index.html and greetings.js) in the same directory on your computer and edit them with the code in listings 7.2 and 7.3, respectively.

> **TIP**   If your web browser supports a developer mode with an error console, activate that feature now. It's useful for debugging and understanding what's happening if something goes wrong. For example, in Chrome in the View menu, you have a Developer section where you can select the JavaScript Console. In Firefox, in the Tools menu, you have a Web Developer section where

you can enable the Web Console. In Safari, in the Advanced Preferences, you can enable the Develop menu and then select Show Error Console there.

Listing 7.2　`GreetingsOnDemand` **HTML page**

```
<html>
  <head>
    <title>Greetings on Demand</title>
    <script src="https://sdk.amazonaws.com/js/aws-sdk-2.2.32.min.js"></
      script>
  </head>
  <body>
    <h1>Greetings on Demand</h1>\
    <p>This is an example of calling an AWS Lambda function
        from a web page via JavaScript.</p>
    <p>Provide a name, and you will receive your greetings.</p>
    <p>Try without a name, too.</p>
    <form role="form" id="greetingsForm">
      <label for="name">Name:</label>
      <input type="text" id="name">
      <button type="submit" id="submitButton">Greet</button>
    </form>
    <div id="result"></div>
    <script src="greetings.js"></script>
  </body>
</html>
```

> To load the AWS SDK for JavaScript in the browser

> The input text field to get a "name" for the function

> All the logic to call the Lambda function and get the result back is in this script.

Listing 7.3　`greetings.js` **(JavaScript in the browser)**

> You need to specify the AWS region to the SDK.

```
AWS.config.region = '<REGION>';
AWS.config.credentials = new AWS.CognitoIdentityCredentials({
  IdentityPoolId: '<IDENTITY-POOL-ID>',
});

var lambda = new AWS.Lambda();

function returnGreetings() {
  document.getElementById('submitButton').disabled = true;
  var name = document.getElementById('name');
  var input;
  if (name.value == null || name.value == '') {
    input = {};
  } else {
    input = {
      name: name.value
    };
  }
  lambda.invoke({
    FunctionName: 'greetingsOnDemand',
    Payload: JSON.stringify(input)
  }, function(err, data) {
    var result = document.getElementById('result');
    if (err) {
      console.log(err, err.stack);
      result.innerHTML = err;
```

> Get AWS credentials for an unauthenticated identity (no login is provided).

> Get the AWS Lambda service interface object.

> This is how to invoke a Lambda function from JavaScript.

> The name of the function to invoke

> The payload is the input event; you need to convert the JSON object in string format.

> In case of error, you show it as a result.

Get the output of the function and convert it from string to JSON format (if required).

```
    } else {
        var output = JSON.parse(data.Payload);
        result.innerHTML = output;
    }
    document.getElementById('submitButton').disabled = false;
  });
}
var form = document.getElementById('greetingsForm');
form.addEventListener('submit', function(evt) {
  evt.preventDefault();
  returnGreetings();
});
```

The result returned by the function is shown.

Add a listener to the submit event from the HMTL form.

Avoid the default behavior in case of form submit.

Call this JavaScript function in case of form submit.

TIP You may want to use a more recent version of the AWS JavaScript SDK. You can find an updated example of how to load the SDK in a browser at http://docs.aws.amazon.com/AWSJavaScriptSDK/guide/browser-intro.html.

In the code of listing 7.3, remember to replace the AWS region you're using and the Cognito identity pool ID you created, as described by the sample code on the Cognito console; for example, your identity pool ID will be different:

```
AWS.config.region = 'us-east-1';
AWS.config.credentials = new AWS.CognitoIdentityCredentials({
    IdentityPoolId: 'us-east-1:a1b2c3d4-1234-1234-a123-12f34f56f78f',
});
```

Now open the index.html file in a web browser to test the code. You should see a screen similar to what's shown in figure 7.10.

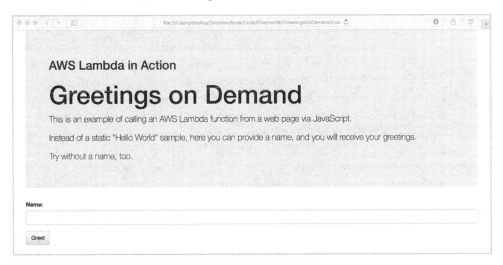

Figure 7.10 The web interface you built for the `greetingsOnDemand` Lambda function. This screenshot is taken form the code accompanying the book, which includes formatting tools. If you use the base HTML examples in the book, the visual rendering will be different.

NOTE   I'm using bare HTML in the examples in the book to make it easy to learn. In the source code accompanying the book, I'm using Bootstrap to enhance the visual result and make it responsive on mobile platforms. Bootstrap is a popular HTML, CSS, and JS framework for developing responsive and mobile-ready web projects originally created by a designer and a developer at Twitter. For more information on Bootstrap, see http://getbootstrap.com.

Type a Name and click the Greet button to see the result. For example, if you used "John" as a name, you should see "Hello John!" on a green background. If an error occurs, it will be printed on a red background. Try clicking "Greet" with no name provided. You should see "Hello World!" When no name is provided, the JavaScript code manages it by sending an empty input event, "{}" in JSON, to the function.

You're now using the Lambda function as the back end of your web application. The current example is basic, but it gives you an idea of how you can use it to add more capabilities to your application.

TIP   To create a public website out of this example, you can upload those two files to a public hosting website or to a cloud storage website that can provide public web access, such as Amazon S3. To optimize performance, you can deliver those two files using a Content Delivery Network (CDN), such as Amazon CloudFront.

7.2   *Calling functions from a mobile app*

NOTE   This section is focused on using Lambda functions from native mobile apps. You can skip this section without any impact on the remaining content of the book.

Mobile developers don't need to be cloud experts. That's one of the reasons why the AWS Mobile Hub service has been released. Using this service, you can choose which features (from a mobile developer perspective) you need to enable for your application, and it will build a custom mobile application for you, implementing those features and provisioning and configuring the necessary AWS services to support them. Both iOS and Android are supported. As you'll see, one of those features integrates Amazon Cognito to manage logins in your application. Another allows you to call Lambda functions from your mobile app.

Open your browser and go to https://console.aws.amazon.com/. Log in with your AWS credentials and select Mobile Hub from the Mobile Services section. Create a new mobile project and give it a name; for example, "AWS Lambda in Action."

A panel appears with all the features that you can enable in your application (figure 7.11). If you look closely, the bottom of every feature has an indication of which AWS services are used in the back end to implement that feature in the mobile application.

Here you can enable sign-in to your application using an external identity provider, such as Facebook or Google, using Amazon Cognito.

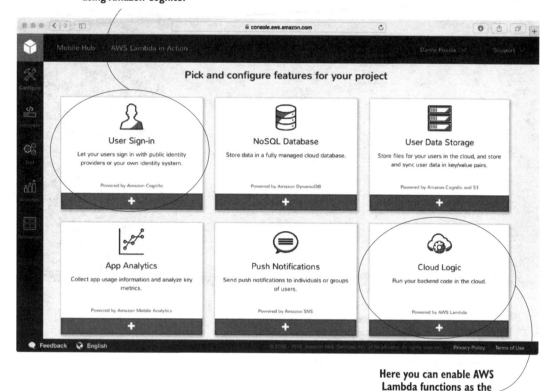

Here you can enable AWS Lambda functions as the back end logic of your mobile application.

Figure 7.11 When creating a new project with AWS Mobile Hub, you can pick up which features to include in your mobile application. The features will be included in the code and the required AWS services will be configured automatically.

For example, if you select User Sign-in, you can choose whether you want to have sign-in enabled for your application. Sign-in can be mandatory to access the app, or it can be optional, to enable more features in the app. AWS configurations are managed by the service, in this case the setup of the Amazon Cognito identity pool. Instructions are provided in the right pane of the window for configuring an external identity service to manage authentication; for example, Facebook or Google.

To use AWS Lambda functions as the back end of your application, choose Cloud Logic. There, you can select "Enable logic" (figure 7.12).

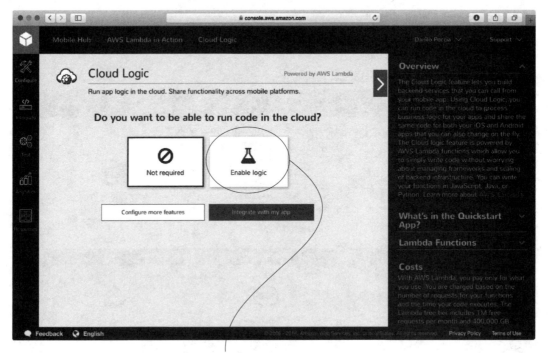

**Enable logic to allow the invocations of
AWS Lambda functions from the mobile
app built by AWS Mobile Hub.**

Figure 7.12 When you select the Cloud Logic feature, you can choose to enable (or disable) the logic.

You can now select which AWS Lambda functions—available in the same region you're using for AWS Mobile Hub—you want to use in the mobile app (figure 7.13). This step will also configure the necessary permissions to call the Lambda function from the mobile app. A sample Hello World function is also created for you to simplify a quick test in the mobile app.

Now select the Integrate tab on the left of the window (it used to be called the Build tab) and download the custom source code, which is prepared based on your configurations for iOS and Android. All the instructions to install the development environments (Xcode, for iOS, and Android Studio), import the code, and execute the mobile app are provided in the AWS Mobile Hub console when you select which platform you want to download.

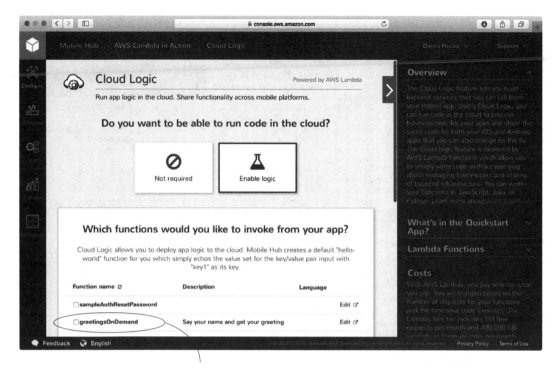

From the list of your Lambda functions you can
choose which ones to call from the mobile app.
A sample "hello-world" function is created
for you by AWS Mobile Hub.

Figure 7.13 After you enable the logic, you can choose which Lambda functions can be invoked by the mobile app. A default `hello-world` function is created for you as a basic example.

You can then test the Cloud Logic functionality (figure 7.14). The behavior of the mobile app is similar for the different supported environments, and calling a Lambda function has the same effect as when you used the AWS CLI or JavaScript via a web interface.

TIP AWS Mobile Hub is provisioning the back end AWS services required to support the features you selected. You can select the Resources tab to see which resources have been created.

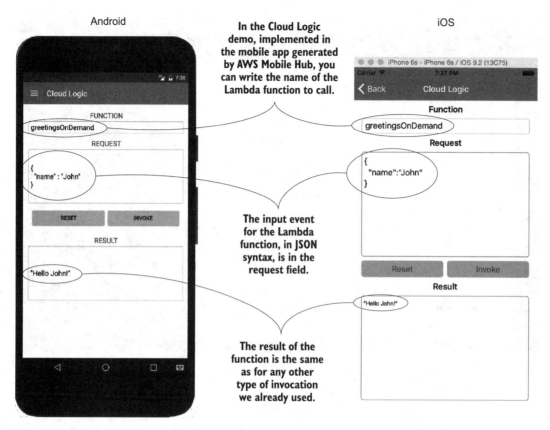

Figure 7.14   In the mobile app generated by AWS Mobile Hub, you can write any function name, but you're allowed to invoke only those that you chose in the configuration of the Cloud Logic feature.

7.2.1   *Sample code for native mobile apps*

The code (using AWS Mobile Hub helper objects) to call Lambda functions from iOS, in Objective C or Swift, is provided in listings 7.4, 7.5, and 7.6, respectively.

Listing 7.4   Calling Lambda functions from iOS (Objective C)

```
[[AWSCloudLogic sharedInstance]
invokeFunction:functionName
withParameters:parameters
withCompletionBlock:^(id result, NSError *error) {
// Use the result of the invocation here
}];
```

Listing 7.5 Calling Lambda functions from iOS (Swift)

```
AWSCloudLogic.defaultCloudLogic().invokeFunction(functionName,
    withParameters: parameters, completionBlock: {(result: AnyObject?, error:
    NSError?) -> Void in
        if let result = result {
// Use the result of the invocation here
        }
        if let error = error {
// Manage the error of the invocation here
        }
})
```

To call Lambda functions from Android, you can use the `InvokeRequest` and `Invoke-Result` objects (as shown in the next listing).

Listing 7.6 Calling Lambda functions from Android

```
final InvokeRequest invokeRequest =
    new InvokeRequest()
        .withFunctionName(functionName)
        .withInvocationType(InvocationType.RequestResponse)
        .withPayload(payload);

final InvokeResult invokeResult =
    AWSMobileClient
        .defaultMobileClient()
        .getCloudFunctionClient()
        .invoke(invokeRequest);

// Use invokeResult here
```

When developing for the Android platform, you can also use annotations to simplify the syntax to call a remote Lambda function from the mobile app the same way you'd call a local function. For example, to call the `faceDetection` Lambda function from an Android mobile app, you can use the following syntax:

```
@LambdaFunction
FacesResult faceDetection(String imageUrl);
```

Now any reference to the `faceDetection` function in the Android code will call the Lambda function remotely. If the name of the Lambda function is different from the name of the Java function in the Android code, you can specify that in the annotation. For example, to call the `faceDetection` Lambda function using the `detectFaces` Java function in the Android code, you can use:

```
@LambdaFunction(functionName = "faceDetection")
FacesResult detectFaces(String imageUrl);
```

If you're a mobile developer, you can use Lambda functions for your back end quickly with AWS Mobile Hub. This way, you can implement a serverless back end for your mobile app and share the same back-end calls with other clients, such as web applications.

7.3   *Calling functions from a web browser*

When configuring the Amazon API Gateway to use Lambda functions, you can choose to have no authentication and leave the API publicly available. Using this option together with the HTTP GET method allows your API to be called by a web browser. You need to return the expected content type for HTML (text/html) to implement a public website.

The architectural configuration we're using in this example is in figure 7.15. The client application is a web browser, and AWS Lambda and Amazon API Gateway are used to distribute a public website on the internet. The advantage compared with a static website hosting, such as what you can easily set up with Amazon S3, is that the Lambda function can generate server-side dynamic content.

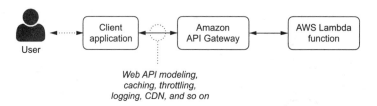

Figure 7.15   You can serve web content from a Lambda function using the Amazon API Gateway and expose the function via HTTP GET. When configuring the integration, you need to be careful to return the right HTTP Content-Type; for example, text/html for HTML.

As an example, let's create a simple website using Embedded JavaScript (EJS) templates[1] that are dynamically served to the end users. I'm using EJS templates in this example, but any kind of server-side technology would work. You need a single Lambda function, ejsWebsite (listing 7.7), that you can integrate with multiple resources in the Amazon API Gateway. For example, the root resource of the API (/) and a resource parameter that can be used for any single-level paths (/{path}). Calling this function will return HTML content.

NOTE   This example is available in Node.js only because it uses EJS templates.

---

[1] For more information on EJS templates, please look at http://www.embeddedjs.com.

Listing 7.7 `ejsWebsite` (Node.js)

```
console.log('Loading function');

const fs = require('fs');
const ejs = require('ejs');

exports.handler = (event, context, callback) => {
  console.log('Received event:', JSON.stringify(event, null, 2));
  var fileName = './content' + event.path + 'index.ejs';
  console.log(fileName)
  fs.readFile(fileName, function(err, data) {
    if (err) {
      callback("Error 404");
    } else {
      var html = ejs.render(data.toString());
      callback(null, { data: html });
    }
  });
};
```

Build a local file name, included in the function deployment package, based on the path in the event.

If the file is missing, fail returning an error string that the Amazon API Gateway can intercept and manage to return HTTP 404 status.

Interpret the EJS template server-side to produce HTML content.

Return the HTML wrapped in JSON to preserve encoding.

Create the `ejsTemplate` Lambda function, using the basic execution role and all default parameters. Because the `ejs` module is required, you need to install it with `npm` and create a ZIP archive to upload your deployment package. In the ZIP archive, include a content folder with sample EJS templates to be interpreted by the Lambda function. For example, for a tiny website with About and Contact pages, you can include the following files:

```
content/index.ejs
content/about/index.ejs
content/contact/index.ejs
```

Each of those files is described in listings 7.8, 7.9, and 7.10, respectively. As you can see, those files are similar to each other and contain dynamic content that's evaluated on the server by the Lambda function before the result is returned by the Amazon API Gateway to the browser.

Listing 7.8 Root EJS template

```
<html>
  <head>
    <title>Home Page</title>
  </head>
  <body>
    <h1>Home Page</h1>
    <p>The home page at <strong><%= new Date() %></strong></p>
    <ul>
      <li><a href="about/">About</a></li>
      <li><a href="contact/">Contact</a></li>
    </ul>
  </body>
</html>
```

The JavaScript code between <%= and %> is interpreted server-side by the Lambda function.

Listing 7.9   About EJS template

```html
<html>
  <head>
    <title>About</title>
  </head>
  <body>
    <h1>Home Page</h1>
    <p>The about page at <strong><%= new Date() %></strong></p>
    <ul>
      <li><a href="../">Home Page</a></li>
      <li><a href="../contact/">Contact</a></li>
    </ul>
  </body>
</html>
```

> The JavaScript code between <%= and %> is interpreted server-side by the Lambda function.

Listing 7.10   Contact EJS template

```html
<html>
  <head>
    <title>Contact</title>
  </head>
  <body>
    <h1>Home Page</h1>
    <p>The contact page at <strong><%= new Date() %></strong></p>
    <ul>
      <li><a href="../">Home Page</a></li>
      <li><a href="../about/">About</a></li>
    </ul>
  </body>
</html>
```

> The JavaScript code between <%= and %> is interpreted server-side by the Lambda function.

This part of the template is using the EJS template syntax to get the current date and time and replace it server-side:

```
<%= new Date() %>
```

7.3.1   Integrating the Lambda functions with the Amazon API Gateway

You now need to integrate this Lambda function with the Amazon API Gateway. From the API Gateway console, create a Simple Website API. This won't be a normal Web API, but it will be used as a public website.

Create a Method for the root (/) resource. Your code needs to answer only the HTTP GET request for this simple website, so choose the GET method from the menu. You can easily extend this example to support other HTTP verbs such as POST.

In the Integration Request, select the ejsTemplate Lambda function you created and create a Mapping Template to send the path to the function. Use the application/ json content type and this basic static mapping template:

```
{
  "path": "/"
}
```

You now need to change the default content type returned by the API call to text/ html. In the Method Response, expand the 200 HTTP Status, add the text/html content type with an Empty Model, and remove the default application/json content type. Use the code in the following listing as a mapping template for the text/html content type.

> **Listing 7.11   Mapping template to return the content of the data attribute**

```
#set($inputRoot = $input.path('$'))
$inputRoot.data
```

I used a data attribute in the JSON payload that's returned by the function to embed all the HTML content; this template is extracting the HTML to be the only content returned. If you return HTML content directly, it's escaped with HTML entities and is difficult to use. You can use the Test button to check whether the content and the content type returned by the integration are correct.

A website with only a home page is now implemented, but let's create another integration to manage all single-level paths, such as /about or /contact. Create a new resource with "Page" as the name and {page} as resource path and add a GET method to this resource as well. In the Method Request, you now have the page resource path parameter. In the Integration Request, use the same ejsTemplate function as before, but in the mapping template for the application/json content type, use the following template to pass the page parameter to the function:

```
{
  "path": "/$input.params('page')/"
}
```

In the Integration Response, replace the default application/json content type with text/html and use the same mapping template as before, using the code in listing 7.11.

Now you have to manage possible requests that don't find content (a corresponding EJS template in this case) within the function. To do that, in the Method Response, add a 404 HTTP Status. In the Integration Response, use Add integration response with 404 as Lambda Error Regex to return the 404 HTTP code in case the page (the EJS template) isn't found in the content folder of the Lambda function.

Use the Test button to try different page values—for example, about/ or wrong/— to see what happens when the EJS template is found or not found.

When you deploy this API in a stage (for example home), the website is publicly accessible and you can navigate through the links using a web browser. Remember to use the full path, the domain, and the stage; for example, (the domain will be different in your case):

```
https://123ab12ab1.execute-api.use-east-1.amazonaws.com/home
```

The dates in the EJS templates are evaluated on the server, and you should see the dates being updated as soon as the browser accesses the link again.

TIP   To customize the URL, you can use a custom domain, supported by Amazon API Gateway, or a CDN such as Amazon CloudFront to cache the results and reduce the number of invocations to AWS Lambda functions.

Summary

In this chapter, you learned how to use standalone AWS Lambda functions in different use cases, such as the following:

- Using functions as the back end of a JavaScript web application
- Using AWS Mobile Hub to call functions from a native mobile app
- Using Amazon API Gateway and AWS Lambda to build a public website whose content is generated server-side by functions

In the next chapter, you'll start using multiple functions together to build your first example of an event-driven application: a serverless authentication service.

EXERCISE

At the beginning of this chapter you learned how to build a web page invoking the greetingsOnDemand function. In the same way, build a web page asking for a name and a custom greeting. Use the customGreetingsOnDemand function from chapter 2 to compute the resulting greeting, and display that result on the web page. For your convenience, you can find the code for the function in the following listings.

Function customGreetingsOnDemand **(Node.js)**

```
console.log('Loading function');

exports.handler = (event, context, callback) => {
    console.log('Received event:',
        JSON.stringify(event, null, 2));
    console.log('greet =', event.greet);
    console.log('name =', event.name);
    var greet = '';
    if ('greet' in event) {
        greet = event.greet;
    } else {
        greet = 'Hello';
    };
    var name = '';
    if ('name' in event) {
        name = event.name;
    } else {
        name = 'World';
    }
    var greetings = greet + ' ' + name + '!';
    console.log(greetings);
    callback(null, greetings);
};
```

Function `customGreetingsOnDemand` **(Python)**

```python
import json

print('Loading function')

def lambda_handler(event, context):
    print('Received event: ' +
        json.dumps(event, indent=2))
    if 'greet' in event:
        greet = event['greet']
    else:
        greet = 'Hello'
    if 'name' in event:
        name = event['name']
    else:
        name = 'World'
    greetings = greet + ' ' + name + '!'
    print(greetings)
    return greetings
```

Solution

The HTML page is shown in the following listing.

`CustomGreetingsOnDemand` **HTML page**

```html
<html>
  <head>
    <title>Custom Greetings on Demand</title>
    <script src="https://sdk.amazonaws.com/js/aws-sdk-2.2.32.min.js"></
     script>
  </head>
  <body>
    <h1>Custom Greetings on Demand</h1>
    <p>This is an example of calling an AWS Lambda function
      from a web page via JavaScript.</p>
    <p>Instead of a static Hello World, here you can provide
      a greet and name, and you will receive customized greetings.</p>
    <p>Try without a greet or without a name, too.</p>
      </div>
      <form role="form" id="greetingsForm">
        <label for="greet">Greet:</label>
        <input type="text" class="form-control" id="greet">
        <label for="name">Name:</label>
        <input type="text" class="form-control" id="name">
        <button type="submit" class="btn btn-default">Greet</button>
      </form>
      <div id="result">
      </div>
    </div>
    <script src="customGreetings.js"></script>
  </body>
</html>
```

The JavaScript code running in the browser to call the Lambda function and get the result back is shown in the following listing.

customGreetings.js (JavaScript in the browser)

```javascript
AWS.config.region = '<REGION>';
AWS.config.credentials = new AWS.CognitoIdentityCredentials({
  IdentityPoolId: '<IDENTITY-POOL-ID>',
});

var lambda = new AWS.Lambda();

function returnGreetings() {
  var greet = document.getElementById('greet');
  var name = document.getElementById('name');
  var input = {};
  if (greet.value != null && greet.value != '') {
    input.greet = greet.value;
  }
  if (name.value != null && name.value != '') {
    input.name = name.value;
  }
  lambda.invoke({
    FunctionName: 'customGreetingsOnDemand',
    Payload: JSON.stringify(input)
  }, function(err, data) {
    var result = document.getElementById('result');
    if (err) {
      console.log(err, err.stack);
      result.innerHTML = err;
    } else {
      var output = JSON.parse(data.Payload);
      result.innerHTML = output;
    }
  });
}

var form = document.getElementById('greetingsForm');
form.addEventListener('submit', function(evt) {
  evt.preventDefault();
  returnGreetings();
});
```

Designing an authentication service

In the previous chapter you learned how to use standalone Lambda functions from different client applications:

- A web page, using JavaScript
- A native Mobile App, with the help of the AWS Mobile Hub to generate your starting code
- An Amazon API Gateway to generate server-side dynamic content for web browsers

Now it's time to build your first event-driven serverless application, using multiple functions together to achieve your purpose. Your goal is to implement a sample authentication service that can be used by itself or together with Amazon Cognito with developer-authenticated identities.

NOTE   The authentication service you're going to build is an example of an event-driven serverless application and hasn't been validated by a security audit. If you need such a service, my advice is to use an already built and production-ready implementation, such as Amazon Cognito User Pools.

You'll define the architecture of your serverless back end built with AWS Lambda. In the chapter after this one, you'll implement all the required components. The first step is to define how your users interact with the application.

8.1   *The interaction model*

To make your application easy to use for a broad range of use cases, the main interface for your users is the web browser. Via a web browser, users can access static HTML pages that include JavaScript code, which can call one or more Lambda functions to execute code in the back end. At the end of the chapter, you'll see how it is easy to reuse the same flow and architecture with a mobile app.

Using the Amazon API Gateway

Another option, instead of calling Lambda functions directly from the client application, is to model a RESTful API with the Amazon API Gateway, using features similar to what you learned in chapter 3. The advantage of this approach is the decoupling of the client application from the actual back-end implementation:

- You call a Web API from the client application and not a Lambda function.
- You can easily change the back end implementation to (or from) AWS Lambda at any time, without affecting the development of the client application (for example, a web or mobile app).
- You can potentially open your back end to other services, publishing a public API that can further extend the reach of your application.

The Amazon API Gateway provides other interesting features, such as

- SDK generation
- Caching of function results
- Throttling to withstand traffic spikes

However, for the purpose of this book, I decided to use AWS Lambda directly in the authentication service. This makes the overall implementation simpler to build and more understandable for a first-time learner.

If you're building a new application, I advise you to evaluate the pros and cons of using the Amazon API Gateway as I did and make an informed decision.

The HTML pages, JavaScript code, and any other file required to render the page correctly on the web browser (such as CSS style sheets) can be stored on Amazon S3 as publicly readable objects. To store structured data, such as user profiles and passwords,

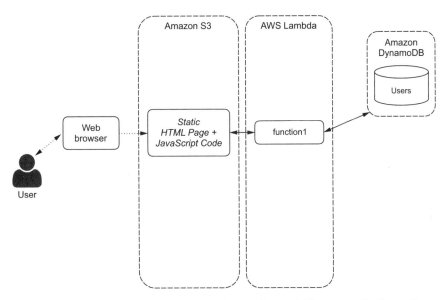

Figure 8.1   The first step in implementing the interaction model for your application: using a web browser to execute back end logic via Lambda functions that can store data on DynamoDB tables

Lambda functions can use DynamoDB tables. A summary of this interaction model is shown in figure 8.1.

> **TIP**   Because the client side of the application is built using HTML pages and JavaScript code, it's relatively easy to repackage it as a hybrid mobile app, using frameworks such as Apache Cordova (formerly PhoneGap). Hybrid apps are popular because you can develop a mobile client once and use it in multiple environments, such as iOS, Android, and Windows Mobile. For more information on using Apache Cordova to implement mobile apps, please look at: https://cordova.apache.org.

It's important for an authentication service to verify contact data provided by users. A common use case is to verify that the email address given by a user is valid. To do that, the Lambda functions in the back end need to send emails to the users. To avoid the complexity of configuring and managing an email server, you can use Amazon Simple Email Services (SES) to send emails. This allows you to extend your interaction model adding this capability (figure 8.2).

> **NOTE**   Amazon SES is a fully managed email service that you can use to send any volume of email, and receive emails that can be automatically stored on Amazon S3 or processed by AWS Lambda. When you receive an email with Amazon SES, you can also send a notification using Amazon Simple Notification Service (SNS). For more information on Amazon SES, see https://aws.amazon.com/ses/.

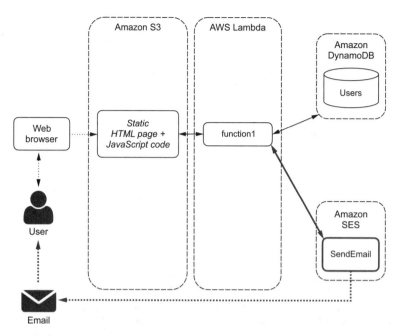

Figure 8.2   Adding the capability for Lambda functions to send emails to the users, via Amazon SES. In this way you can verify the validity of email addresses provided by users.

When a user receives an email sent by Amazon SES, you need a way of interacting with your back end to complete the verification process. To do that, you can include in the body of the email a link to the URL of another static HTML page on Amazon S3. When the user clicks the link, the web browser will open that page and execute the JavaScript code that's embedded in the page. The execution includes the invocation of another Lambda function that can interact with the data stored in Amazon DynamoDB (figure 8.3).

Now that you know how to interact with your users using a web browser or by sending emails, you can design the overall architecture of the authentication service.

8.2   *The event-driven architecture*

Every static HTML page you put on Amazon S3 can potentially be used as an *interactive step* to engage the user. If you compare this with a native mobile app, each of those pages can behave similarly to an *activity* in Android or a *scene* in iOS.

As the first step, you'll implement a menu of all possible actions users can perform (such as sign-up, login, or change password) and put that in an `index.html` page (figure 8.4). For now, this page doesn't require any client logic, so you have no JavaScript code to execute; it's a list of actions linking to other HTML pages.

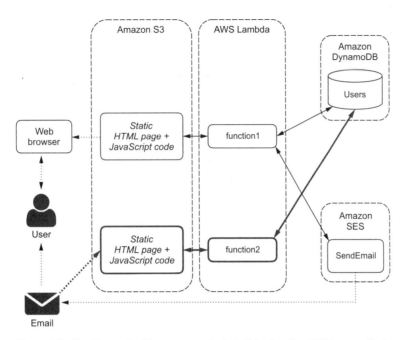

Figure 8.3 Emails received by users can include links to other HTML pages that can execute JavaScript code and invoke other Lambda function to interact with back-end data repositories such as DynamoDB tables.

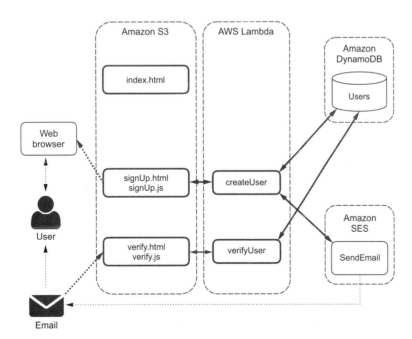

Figure 8.4 The first HTML pages, JavaScript files, and Lambda functions required to sign up new users and verify their email addresses

Next, you'll want users to sign up and create a new account using a `signUp.html` page. This page needs JavaScript code to invoke the `createUser` Lambda function (see figure 8.4).

> **TIP** To simplify separate management of the user interface (in the HTML page) and the client-side login (in the JavaScript code), put the JavaScript code in a separate file, with the same name as the HMTL page, but with the .js extension (for example, signUp.js in this case).

The `createUser` Lambda function takes as input all the information provided by a new user (such as the email and the password) and stores it in the `Users` DynamoDB table. A new user is flagged as unverified on the table because you don't know if the provided email address is correct. To verify that the email address given by the user is valid and that the user can receive emails at that address, the `createUser` function sends an email to the user (via Amazon SES).

The email sent to the user has a link to the `verify.html` page that includes a query parameter with a unique identifier (for example, a `token`) that's randomly generated for that specific user and stored in the `Users` DynamoDB table. For example, the link in the HTML page would be similar to the following:

```
http://some.domain/verify.html?token=<some unique identifier>
```

The JavaScript code in the `verify.html` page can read the unique identifier (`token`) from the URL and send it as input (as part of the event) to the `verifyUser` Lambda function. The function can check the validity of the `token` and change the status of the user to "verified" on the DynamoDB table.

A verified user can log in using the provided credentials (email, password). You can use a `login.html` page and a `login` Lambda function to check in the User table that the user is verified and the credentials are correct (figure 8.5). At first, this function can return the login status as a Boolean value (`true` or `false`). You'll learn later in this chapter how to federate the authentication service you're building with Amazon Cognito as a developer-authenticated identity.

Another important capability is for your users to change their passwords. Changing passwords periodically (for example, every few months) is a good practice to reduce the risk associated with compromised credentials.

You can add a `changePassword.html` page that can use a `changePassword` Lambda function to update credentials in the `Users` DynamoDB table (figure 8.6). But this page is different from others: only an authenticated user can change their own password.

There are two possible implementations that you can use for secure access to the `changePassword` function:

1 Add the current password to the input event of the function, to check the authentication of the user before changing the password.
2 Use Amazon Cognito, via the `login` function, to provide an authenticated status to the user.

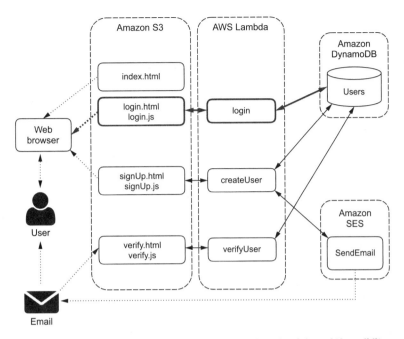

Figure 8.5 Adding a login page to test the provided credentials and the validity of the user in the Users repository

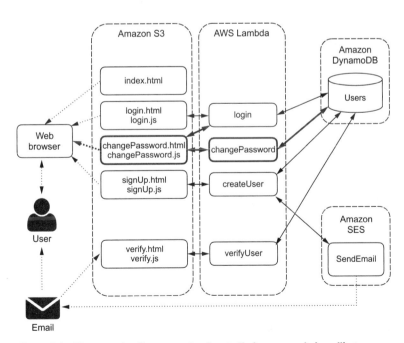

Figure 8.6 The page to allow users to change their passwords is calling a function that must be protected so that only authenticated users can use it.

The first solution is easy to implement (for example, reusing code from the `login` function), but because we're going to federate this authentication service with Amazon Cognito, let's make this example more interesting and go for the second option.

As you may recall, HTML pages need to get AWS credentials from Amazon Cognito to invoke Lambda functions. In all examples so far, we used only unauthenticated users; to allow those users to invoke a Lambda function, we added those functions to the unauthenticated IAM role associated with the Cognito identity pool.

To protect access to the `changePassword` function, you'll add this function to the authenticated IAM role (and not to the unauthenticated role). The same approach will work for any function that needs to be executed by only authenticated users.

Sometimes users need to change passwords because they forgot their current one. In those cases, you can use their email address to validate their request in a way similar to what you did for the initial sign-up: send an email with an embedded link and a unique identifier.

The `lostPassword.html` page is calling a `lostPassword` Lambda function to generate a unique identifier (`resetToken`) that's stored in the `Users` DynamoDB table. The `resetToken` is then sent to the user as a query parameter in a link embedded in a verification email (figure 8.7).

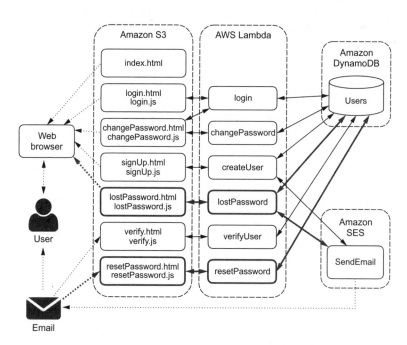

Figure 8.7   In case of a lost password, a lost password page is used to send an email with an embedded link to reset the password. A unique identifier, stored in the DynamoDB table and part of the reset password link, is used to verify that the user making the request to reset the password is the same user who receives the email.

For example, the link can be something similar to the following:

```
http://some.domain/resetPassword?resetToken=<some unique identifier>
```

The user can then open the email and click the link to the `resetPassword.html` page, which will ask for a new password and then call a `resetPassword` Lambda function to check the unique identifier (`resetToken`) in the `Users` DynamoDB table. If the identifier is correct, the function will change the password to the new value.

You've now designed the overall flow and the necessary components to cover the basic functionalities for implementing the authentication service. But before you move into the implementation phase in the next chapter, you'll learn how to *federate* the authentication with Amazon Cognito, and define how to implement other details. By *identity federation* I mean having an authorization service (Amazon Cognito in this case) trusting the authentication of an external service (the sample authentication service you are building).

> **NOTE** Instead of creating multiple Lambda functions, one for each HTML page, you could create a single Lambda function and pass the kind of action (for example `signUp` or `resetPassword`) as part of the input event. You'd have fewer functions to manage (potentially, only one) but the codebase of that function would be larger and more difficult to evolve and extend with further functionalities. Following a microservices approach, my advice is to have multiple smaller functions, each one with a well-defined input/output interface that you can update and deploy separately. However, the right balance between function size and the number of functions to implement depends on your actual use case and programming style. If you need to aggregate multiple functions into a single service call, the Amazon API Gateway is the place to do that instead of the functions themselves.

8.3 Working with Amazon Cognito

To use the authentication service with Amazon Cognito, you need to add to the `login` Lambda function a call to Amazon Cognito to get a token for a developer identity. The `login` function can then return the authentication token for a correct authentication.

The JavaScript code in the page can use that token to authenticate with Amazon Cognito and get AWS temporary credentials for the authenticated role (figure 8.8).

> **WARNING** The AWS credentials returned by Amazon Cognito are temporary and expire after a period of time. You need to manage credential rotation—for example, using the JavaScript `setInterval()` method to periodically call Amazon Cognito to refresh the credentials.

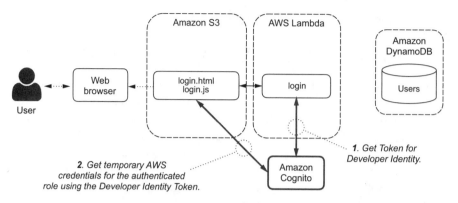

Figure 8.8 Integrating the login function with Cognito Developer Authenticated Identities. The login function gets the token from Amazon Cognito, and then the JavaScript code running in the browser can get AWS Credentials for the authenticated role by passing the token as a login.

8.4 Storing user profiles

To store user profiles, you're using the `Users` DynamoDB table in this sample application. Generally speaking, in a Lambda function you can use any repository reachable via the internet, or that's deployed on AWS in an Amazon Virtual Private Cloud (VPC), or deployed on-premises and connected to an Amazon VPC with a VPN connection. I'm using Amazon DynamoDB because it's a fully-managed NoSQL database service that embraces the serverless approach of this book.

In Amazon DynamoDB, when you create a new table, only the primary key must be declared and must be used in all items in the table. The rest of the table schema is flexible and other attributes can be used (or not) to add more information to any item.

> **NOTE** A DynamoDB item is a collection of attributes, and each attribute has a name and a value. For more details on how to work with items, see https://docs.aws.amazon.com/amazondynamodb/latest/developerguide/WorkingWithItems.html.

The primary key must be unique for an item and can be composed of a single *hash key* (for example, a user ID), or of a hash key together with a *range key* (such as a user ID and a validity date).

For this authentication service, the email of the user is a unique identifier that you can use as hash key, without a range key. If you want to have multiple items for the same users—for example, to keep track of changes and updates in the user profile—you could use a composed primary key with the email as hash key and a validity date in the sort key.

8.5 Adding more data to user profiles

Because Amazon DynamoDB doesn't enforce a schema outside of the primary key, you can freely add more attributes to any item in a table. Different items can have different attributes. For example, to flag newly created users as unverified, you can add an `unverified` attribute equal to `true`.

When a user email is verified, instead of keeping the `unverified` attribute with a `false` value, you can remove it from the item using the assumption that if the `unverified` attribute isn't present, the user is verified. This approach (that can be easily used with Boolean values) provides a compact and efficient usage of the database storage, especially if you create an index on the `unverified` attribute, because only items with that attribute are part of the index.

Amazon DynamoDB also supports a JSON Document Model, so that the value of an attribute can be a JSON document. In this way, you can further extend the possibility of storing data in a hierarchical and structured way. For example, in the AWS JavaScript SDK, you can use the document client to have native JavaScript data types mapped to and from DynamoDB attributes.

For more information on the document client in the AWS JavaScript SDK, see http://docs.aws.amazon.com/AWSJavaScriptSDK/latest/AWS/DynamoDB/Document-Client.html.

8.6   *Encrypting passwords*

When managing passwords, certain interactions are critical and must be secured. For example, the following are not secure:

- Storing passwords in plain text in a database table, because any user who has read access to the database table can intercept user credentials
- Sending passwords on an insecure channel, where malicious eavesdropping users can intercept user credentials

For this authentication service, you'll store the password as encrypted using a *salt*. In cryptography, a salt is random data that's generated for each password and used as an additional input to a one-way function that computes a hash of the password that's stored in the user profile, together with the salt:

```
hashingFunction(password, salt) = hash
```

To test the password in a login, the salt is read from the user profile and the same hashing function is used to compare the result with the stored hash. For example,

```
if hashingFunction(inputPassword, salt) == hash then // Logged in...
```

If user profiles are compromised and a malicious user has access to the database content, the use of a salt can protect against dictionary attacks, which use a list of common passwords versus a list of password hashes.

TIP   Common hashing functions, used in the past for salting passwords, were MD5 and SHA1, but they've been demonstrated to not be robust enough to protect against specific attacks. You have to check the robustness of a hashing function at the time you use it.

In the login phase, you send the password over a secure channel, because the AWS API, used by the login.html page to invoke the login Lambda function, is using HTTPS as transport.

> **TIP** This approach is secure enough for a sample implementation, but for a more robust solution you should never send the password as plain text. Use a challenge-response authentication, such as that implemented by the Secure Remote Password (SRP) protocol, used by Amazon Cognito User Pools. For more information on the SRP protocol, see http://srp.stanford.edu.

For a more in-depth analysis of password security in case of remote access, I suggest you to have a look at "Password Security: A Case History" by Robert Morris and Ken Thompson (1978), https://www.bell-labs.com/usr/dmr/www/passwd.ps.

Summary

In this chapter you designed the overall architecture of your first event-driven application, a sample authentication service using AWS lambda to implement the back-end logic.

In particular, you learned how to do the following:

- Interact with a client application via a static HTML page using JavaScript
- Differentiate between authenticated and unauthenticated access
- Send emails and interact using custom links in the email body
- Map application functionality to different components in the architecture
- Federate the custom authentication service with Amazon Cognito
- Use Amazon DynamoDB to store user profiles
- Use encryption to protect passwords from being intercepted and compromised

In the next chapter, you'll implement this sample authentication service.

EXERCISE

1 To send an email from a web page, you can

  a Use JavaScript in the browser to use SMTP

  b Use JavaScript in the browser to use IMAP

  c Use a Lambda function to call Amazon SES

  d Use a Lambda function to call Amazon SQS

2 To give access to a Lambda function only to authenticated users coming from a web or mobile app, you can

  a Use AWS IAM users and groups to give access to the function to authenticated users only

  b Use Amazon Cognito and give access to the function to the authenticated role only c Use AWS IAM users and groups to give access to the function to unauthenticated users only

    d Use Amazon Cognito and give access to the function to the unauthenticated role only

3 The most secure way to validate a user password with a login service is to

    a Use a challenge-response interface such as CAPTCHA

    b Send the password over HTTP

    c Use a challenge-response protocol such as SRP

    d Send the password via email

Solution

1 c

2 b

3 c

Implementing an
authentication service

This chapter covers

- Implementing the serverless architecture for a sample authentication service
- Creating the back end using Lambda functions
- Using HTML with JavaScript running in a browser to implement the client application
- Using AWS CLI to automate initialization and deployment
- Having a central configuration and sharing code among multiple Lambda functions
- Using Amazon SES to send emails without servers to manage

In the previous chapter, you designed the serverless architecture for a sample authentication service that you can use to create new users, validate email, change or reset passwords, and log in as an Amazon Cognito Developer Authenticated Identity.

You learned many things in the previous chapters, and this is the right time to use that knowledge in a more complex scenario. You now know how to create

Lambda functions, call them from client applications, and subscribe their execution to events happening on AWS, such as a new or updated file on Amazon S3 or a file written to a database on Amazon DynamoDB.

It's time to implement such a service using multiple Lambda functions together with Amazon DynamoDB to store user profiles, and Amazon Simple Email Service (SES) to deliver emails for validation, as described in figure 9.1.

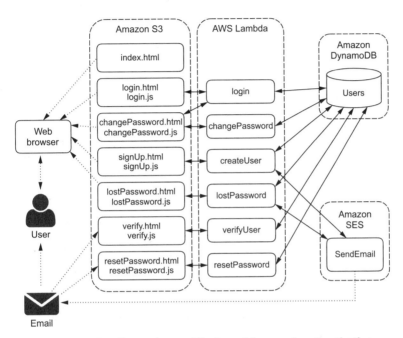

Figure 9.1   The overall serverless architecture of the sample authentication service you're going to implement. HTML and JavaScript files are hosted on Amazon S3, Lambda functions provide the back end logic, a DynamoDB table is used to store user profiles, and Amazon SES sends emails for verification and for password resets.

TIP   When implementing your own projects, if you find that you're creating Lambda functions that could share code, please consider that you can also have a single function and add an additional parameter to act on multiple purposes. For example, imagine you have to manipulate a user with four functions such as `createUser`, `readUser`, `updateUser`, and `deleteUser`. You can optionally create a single `manageUser` function and add an `action` parameter that can have different values, such as `create`, `read`, `update`, and `delete`. The choice depends on your programming style.

NOTE   This example uses both client-side (running in the browser) and server-side (running in Lambda functions) code. Because the code running in the browser is JavaScript, the Lambda function examples are also provided in

JavaScript. The implementation of those functions in Python is left as an exercise for you to do on your own, because it doesn't change the architecture or the logic of the application.

9.1 Managing a centralized configuration

As a developer, it's a good practice to put configuration information outside your code. In the application you're going to build, you'll use a config.json file to store all deployment-specific configurations in JSON format (see the following listing).

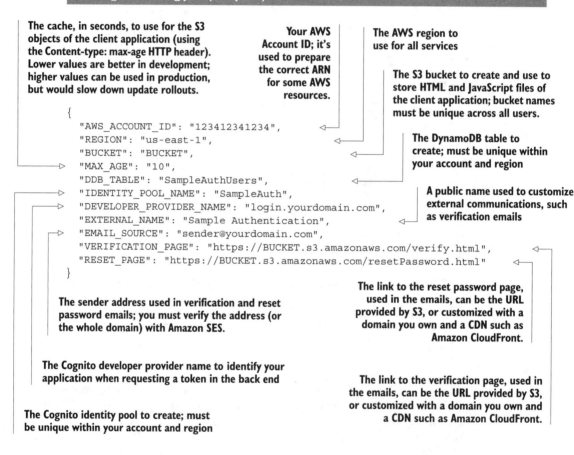

Listing 9.1   config.json (Template)

The cache, in seconds, to use for the S3 objects of the client application (using the Content-type: max-age HTTP header). Lower values are better in development; higher values can be used in production, but would slow down update rollouts.

Your AWS Account ID; it's used to prepare the correct ARN for some AWS resources.

The AWS region to use for all services

The S3 bucket to create and use to store HTML and JavaScript files of the client application; bucket names must be unique across all users.

The DynamoDB table to create; must be unique within your account and region

A public name used to customize external communications, such as verification emails

```json
{
    "AWS_ACCOUNT_ID": "123412341234",
    "REGION": "us-east-1",
    "BUCKET": "BUCKET",
    "MAX_AGE": "10",
    "DDB_TABLE": "SampleAuthUsers",
    "IDENTITY_POOL_NAME": "SampleAuth",
    "DEVELOPER_PROVIDER_NAME": "login.yourdomain.com",
    "EXTERNAL_NAME": "Sample Authentication",
    "EMAIL_SOURCE": "sender@yourdomain.com",
    "VERIFICATION_PAGE": "https://BUCKET.s3.amazonaws.com/verify.html",
    "RESET_PAGE": "https://BUCKET.s3.amazonaws.com/resetPassword.html"
}
```

The sender address used in verification and reset password emails; you must verify the address (or the whole domain) with Amazon SES.

The link to the reset password page, used in the emails, can be the URL provided by S3, or customized with a domain you own and a CDN such as Amazon CloudFront.

The Cognito developer provider name to identify your application when requesting a token in the back end

The Cognito identity pool to create; must be unique within your account and region

The link to the verification page, used in the emails, can be the URL provided by S3, or customized with a domain you own and a CDN such as Amazon CloudFront.

INFO   To initialize and deploy the sample authentication service, you can use any AWS region where all the services you need are available. At the time of writing this book, you can choose between US East (N. Virginia) us-east-1, and EU West (Ireland) eu-west-1. Through some customizations, you can use a different region for certain services (such as Amazon SES) and choose among more regions.

TIP You can optionally use an AWS CLI profile by adding `CLI_PROFILE` to the config.json file. For example, add `"CLI_PROFILE": "personal"` to use your "personal" profile when creating and deploying the application.

WARNING To protect AWS customers from fraud and abuse, and to help establish trustworthiness for ISPs and email recipients when sending emails, the first time you use Amazon SES in a region, your account has sandbox access. With sandbox access, you can send emails only if both the sender and the destination are verified by Amazon SES, on the specific email address, or as a whole domain. You can verify a few specific addresses for test and development using the Amazon SES console at https://console.aws.amazon.com/ses. Remember to verify that you're using the same region as the region in the config.json file. You can ask for production access for Amazon SES to avoid costs. With production access, only the sender address must be verified. Follow the procedure described at http://docs.aws.amazon.com/ses/latest/DeveloperGuide/request-production-access.html.

9.2 *Automating initialization and deployment*

The implementation of the sample authentication service requires that multiple AWS resources be created:

- 6 Lambda functions, to implement the required back end interactions
- 6 IAM policies, to create an IAM role for each of the Lambda functions
- 1 DynamoDB table, to store user profiles
- 1 Cognito identity pool, to federate this authentication service
- 2 IAM policies, for the authenticated and unauthenticated roles of the Cognito identity pool
- 1 S3 bucket to store the client application, built using HTML and JavaScript files
- 3 IAM trust policies, for the authenticated and unauthenticated roles of the Cognito identity pool and for the Lambda functions

Creating all those resources from the web console may be a useful exercise, but it can also be slow and error-prone. To automate all those steps, I created two Bash[1] scripts that you can use:

- `init.sh`, to create and initialize all the required resources, so you don't need to create anything on the web console
- `deploy.sh`, to redeploy and update all back-end and front-end code (Lambda functions and HTML/JavaScript for the client application)

---

[1] Bash is the "Bourne Again Shell" incorporating useful features from the Korn shell (ksh) and C shell (csh). For more information on Bash, see https://www.gnu.org/software/bash/.

NOTE Before using the scripts, read the next section to understand how to manage the configuration. Both scripts require the AWS CLI to be installed and configured on the system. To manipulate JSON content, the scripts use the jq utility, which you can find at https://stedolan.github.io/jq.

The scripts are included in the source code repository for this book. You can use the Bash scripts natively on Linux or Mac. You can also use a small Linux Amazon EC2 instance, such as a t2.micro or t2.nano. On Windows platforms, you can run Bash scripts using either of the following:

- The open source Cygwin project, which includes a large collection of open source tools that can run on Windows. For more information, see https://www.cygwin.com.
- The new native Bash available for Windows 10. For installation and usage, see https://msdn.microsoft.com/commandline.

TIP Consider the Bash scripts as an example of how you can use the AWS CLI to automate your activities on AWS. Any other automation tool that can execute AWS CLI commands or use an AWS SDK, such as those for Ruby or Python, would work. In your projects, you should use the tool that you're most comfortable with.

The config.json file is uploaded with all Lambda functions and is used by the init.sh and deploy.sh scripts to customize the code in the Lambda functions and in the IAM roles, and also during certain deployment steps, such as when uploading to Amazon S3.

After you customize the config.json file, you can use the init.sh script to initialize the application and then deploy.sh to update back end and front end code. You should run init.sh once, and then you can use deploy.sh to update your environment.

9.3 *Having shared code*

Every time you create a Lambda function or update its code, you have to upload all of the code (and binaries) used by the function. But that doesn't mean that you can't manage shared code when developing your application. The "don't repeat yourself" (DRY) principle applies. You do need a way to package the code before uploading to AWS Lambda.

In this case, I'm using a lib folder in the root of the project to hold all the shared code. The init.sh and deploy.sh scripts will automatically include the lib folder with all functions, together with the configuration file, when building a ZIP file to upload.

For example, in the sample authentication application, we're using a salting function to encrypt all passwords stored in the database. To check if a user is providing the correct password—for example, during login—the same function is used again to compare the results. This function is required in more than one function and is the perfect candidate for a shared library, implemented in the cryptoUtils.js file (see the following listing).

Listing 9.2   cryptoUtils.js Shared Library (Node.js)

This function requires the crypto module.

Declaring the computeHash() function with three arguments

```
var crypto = require('crypto');
```

The byte size of the resulting salted password

The digest function to use; SHA512 in this case

```
function computeHash(password, salt, fn) {
  var len = 512;
  var iterations = 4096;
  var digest = 'sha512';
```

The number of iterations to secure the one-way hashing (the actual value should be evaluated with a security expert).

If the function is invoked with three arguments (password, salt, and callback function), proceed with computing the salted password (derivedKey).

```
  if (3 == arguments.length) {
    crypto.pbkdf2(password, salt, iterations, len, digest, function(err,
      derivedKey) {
      if (err) return fn(err);
      else fn(null, salt, derivedKey.toString('base64'));
    });
  } else {
    fn = salt;
    crypto.randomBytes(len, function(err, salt) {
      if (err) return fn(err);
      salt = salt.toString('base64');
      computeHash(password, salt, fn);
    });
  }
}

module.exports.computeHash = computeHash;
```

Passing the return value (salt and derivedKey) or the error to the callback function

If the function is invoked with two arguments (password and callback function), the salt is generated randomly. This is used the first time a password is provided, and the random salt is part of the return value.

When the random salt is generated, the function is invoked recursively with all three arguments.

The function is exported as part of a module.

TIP   In a production environment, the values of byte size, iterations, and the choice of the digest algorithm should be evaluated with a security expert.

9.4   *Creating the home page*

As an entry point for the users, you can create a simple index.html home page with all available options (figure 9.2).

The HTML page in listing 9.3 is a static page, with no JavaScript code.

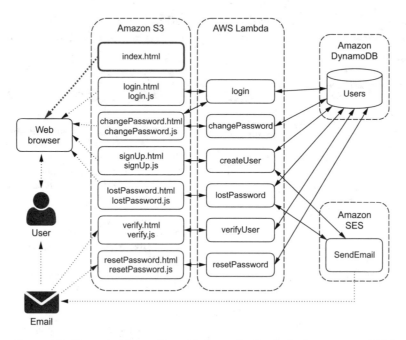

Figure 9.2   Users start interacting with the application in the home page, which acts as an index for all the available functionalities.

Listing 9.3   `index.html` (Home Page)

```html
<html>
<head>
  <title>Index - Sample Authentication Service</title>
</head>
<body>
  <h2>Sample Authentication Service</h2>
  <h1>Index</h1>
  <p>Choose Your Option:</p>
  <a href="signUp.html">Sign Up</a>
  <a href="login.html">Login</a>
  <a href="changePassword.html">Change Password</a>
  <a href="lostPassword.html">Reset Password</a>
</body>
</html>
```

The home page is a static HTML file with links to other HTML pages implementing different functionalities, such as creating new users, changing password, and so on.

NOTE I use bare HTML in these examples to make it easy to learn. In the source code accompanying the book, I use Bootstrap to enhance the visual result and make it responsive on mobile platforms. Bootstrap, originally created by a designer and a developer at Twitter, is a popular HTML, CSS, and JavaScript framework for developing responsive and mobile-ready web projects. For more information about Bootstrap, see http://getbootstrap.com.

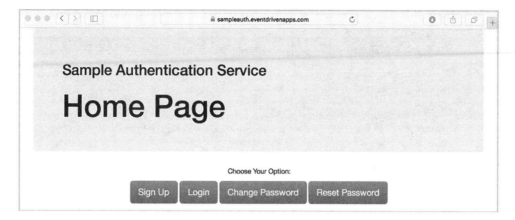

Figure 9.3 **The home page for the sample authentication application, with links to the options to sign up a new user, log in, change a password, or reset a lost password**

A sample screenshot of the home page is shown in figure 9.3.

9.5 Signing up new users

The first step for the user is to sign up and create a new user (figure 9.4).

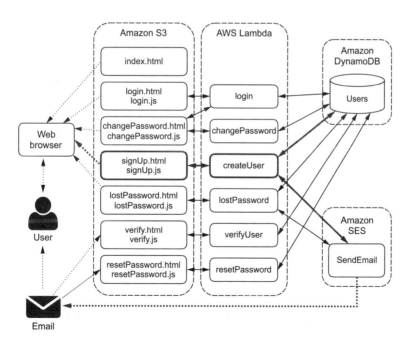

Figure 9.4 **The Sign Up page is creating a new user on the database and sending a validation email back to the user.**

The code for the `signUp.html` page is shown in the following listing.

Listing 9.4   `signUp.html` (Sign Up Page)

Including the AWS
JavaScript SDK in
the Browser

```html
<html>
<head>
  <title>Sign Up - Sample Authentication Service</title>
  <script src="https://sdk.amazonaws.com/js/aws-sdk-2.3.16.min.js"></script>   ◁
</head>
<body>
  <h2>Sample Authentication Service</h2>
  <h1>Sign Up</h1>
  <form role="form" id="signup-form">          ◁─┐   The HTML form to get
    <div>                                            input parameters to
      <label for="email">Email:</label>              create a new user
      <input type="email" id="email">
    </div>
    <div>
      <label for="password">Password:</label>
      <input type="password" id="password">
    </div>
    <div>
      <label for="password">Verify Password:</label>
      <input type="password" id="verify-password">
    </div>
    <button type="submit" id="signup-button">Sign Up</button>
    </form>
  <div id="result">
  </div>                                 ◁──┐  A link back to
  <a href="index.html">Back</a>              the home page
  <script src="js/signUp.js"></script>   ◁──┐  The JavaScript code
</body>                                         running in the browser
</html>                                         for this page
```

TIP   You may want to use a more recent version of the AWS JavaScript SDK
than the one available at the time of writing the book. You can find an
updated example on how to load the SDK in a browser at http://docs.aws
.amazon.com/AWSJavaScriptSDK/guide/browser-intro.html.

The JavaScript code running in the browser for the `signUp.html` page is in the
signUp.js file (see the following listing). The IAM role for unauthenticated users of
the Cognito identity pool is shown in listing 9.6.

Listing 9.5   signUp.js (JavaScript in the Browser)

```javascript
AWS.config.region = '<REGION>';
AWS.config.credentials = new AWS.CognitoIdentityCredentials({
  IdentityPoolId: '<IDENTITY_POOL_ID>'
});
```

Getting AWS
credentials from
Amazon Cognito for
the unauthenticated
IAM role

The AWS region to use

```
var lambda = new AWS.Lambda();
```
Getting the AWS Lambda service object from the SDK

Declaring a signup() function
```
function signup() {

  var result = document.getElementById('result');
  var email = document.getElementById('email');
  var password = document.getElementById('password');
  var verifyPassword = document.getElementById('verify-password');
```
Getting input parameters from the HTML form

Checking input parameters are correct before invoking the Lambda function; you will need to repeat those checks in the Lambda function to be secure.
```
  result.innerHTML = 'Sign Up...';

  if (email.value == null || email.value == '') {
    result.innerHTML = 'Please specify your email address.';
  } else if (password.value == null || password.value == '') {
    result.innerHTML = 'Please specify a password.';
  } else if (password.value != verifyPassword.value) {
    result.innerHTML = 'Passwords are <b>different</b>, please check.';
  } else {

    var input = {
      email: email.value,
      password: password.value,
    };
```
Preparing the input JSON for the Lambda function

Specifying the function name

Invoking the function synchronously using the Lambda service object
```
    lambda.invoke({
      FunctionName: 'sampleAuthCreateUser',
      Payload: JSON.stringify(input)
    }, function(err, data) {
      if (err) console.log(err, err.stack);
      else {
        var output = JSON.parse(data.Payload);
        if (output.created) {
          result.innerHTML = 'User ' + input.email + ' created. Please check
    your email to validate the user and enable login.';
        } else {
          result.innerHTML = 'User <b>not</b> created.';
        }
      }
    });
  }
}
```
The JSON input object must be transformed to a text string before invoking the function.

The anonymous callback function receiving the return value from the synchronous invocation

The Lambda function returns a Boolean value ("created") to tell the client application whether the user has been created or not.

```
  var form = document.getElementById('signup-form');
  form.addEventListener('submit', function(evt) {
    evt.preventDefault();
    signup();
  });
```
Automatically executes the signup() function when the form is submitted

The return value is a string in data. Payload—in this case the function output—can be parsed as JSON, but this depends on how you write the function. You can send a sample string as a return value.

NOTE If you use the init.sh and deploy.sh scripts, you don't need to replace in the source code the options between angle brackets, such as <REGION> or <IDENTITY_POOL_ID>, as you did for the previous examples in this book. The init.sh and deploy.sh scripts will automatically replace those options with the correct ones, based on the current configuration.

Listing 9.6 Policy_Cognito_Unauthenticated_Role

```
{
    "Version": "2012-10-17",
    "Statement": [
        {
            "Effect": "Allow",
            "Action": [
                "mobileanalytics:PutEvents",
                "cognito-sync:*"
            ],
            "Resource": [
                "*"
            ]
        },
        {
            "Effect": "Allow",
            "Action": [
                "lambda:InvokeFunction"          ⟵  Gives access to the
            ],                                        Lambda functions used by
            "Resource": [                             the client application
                "arn:aws:lambda:<REGION>:<ACCOUNT>:function:createUser",
                "arn:aws:lambda:<REGION>:<ACCOUNT>:function:verifyUser",
                "arn:aws:lambda:<REGION>:<ACCOUNT>:function:lostPassword",
                "arn:aws:lambda:<REGION>:<ACCOUNT>:function:resetPassword",
                "arn:aws:lambda:<REGION>:<ACCOUNT>:function:login"
            ]
        }
    ]
}
```

The code for the createUser Lambda function is shown in the following listing, and the IAM role used by the function is shown in listing 9.8.

Listing 9.7 createUser Lambda Function (Node.js)

```
console.log('Loading function');          Loading standard       Loading the crytoUtils.js
                                           modules, such as crypto  module shared code,
var AWS = require('aws-sdk');              and the AWS SDK          included in the uploaded
var crypto = require('crypto');                                    ZIP archive
var cryptoUtils = require('./lib/cryptoUtils');   ⟵
var config = require('./config');
                                                  Loading the
var dynamodb = new AWS.DynamoDB();                configuration in the
var ses = new AWS.SES();           ⟵             config.json file,
                                    Getting the   included in the
                                    Amazon SES     uploaded ZIP archive
                                    service object
```

Getting the Amazon DynamoDB service object ⟶ (var dynamodb = new AWS.DynamoDB();)

Putting an item in the DynamoDB table

The table name is taken from the config.json configuration file.

```
function storeUser(email, password, salt, fn) {
  var len = 128;
  crypto.randomBytes(len, function(err, token) {
    if (err) return fn(err);
    token = token.toString('hex');
    dynamodb.putItem({
      TableName: config.DDB_TABLE,
      Item: {
        email: {
          S: email
        },
        passwordHash: {
          S: password
        },
        passwordSalt: {
          S: salt
        },
        verified: {
          BOOL: false
        },
        verifyToken: {
          S: token
        }
      },
      ConditionExpression: 'attribute_not_exists (email)'
    }, function(err, data) {
      if (err) return fn(err);
      else fn(null, token);
    });
  });
}
```

The storeUser() function stores the new user in the DynamoDB table.

A random token sent in the validation email and used to validate a user

Most of the data is string ("S"), but the verified attribute is Boolean ("BOOL"), new users aren't verified (false), and the randomly generated token is stored in the "verifyToken" attribute.

This condition avoids overwriting existing users (with the same email).

The storeUser() function returns the randomly generated token.

```
function sendVerificationEmail(email, token, fn) {
  var subject = 'Verification Email for ' + config.EXTERNAL_NAME;
  var verificationLink = config.VERIFICATION_PAGE + '?email=' +
    encodeURIComponent(email) + '&verify=' + token;
  ses.sendEmail({
    Source: config.EMAIL_SOURCE,
    Destination: {
      ToAddresses: [
        email
      ]
    },
    Message: {
      Subject: {
        Data: subject
      },
      Body: {
        Html: {
          Data: '<html><head>'
          + '<meta http-equiv="Content-Type" content="text/html; charset=UTF-8" />'
          + '<title>' + subject + '</title>'
          + '</head><body>'
```

The send-VerificationEmail() function sends the verification email to the new user.

Sending the email in HTML format

The verification link, to the verify.html page, passes the randomly generated token as a query parameter.

```
                        + 'Please <a href="' + verificationLink + '">click here to verify
                  your email address</a> or copy & paste the following link in a browser:'
                        + '<br><br>'
                        + '<a href="' + verificationLink + '">' + verificationLink + '</a>'
                        + '</body></html>'
                  }
                }
              }
            }, fn);
          }

          exports.handler = (event, context, callback) => {
            var email = event.email;
            var clearPassword = event.password;

            cryptoUtils.computeHash(clearPassword, function(err, salt, hash) {
              if (err) {
                callback('Error in hash: ' + err);
              } else {
                storeUser(email, hash, salt, function(err, token) {
                  if (err) {
                    if (err.code == 'ConditionalCheckFailedException') {
                      // userId already found
                      callback(null, { created: false });
                    } else {
                      callback('Error in storeUser: ' + err);
                    }
                  } else {
                    sendVerificationEmail(email, token, function(err, data) {
                      if (err) {
                        callback('Error in sendVerificationEmail: ' + err);
                      } else {
                        callback(null, { created: true });
                      }
                    });
                  }
                });
              }
            });
          }
```

The function that's exported and can be invoked using AWS Lambda as createUser.

Getting the input parameters (email, password) from the event

Using computeHash() from crytoUtils.js to salt the password

Storing the user via the storeUser() function

Checking if the database error is due to the email being already present in the database

Sending the verification email

TIP In the source code of the book, I added sampleAuth at the beginning of all Lambda function names. For example, the `createUser` function is called `sampleAuthCreateUser`. It's a good practice to logically group your functions to make it easier to find and manage them using the AWS Lambda console or the AWS CLI.

Listing 9.8   Policy_Lambda_createUser

```
{
    "Version": "2012-10-17",
    "Statement": [
        {
            "Action": [
                "dynamodb:PutItem"
```

Putting a new item in the DynamoDB table (for a new user)

```
        ],
        "Effect": "Allow",
        "Resource": "arn:aws:dynamodb:<REGION>:<AWS_ACCOUNT_ID>:table/
    <DYNAMODB_TABLE>"
    },
    {
        "Effect": "Allow",
        "Action": [
            "ses:SendEmail",          Sending the validation
            "ses:SendRawEmail"        email using Amazon SES
        ],
        "Resource": "*"
    },
    {
        "Sid": "",
        "Resource": "*",
        "Action": [
            "logs:*"
        ],
        "Effect": "Allow"
    }
  ]
}
```

A screenshot of the signUp.html page is shown in figure 9.5.

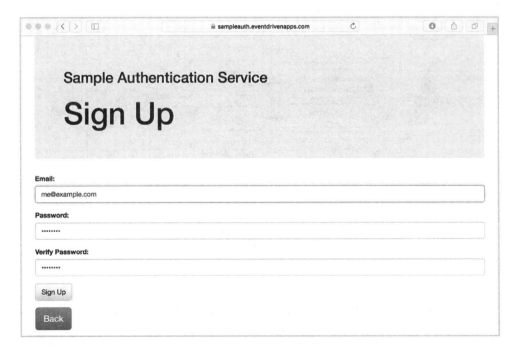

Figure 9.5 The Sign Up page, where users give their email and password to create a new account

9.6   *Validating user emails*

After a user has been created, a validation email is sent to the provided address. The
email contains a link. For example, a validation email will be similar to the following:

Subject: Verification Email for Sample Authentication

Please <u>click here to verify your email address</u> or copy & paste the following
link in a browser:

<u>https://sampleauth.eventdrivenapps.com/</u>
<u>verify.html?email=me%40example.com&verify=1073eac77cd4959c45a16e656398321b275</u>
<u>f84ea3394c74921771782086662c1c0fd44e21179d424436e9d0900c308298d2339ec16657a26</u>
<u>ce69754013f562003bf8595eca4770bfaf0e3d1bd73a502085f1ba330b0a12331c4cdef6ba333</u>
<u>dec52202cc11ecf357a8d6e4b7c9572bab8eafcb57fc2be6fd3061e908140ed8f27</u>

The link in the validation email opens the verify.html page (figure 9.6), passing a
verify token as query parameter (listing 9.9).

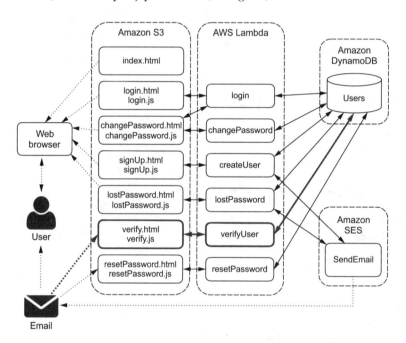

**Figure 9.6   Clicking on the link in the validation email opens the verify.html
page, which uses the verifyUser Lambda function to check if the token in the
link is correct.**

Listing 9.9   verify.html (Verify Page)

```html
<html>
<head>
  <title>Verify - Sample Authentication Service</title>
  <script src="https://sdk.amazonaws.com/js/aws-sdk-2.3.16.min.js"></script>
</head>
```

```
<body>
  <h2>Sample Authentication Service</h2>
  <h1>Verify</h1>
  <div id="result">
  </div>
  <a class="btn btn-info btn-lg" href="index.html">Back</a>
  <script src="js/verify.js"></script>    ◁────
</body>
</html>
```

> The verify.js script will execute automatically on page load to grab the token from the URL (query parameter) and use it to invoke the verifyUser Lambda function.

The query parameter is read client-side by the JavaScript code in verify.js (see the following listing) and then used to invoke the verifyUser Lambda function to validate (or not) the user (listing 9.11). The IAM role used by the function is shown in listing 9.12.

Listing 9.10   verify.js (JavaScript in the Browser)

```
AWS.config.region = '<REGION>';
AWS.config.credentials = new AWS.CognitoIdentityCredentials({
  IdentityPoolId: '<IDENTITY_POOL_ID>'
});

var lambda = new AWS.Lambda();

var result = document.getElementById('result');

function getUrlParams() {
  var p = {};
  var match,
    pl     = /\+/g,
    search = /([^&=]+)=?([^&]*)/g,
    decode = function (s) { return decodeURIComponent(s.replace(pl, " ")); },
    query = window.location.search.substring(1);
  while (match = search.exec(query))
    p[decode(match[1])] = decode(match[2]);
  return p;
}

function init() {
  var urlParams = getUrlParams();
  if (!('email' in urlParams) || !('verify' in urlParams)) {
    result.innerHTML = 'Please specify email and verify token in the URL.';
  } else {
    result.innerHTML = 'Verifying...';
    var input = {
      email: urlParams['email'],
      verify: urlParams['verify']
    };
    lambda.invoke({
      FunctionName: 'sampleAuthVerifyUser',
      Payload: JSON.stringify(input)
    }, function(err, data) {
```

> The getUrlParams() function reads query parameters from the URL.

> Regex for replacing addition symbol with a space

> The init() function executes all the validation logic.

> Check the parameters are in the URL.

Get the parameters from the URL.

> Prepare the input parameters for the Lambda function.

Get the result of the Lambda function.

> Invoke the verifyUser Lambda function.

```
        if (err) console.log(err, err.stack);
        else {
          var output = JSON.parse(data.Payload);
          if (output.verified) {
            result.innerHTML = 'User ' + input.email +
                          ' has been <b>Verified</b>, thanks!';
          } else {
            result.innerHTML = 'User ' + input.email +
                          ' has <b>not</b> been Verified, sorry.';
          }
        }
      });
    }
  }
window.onload = init();
```

Parse the return value and check if the user has been verified (or not).

Execute the init() function automatically when the page loads.

Listing 9.11 `verifyUser Lambda function (Node.js)`

```
console.log('Loading function');

var AWS = require('aws-sdk');
var config = require('./config');

var dynamodb = new AWS.DynamoDB();

function getUser(email, fn) {
  dynamodb.getItem({
    TableName: config.DDB_TABLE,
    Key: {
      email: {
        S: email
      }
    }
  }, function(err, data) {
    if (err) return fn(err);
    else {
      if ('Item' in data) {
        var verified = data.Item.verified.BOOL;
        var verifyToken = null;
        if (!verified) {
          verifyToken = data.Item.verifyToken.S;
        }
        fn(null, verified, verifyToken);
      } else {
        fn(null, null);
      }
    }
  });
}

function updateUser(email, fn) {
  dynamodb.updateItem({
      TableName: config.DDB_TABLE,
      Key: {
```

The getUser() function looks up the user in the database and returns the verification status.

If there is an "Item" in data, the user with that email has been found in the database.

Get the verification status.

If the user is not verified, get the token.

User not found

The updateUser() function changes the verification status on the database.

```
        email: {
          S: email
        }
      },
    AttributeUpdates: {
      verified: {
        Action: 'PUT',
        Value: {
          BOOL: true
        }
      },
      verifyToken: {
        Action: 'DELETE'
      }
    }
  },
  fn);
}
exports.handler = (event, context, callback) => {
  var email = event.email;
  var verifyToken = event.verify;

  getUser(email, function(err, verified, correctToken) {
    if (err) {
      callback('Error in getUser: ' + err);
    } else if (verified) {
      console.log('User already verified: ' + email);
      callback(null, { verified: true });
    } else if (verifyToken == correctToken) {
      updateUser(email, function(err, data) {
        if (err) {
          callback('Error in updateUser: ' + err);
        } else {
          console.log('User verified: ' + email);
          callback(null, { verified: true });
        }
      });
    } else {
      console.log('User not verified: ' + email);
      callback(null, { verified: false });
    }
  });
}
```

- Set verified attribute to true.
- Delete the token attribute.
- The function exported to AWS Lambda as verifyUser
- Look up the user in the database (by email).
- If already verified, do nothing.
- If the token in the URL is the same as the one on the database, flag the user as verified.
- Update verification status on the database (and remove token).
- Unable to verify the user (for example, the token is wrong)

Listing 9.12 Policy_Lambda_verifyUser

```
{
    "Version": "2012-10-17",
    "Statement": [
        {
            "Action": [
                "dynamodb:GetItem",
                "dynamodb:UpdateItem"
            ],
```

- Getting an item (by primary key—the email in this case)
- Updating an item (to flag as verified)

```
        "Effect": "Allow",
        "Resource": "arn:aws:dynamodb:<REGION>:<AWS_ACCOUNT_ID>:table/
    <DYNAMODB_TABLE>"
      },
      {
        "Sid": "",
        "Resource": "*",
        "Action": [
            "logs:*"
        ],
        "Effect": "Allow"
      }
    ]
}
```

The output of the `verify.html` page is shown in figure 9.7.

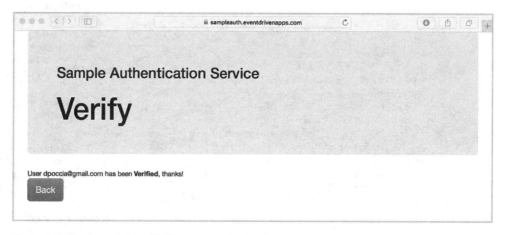

Figure 9.7   The output of the Verify page, confirming that the user has been validated

Summary

In this chapter you built a sample authentication service with a web client application. In particular, you learned about the following:

- Using multiple Lambda functions to implement your back end
- Using HTML with JavaScript to implement a web client application
- Using the AWS CLI to automate resource creation and updates on AWS
- Managing a central configuration and shared code in your application
- Sending emails using Amazon SES

In the next chapter, you'll add more advanced features to the authentication service, such as changing and resetting passwords, and using the login together with Amazon Cognito to get AWS credentials for authenticated users.

EXERCISE

Add a name field to the Sign Up page and have the name stored on the DynamoDB table and in the validation email.

> **TIP** In Amazon DynamoDB, you need to specify only the primary key (the `email` in this case), and you can add different attributes in any item of the table. As a consequence, no changes in the IAM role used by the Lambda function are required.

Solution

To add a name, you need to change the HTML page (`signUp.html`), the client-side JavaScript file (signUp.js), and the Lambda function (`createUser`). A possible solution is presented in **bold** in the following listings, with the changes compared to the standard implementation.

`signUpWithName.html` **(Sign Up page)**

```html
<html>
<head>
  <title>Sign Up - Sample Authentication Service</title>
  <script src="https://sdk.amazonaws.com/js/aws-sdk-2.3.16.min.js"></script>
</head>
<body>
  <h2>Sample Authentication Service</h2>
  <h1>Sign Up</h1>
  <form role="form" id="signup-form">
    <div>
      <label for="email">Email:</label>
      <input type="email" id="email">
    </div>
    <div>
      <label for="name">Email:</label>
      <input type="text" id="name">
    </div>
    <div>
      <label for="password">Password:</label>
      <input type="password" id="password">
    </div>
    <div>
      <label for="password">Verify Password:</label>
      <input type="password" id="verify-password">
    </div>
    <button type="submit" id="signup-button">Sign Up</button>
  </form>
  <div id="result">
  </div>
  <a href="index.html">Back</a>
  <script src="js/signUp.js"></script>
</body>
</html>
```

signUpWithName.js (JavaScript in the browser)

```javascript
AWS.config.region = '<REGION>';
AWS.config.credentials = new AWS.CognitoIdentityCredentials({
  IdentityPoolId: '<IDENTITY_POOL_ID>'
});

var lambda = new AWS.Lambda();

function signup() {

  var result = document.getElementById('result');
  var email = document.getElementById('email');
  var name = document.getElementById('name');
  var password = document.getElementById('password');
  var verifyPassword = document.getElementById('verify-password');

  result.innerHTML = 'Sign Up...';

  if (email.value == null || email.value == '') {
    result.innerHTML = 'Please specify your email address.';
  } else if (name.value == null || name.value == '') {
    result.innerHTML = 'Please specify your name.';
  } else if (password.value == null || password.value == '') {
    result.innerHTML = 'Please specify a password.';
  } else if (password.value != verifyPassword.value) {
    result.innerHTML = 'Passwords are <b>different</b>, please check.';
  } else {

    var input = {
      email: email.value,
      name: name.value,
      password: password.value,
    };

    lambda.invoke({
      FunctionName: 'sampleAuthCreateUser',
      Payload: JSON.stringify(input)
    }, function(err, data) {
      if (err) console.log(err, err.stack);
      else {
        var output = JSON.parse(data.Payload);
        if (output.created) {
          result.innerHTML = 'User ' + input.email + ' created. Please check
    your email to validate the user and enable login.';
        } else {
          result.innerHTML = 'User <b>not</b> created.';
        }
      }
    });

  }
}

var form = document.getElementById('signup-form');
form.addEventListener('submit', function(evt) {
  evt.preventDefault();
  signup();
});
```

createUser Lambda Function (Node.js)

```javascript
console.log('Loading function');

var AWS = require('aws-sdk');
var crypto = require('crypto');
var cryptoUtils = require('./lib/cryptoUtils');
var config = require('./config');

var dynamodb = new AWS.DynamoDB();
var ses = new AWS.SES();

function storeUser(email, name, password, salt, fn) {
  var len = 128;
  crypto.randomBytes(len, function(err, token) {
    if (err) return fn(err);
    token = token.toString('hex');
    dynamodb.putItem({
      TableName: config.DDB_TABLE,
      Item: {
        email: {
          S: email
        },
        name: {
          S: name
        },
        passwordHash: {
          S: password
        },
        passwordSalt: {
          S: salt
        },
        verified: {
          BOOL: false
        },
        verifyToken: {
          S: token
        }
      },
      ConditionExpression: 'attribute_not_exists (email)'
    }, function(err, data) {
      if (err) return fn(err);
      else fn(null, token);
    });
  });
}

function sendVerificationEmail(email, name, token, fn) {
  var subject = 'Verification Email for ' + config.EXTERNAL_NAME;
  var verificationLink = config.VERIFICATION_PAGE + '?email=' +
    encodeURIComponent(email) + '&verify=' + token;
  ses.sendEmail({
    Source: config.EMAIL_SOURCE,
    Destination: {
      ToAddresses: [
        email
      ]
```

```
        },
      Message: {
        Subject: {
          Data: subject
        },
        Body: {
          Html: {
            Data: '<html><head>'
            + '<meta http-equiv="Content-Type" content="text/html; charset=UTF-
      8" />'
            + '<title>' + subject + '</title>'
            + '</head><body>'
            + 'Hello ' + name + ', please <a href="' + verificationLink +
      '">click here to verify your email address</a> or copy & paste the
      following link in a browser:'
            + '<br><br>'
            + '<a href="' + verificationLink + '">' + verificationLink + '</a>'
            + '</body></html>'
          }
        }
      }
    }, fn);
}

exports.handler = (event, context, callback) => {
  var email = event.email;
  var name = event.name;
  var clearPassword = event.password;

  cryptoUtils.computeHash(clearPassword, function(err, salt, hash) {
    if (err) {
      callback('Error in hash: ' + err);
    } else {
      storeUser(email, name, hash, salt, function(err, token) {
        if (err) {
          if (err.code == 'ConditionalCheckFailedException') {
            // userId already found
            callback(null, { created: false });
          } else {
            callback('Error in storeUser: ' + err);
          }
        } else {
          sendVerificationEmail(email, name, token, function(err, data) {
            if (err) {
              callback('Error in sendVerificationEmail: ' + err);
            } else {
              callback(null, { created: true });
            }
          });
        }
      });
    }
  });
}
```

Adding more features to the authentication service

10

This chapter covers

- Managing more use cases, such as resetting and changing passwords
- Integrating the login process with Amazon Cognito
- Using the login to get AWS credentials as an authenticated user
- Allowing access to Lambda functions to only authenticated users

In the previous chapter, you started implementing the serverless architecture for a sample authentication service (figure 10.1) capable of creating new users and validating the email address. In this chapter, you're going to add more interesting features, such as the ability to change or reset the password, and log in as an Amazon Cognito developer authenticated identity.

> **NOTE** This example uses both client-side (running in the browser) and server-side (running in Lambda functions) code. Because the code running in the browser is JavaScript, the Lambda function examples are also

provided in JavaScript. The implementation of those functions in Python is left as an exercise for you to do on your own, because it doesn't change the architecture or the logic of the application.

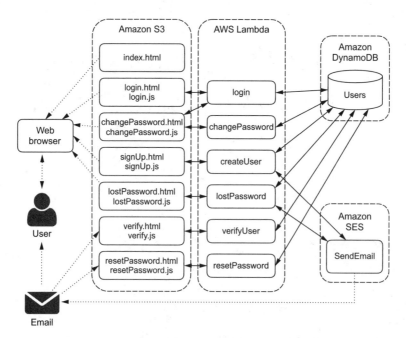

Figure 10.1   The overall serverless architecture of the sample authentication service you're implementing in this chapter. HTML and JavaScript files are hosted on Amazon S3. Lambda functions provide the back end logic. A DynamoDB table is used to store user profiles. Amazon SES sends emails for verification and for password resets.

10.1   *Reporting lost passwords*

With a flow similar to that of the create and validate user pages, you can implement a reset password process using an email with a random token to validate the user.

> **NOTE**   For the sake of simplicity, we'll call this functionality "lost password," even though it can cover different use cases. For example, if the user suspects their credentials have been compromised, asking for a password reset is a good option.

First, the user reports the lost password in the `lostPassword.html` page (figure 10.2). The code for the `lostPassword.html` page is shown in listing 10.1.

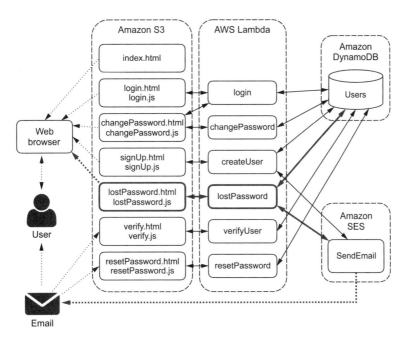

Figure 10.2 To reset a password, the user first has to report that he has lost the password. The `lostPassword` Lambda function sends an email with a random token to validate the request.

Listing 10.1 `lostPassword.html` (Lost Password page)

```html
<html>
<head>
  <title>Change Password - Sample Authentication Service</title>
  <meta charset="utf-8">
  <script src="https://sdk.amazonaws.com/js/aws-sdk-2.3.16.min.js">
  </script>
</head>
<body>
  <h2>Sample Authentication Service</h2>
  <h1>Lost Password</h1>
  <form role="form" id="lost-password-form">
    <div>
      <label for="email">Email:</label>
      <input type="text" class="form-control" id="email">
    </div>
    <button type="submit" class="btn btn-default" id="lost-password-
button">
      Lost Password
    </button>
  </form>
  <div id="result">
  </div>
  <a class="btn btn-info btn-lg" href="index.html">Back</a>
```

```
    <script src="js/lostPassword.js"></script>
</body>
</html>
```

The client logic is in this
JavaScript code, running
in the browser.

The lostPassword.js JavaScript code (see the following listing), running in the browser,
calls the lostPassword Lambda function to initiate the reset password process.

Listing 10.2   lostPassword.js (JavaScript in the browser)

```
AWS.config.region = '<REGION>';
AWS.config.credentials = new AWS.CognitoIdentityCredentials({
  IdentityPoolId: '<IDENTITY_POOL_ID>'
});

var lambda = new AWS.Lambda();

function lostPassword() {

  var result = document.getElementById('result');
  var email = document.getElementById('email');

  result.innerHTML = 'Password Lost...';

  if (email.value == null || email.value == '') {
    result.innerHTML = 'Please specify your email address.';
  } else {

    var input = {
      email: email.value
    };

    lambda.invoke({
      FunctionName: 'sampleAuthLostPassword',
      Payload: JSON.stringify(input)
    }, function(err, data) {
      if (err) console.log(err, err.stack);
      else {
        var output = JSON.parse(data.Payload);
        if (output.sent) {
          result.innerHTML =
            'Email sent. Please check your email to reset your password.';
        } else {
          result.innerHTML = 'Email <b>not</b> sent.';
        }
      }
    });

  }
}

var form = document.getElementById('lost-password-form');
form.addEventListener('submit', function(evt) {
  evt.preventDefault();
  lostPassword();
});
```

Only the email address is
required to initiate the
reset password process.

The back end Lambda
function to call, passing
the email address in
the input event

The lostPassword Lambda function (listing 10.3) generates a random reset token that's stored in the database and sent as a query parameter in the link embedded in the reset email message. The IAM role used by the function is shown in listing 10.4. For example, the reset email message will look similar to the following:

Subject: Password Lost for Sample Authentication

Please <u>click here to reset your password</u> or copy & paste the following link in a browser:

<u>https://sampleauth.eventdrivenapps.com/</u>
<u>resetPassword.html?email=you@example.com&lost=7d66118778f1c222f51ca68802652e6</u>
<u>d569216a5e4b5ad93756bed9cb680755b3ef45be06714c17a62368d4853db408658223821aa02</u>
<u>08d9ef50e59460d7617995ac291b1973dd5dfae5bb15ebfd6eb3e1ae5f13c5339af0d8e4680af</u>
<u>42f96766c4b33933008e5c66e8fce32c05be2d089502779ca2112cfd09aba7890896155</u>

Listing 10.3 lostPassword Lambda function (Node.js)

```
console.log('Loading function');

var AWS = require('aws-sdk');
var crypto = require('crypto');
var config = require('./config.json');

var dynamodb = new AWS.DynamoDB();
var ses = new AWS.SES();

function getUser(email, fn) {            ◄──  The getUser() function
  dynamodb.getItem({                          reads all the user data from
    TableName: config.DDB_TABLE,              the DynamoDB table; the
    Key: {                                    email is the hash key.
      email: {
        S: email
      }
    }
  }, function(err, data) {
    if (err) return fn(err);
    else {
      if ('Item' in data) {
        fn(null, email);
      } else {                         ┐ User not
        fn(null, null);          ◄──  ┘ found
      }
    }
  });
}
                                       The storeLostToken() function
                                       generates a random token and
                                       stores the value in the lostToken
function storeLostToken(email, fn) {   ◄──  attribute of the DynamoDB table.
  var len = 128;
  crypto.randomBytes(len, function(err, token) {   ◄─  Bytesize
    if (err) return fn(err);
    token = token.toString('hex');
    dynamodb.updateItem({
        TableName: config.DDB_TABLE,
        Key: {
```

```
            email: {
              S: email
            }
          },
          AttributeUpdates: {
            lostToken: {
              Action: 'PUT',
              Value: {
                S: token
              }
            }
          }
        },
      function(err, data) {
        if (err) return fn(err);
        else fn(null, token);
      });
    });
  }
```

The sendLostPassword-
Email() function sends
the reset email message
to the user.

```
function sendLostPasswordEmail(email, token, fn) {
  var subject = 'Password Lost for ' + config.EXTERNAL_NAME;
  var lostLink = config.RESET_PAGE +
    '?email=' + email + '&lost=' + token;
  ses.sendEmail({
    Source: config.EMAIL_SOURCE,
    Destination: {
      ToAddresses: [
        email
      ]
    },
    Message: {
      Subject: {
        Data: subject
      },
      Body: {
        Html: {
          Data: '<html><head>'
          + '<meta http-equiv="Content-Type"
            content="text/html; charset=UTF-8" />'
          + '<title>' + subject + '</title>'
          + '</head><body>'
          + 'Please <a href="' + lostLink + '">'
          + 'click here to reset your password</a>'
          + ' or copy & paste the following link in a browser:'
          + '<br><br>'
          + '<a href="' + lostLink + '">' + lostLink + '</a>'
          + '</body></html>'
        }
      }
    }
  }, fn);
}
```

The randomly generated
token is used as a query
parameter in the link to the
resetPassword.html page.

Amazon SES is used to
send the reset email.

```
exports.handler = (event, context, callback) => {          ◄─┐    The exported function
  var email = event.email;                                   │    that will be invoked by
                                                             │    using AWS Lambda
  getUser(email, function(err, emailFound) {        ◄────────┘
    if (err) {
      callback('Error in getUserFromEmail: ' + err);      The user data is
    } else if (!emailFound) {                             read from the
      console.log('User not found: ' + email);            database.
      callback(null, { sent: false });
    } else {                                                      The random
      storeLostToken(email, function(err, token) {   ◄───┐       token is stored in
        if (err) {                                        │       the database.
          callback('Error in storeLostToken: ' + err);
        } else {
          sendLostPasswordEmail(email, token, function(err, data) {  ◄─┐  The reset
            if (err) {                                                 │  email
              callback('Error in sendLostPasswordEmail: ' + err);     │  message
            } else {                                                  │  is sent to
              console.log('User found: ' + email);                    │  the user.
              callback(null, { sent: true });
            }
          });
        }
      });
    }
  });
}
```

Listing 10.4 Policy_Lambda_lostPassword

```
{
    "Version": "2012-10-17",
    "Statement": [
        {
            "Action": [
                "dynamodb:GetItem",             Reading and
                "dynamodb:UpdateItem"           updating an item
            ],
            "Effect": "Allow",
            "Resource": "arn:aws:dynamodb:<REGION>:<ACCOUNT>:table/<TABLE>"
        },
        {
            "Effect": "Allow",
            "Action": [
                "ses:SendEmail",                Sending the reset email
                "ses:SendRawEmail"              using Amazon SES
            ],
            "Resource": "*"
        },
        {
            "Sid": "",
            "Resource": "*",
```

```
        "Action": [
            "logs:*"
        ],
        "Effect": "Allow"
    }
  ]
}
```

A screenshot of the `lostPassword.html` page is shown in figure 10.3. The user has to provide the email address to start the reset password procedure and receive a reset email message.

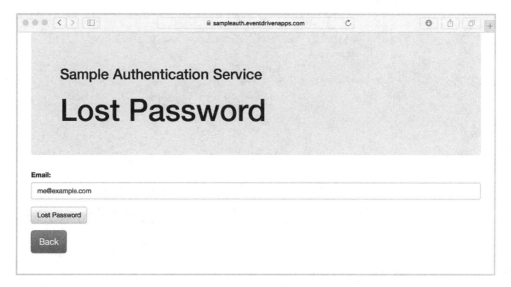

Figure 10.3   The output of the Lost Password page. When submitted, the reset email message is sent to the user.

10.2   *Resetting passwords*

After a password has been reported lost, the user receives a reset email message. Clicking the link in the reset email message opens the `resetPassword.html` page (listing 10.5), passing the `lost` token in the URL (figure 10.4).

The reset password token is read by the JavaScript code in the resetPassword.js file (listing 10.6), executed in the browser, and passed to the `resetPassword` Lambda function (listing 10.7), together with the new password. The IAM role used by the function is shown in listing 10.8.

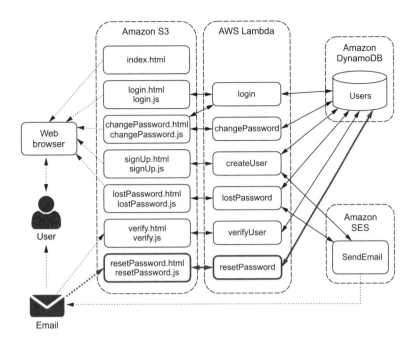

Figure 10.4 The second part of the lost password process: the link in the reset email message opens the `resetPassword.html` page that asks for a new password and calls the `resetPassword` Lambda function passing the lost password token. If the lost password token is correct, checking on the database, the Lambda function changes the password to the new one.

Listing 10.5 `resetPassword.html` (Reset Password page)

```
<html>
<head>
  <title>Reset Password - Sample Authentication Service</title>
  <script src="https://sdk.amazonaws.com/js/aws-sdk-
2.3.16.min.js"></script>
</head>
<body>
  <h2>Sample Authentication Service</h2>
  <h1>Reset Password</h1>
  <form role="form" id="reset-password-form">
    <div>
      <label for="password">New Password:</label>
      <input type="password" class="form-control" id="new-password">
    </div>
    <div >
      <label for="password">Verify New Password:</label>
      <input type="password" class="form-control" id="verify-new-password">
    </div>
    <button type="submit" id="reset-password-button">
      Reset Password
    </button>
```

```
  </form>
  <div id="result">
  </div>
  <a href="index.html">Back</a>
  <script src="js/resetPassword.js"></script>
</body>
</html>
```

The client logic is in this
JavaScript code, running
in the browser.

Listing 10.6   resetPassword.js (JavaScript in the browser)

```
AWS.config.region = '<REGION>';
AWS.config.credentials = new AWS.CognitoIdentityCredentials({
  IdentityPoolId: '<IDENTITY_POOL_ID>'
});

var lambda = new AWS.Lambda();

function getUrlParams() {
  var p = {};
  var match,
    pl     = /\+/g,
    search = /([^&=]+)=?([^&]*)/g,
    decode = function (s)
      { return decodeURIComponent(s.replace(pl, " ")); },
    query  = window.location.search.substring(1);
  while (match = search.exec(query))
    p[decode(match[1])] = decode(match[2]);
  return p;
}

function resetPassword() {

  var result = document.getElementById('result');
  var password = document.getElementById('new-password');
  var verifyPassword = document.getElementById('verify-new-password');

  var urlParams = getUrlParams();
  var email = urlParams['email'] || null;
  var lost = urlParams['lost'] || null;

  if (password.value == null || password.value == '') {
    result.innerHTML = 'Please specify a password.';
  } else if (password.value != verifyPassword.value) {
    result.innerHTML = 'Passwords are <b>not</b> the same, please check.';
  } else {
    if ((!email)||(!lost)) {
      result.innerHTML = 'Please specify email and lost token in the URL.';
    } else {
      result.innerHTML = 'Trying to reset password for user ' +
        email + ' ...';

      var input = {
        email: email,
        lost: lost,
        password: password.value
      };
```

The getUrlParams()
function reads query
parameters from the URL.

Regex for replacing addition
symbol with a space

The resetPassword()
function is executed when
the form is submitted.

The input event for the Lambda
function contains the email, the
lost token, and the new password.

```
        lambda.invoke({
          FunctionName: 'sampleAuthResetPassword',
          Payload: JSON.stringify(input)
        }, function(err, data) {
          if (err) console.log(err, err.stack);
          else {
            var output = JSON.parse(data.Payload);
            if (output.changed) {
              result.innerHTML = 'Password changed for user ' + email;
            } else {
              result.innerHTML = 'Password <b>not</b> changed.';
            }
          }
        });
      }
    }
}

function init() {
  if (email) {
    result.innerHTML = 'Type your new password for user ' + email;
  }
}

var form = document.getElementById('reset-password-form');
form.addEventListener('submit', function(evt) {
  evt.preventDefault();
  resetPassword();
});

window.onload = init();
```

- The resetPassword Lambda function is invoked.
- Check if the password was changed (or not) by the resetPassword Lambda function.
- The init() function is used to customize the result message on the HTML page.
- The init() function is executed automatically on page load.

Listing 10.7 resetPassword Lambda function (Node.js)

```
console.log('Loading function');

var AWS = require('aws-sdk');
var cryptoUtils = require('./lib/cryptoUtils');
var config = require('./config');

var dynamodb = new AWS.DynamoDB();

function getUser(email, fn) {
  dynamodb.getItem({
    TableName: config.DDB_TABLE,
    Key: {
      email: {
        S: email
      }
    }
  }, function(err, data) {
    if (err) return fn(err);
    else {
      if (('Item' in data) && ('lostToken' in data.Item)) {
        var lostToken = data.Item.lostToken.S;
```

- The getUser() function is reading the user data from the database, including the lost token written by the lostPassword Lambda function.

```
                fn(null, lostToken);
            } else {
                fn(null, null); // User or token not found
            }
        }
    });
}

function updateUser(email, password, salt, fn) {        ◁──
    dynamodb.updateItem({
        TableName: config.DDB_TABLE,
        Key: {
            email: {
                S: email
            }
        },
        AttributeUpdates: {
            passwordHash: {
                Action: 'PUT',
                Value: {
                    S: password
                }
            },
            passwordSalt: {
                Action: 'PUT',
                Value: {
                    S: salt
                }
            },
            lostToken: {
                Action: 'DELETE'
            }
        }
    },
    fn);
}

exports.handler = (event, context, callback) => {      ◁──
    var email = event.email;
    var lostToken = event.lost;
    var newPassword = event.password;

    getUser(email, function(err, correctToken) {       ◁──
        if (err) {
            callback('Error in getUser: ' + err);
        } else if (!correctToken) {                    ◁──
            console.log('No lostToken for user: ' + email);
            callback(null, { changed: false });
        } else if (lostToken != correctToken) {        ◁──
            // Wrong token, no password lost
            console.log('Wrong lostToken for user: ' + email);
            callback(null, { changed: false });
        } else {
            console.log('User logged in: ' + email);
            cryptoUtils.computeHash(newPassword,
```

The updateUser() function is updating the user data in the database, updating the (salted) password, and deleting the lost password token.

The function exported to AWS Lambda for invocation

Read the lost password token from the database.

If there's no lost password token in the database, the user didn't ask to reset the password (or the user wasn't found).

If the lost password token in the database is different from the one given to the Lambda function, the password isn't changed.

If the lost password token is the correct one, compute the new salted password and update the database.

```
              function(err, newSalt, newHash) {
          if (err) {
            callback('Error in computeHash: ' + err);
          } else {
            updateUser(email, newHash, newSalt, function(err, data) {
              if (err) {
                callback('Error in updateUser: ' + err);
              } else {
                console.log('User password changed: ' + email);
                callback(null, { changed: true });
              }
            });
          }
        });
      }
    });
}
```

Listing 10.8 Policy_Lambda_resetPassword

```
{
  "Version": "2012-10-17",
  "Statement": [
    {
      "Action": [
        "dynamodb:GetItem",              To read and update
        "dynamodb:UpdateItem"            items in the database
      ],
      "Effect": "Allow",
      "Resource": "arn:aws:dynamodb:<REGION>:<ACCOUNT>:table/<TABLE>"
    },
    {
      "Sid": "",
      "Resource": "*",
      "Action": [
        "logs:*"
      ],
      "Effect": "Allow"
    }
  ]
}
```

The output of the resetPassword.html page is shown in figure 10.5.

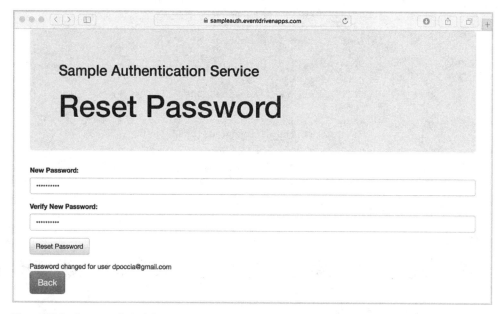

Figure 10.5   A screenshot of the `resetPassword.html` **page, reporting if the password reset was successful or not**

10.3   *Logging in users*

Probably the most important feature of an authentication service is to provide the option to log in (figure 10.6). The `login.html` (listing 10.9) page uses the JavaScript code in the login.js file (listing 10.10) to call the `login` Lambda function (listing 10.11) with the user credentials (email and password) to authenticate the user. The IAM role used by the function is shown in listing 10.12.

Listing 10.9   `login.html` (Login Page)

```
<html>
<head>
  <title>Login - Sample Authentication Service</title>
  <script src="https://sdk.amazonaws.com/js/aws-sdk-2.3.16.min.js">
  </script>
</head>
<body>
  <h2>Sample Authentication Service</h2>
  <h1>Login</h1>
  <form role="form" id="login-form">
    <div>
      <label for="email">Email:</label>
      <input type="text" class="form-control" id="email">
    </div>
    <div>
      <label for="password">Password:</label>
      <input type="password" class="form-control" id="password">
```

```
        </div>
        <button type="submit" id="login-button">Login</button>
      </form>
      <div id="result">
      </div>
      <a href="index.html">Back</a>
      <script src="js/login.js"></script>
    </body>
</html>
```

The client logic is in the login.js JavaScript file.

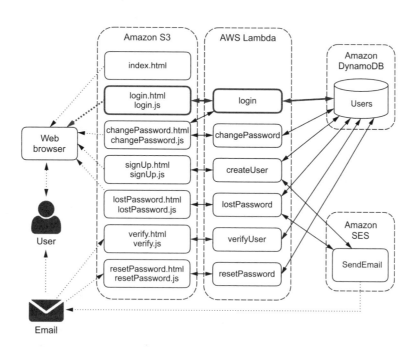

Figure 10.6 The login process checks the user credentials on the database and returns a confirmation for the login and a Cognito Developer Authenticated Identity token that can be used to get AWS credentials for authenticating users.

Listing 10.10 login.js (JavaScript in the browser)

```
AWS.config.region = '<REGION>';
AWS.config.credentials = new AWS.CognitoIdentityCredentials({
  IdentityPoolId: '<IDENTITY_POOL_ID>'
});

var lambda = new AWS.Lambda();

function login() {

  var result = document.getElementById('result');
  var email = document.getElementById('email');
  var password = document.getElementById('password');
```

```
      result.innerHTML = 'Login...';

    if (email.value == null || email.value == '') {
      result.innerHTML = 'Please specify your email address.';
    } else if (password.value == null || password.value == '') {
      result.innerHTML = 'Please specify a password.';
    } else {

      var input = {
        email: email.value,
        password: password.value
      };

      lambda.invoke({
        FunctionName: 'sampleAuthLogin',
        Payload: JSON.stringify(input)
      }, function(err, data) {
        if (err) console.log(err, err.stack);
        else {
          var output = JSON.parse(data.Payload);
          if (!output.login) {
            result.innerHTML = '<b>Not</b> logged in';
          } else {
            result.innerHTML = 'Logged in with IdentityId: '
              + output.identityId + '<br>';

            var creds = AWS.config.credentials;
            creds.params.IdentityId = output.identityId;
            creds.params.Logins = {
              'cognito-identity.amazonaws.com': output.token
            };
            creds.expired = true;

            // Do something with the authenticated role

          }
        }
      });

    }
  }

var form = document.getElementById('login-form');
form.addEventListener('submit', function(evt) {
  evt.preventDefault();
  login();
});
```

> Email and password are in the input event for the login Lambda function.

> The login Lambda function is invoked, with the user credentials in the input event.

> Check if the login was successful or not.

> Update the AWS credentials with the identity ID and the login token.

> Explicitly expiring the current AWS credentials will force the refresh, this time as an authenticated user.

Listing 10.11   login Lambda function (Node.js)

```
console.log('Loading function');

var AWS = require('aws-sdk');
var config = require('./config.json');
var cryptoUtils = require('./lib/cryptoUtils');

var dynamodb = new AWS.DynamoDB();
var cognitoidentity = new AWS.CognitoIdentity();
```

```
function getUser(email, fn) {
  dynamodb.getItem({
    TableName: config.DDB_TABLE,
    Key: {
      email: {
        S: email
      }
    }
  }, function(err, data) {
    if (err) return fn(err);
    else {
      if ('Item' in data) {
        var hash = data.Item.passwordHash.S;
        var salt = data.Item.passwordSalt.S;
        var verified = data.Item.verified.BOOL;
        fn(null, hash, salt, verified);
      } else {
        fn(null, null); // User not found
      }
    }
  });
}

function getToken(email, fn) {
  var param = {
    IdentityPoolId: config.IDENTITY_POOL_ID,
    Logins: {}
  };
  param.Logins[config.DEVELOPER_PROVIDER_NAME] = email;
  cognitoidentity.getOpenIdTokenForDeveloperIdentity(param,
    function(err, data) {
      if (err) return fn(err);
      else fn(null, data.IdentityId, data.Token);
    });
}

exports.handler = (event, context, callback) => {
  var email = event.email;
  var clearPassword = event.password;

  getUser(email, function(err, correctHash, salt, verified) {
    if (err) {
      callback('Error in getUser: ' + err);
    } else {
      if (correctHash == null) {
        // User not found
        console.log('User not found: ' + email);
        callback(null, { login: false });
      } else if (!verified) {
        // User not verified
        console.log('User not verified: ' + email);
        callback(null, { login: false });
      } else {
        cryptoUtils.computeHash(clearPassword, salt,
          function(err, salt, hash) {
```

The getUser() function reads the salted password (hash and salt) from the database.

The getToken() function gets a token and the Identity ID for the user from Amazon Cognito, using the Developer Provider Name in the config.json configuration file.

The function exported to AWS Lambda for invocation

Get the salted password (hash and salt) from the database.

If no hash exists, the user wasn't found.

If the user is not verified, they cannot log in.

Compute the hash for the password given in input, using the same salt from the database.

If the two hashes (computed and stored in the database) are the same, the user can log in.

Get the token from Amazon Cognito and return it as part of the return value.

```
      if (err) {
        callback('Error in hash: ' + err);
      } else {
        console.log('correctHash: ' + correctHash + ' hash: ' + hash);
        if (hash == correctHash) {
          // Login ok
          console.log('User logged in: ' + email);
          getToken(email, function(err, identityId, token) {
            if (err) {
              callback('Error in getToken: ' + err);
            } else {
              callback(null, {
                login: true,
                identityId: identityId,
                token: token
              });
            }
          });
        } else {
          // Login failed
          console.log('User login failed: ' + email);
          callback(null, { login: false });
        }
      }
    }
  });
}
```

The hashes are different; the input password wasn't the correct one.

Listing 10.12   Policy_Lambda_login

```json
{
  "Version": "2012-10-17",
  "Statement": [
    {
      "Action": [
        "dynamodb:GetItem"
      ],
      "Effect": "Allow",
      "Resource": "arn:aws:dynamodb:<REGION>:<ACCOUNT>:table/<TABLE>"
    },
    {
      "Effect": "Allow",
      "Action": [
        "cognito-identity:GetOpenIdTokenForDeveloperIdentity"
      ],
      "Resource":
        "arn:aws:cognito-identity:<REGION>:<ACCOUNT>:identitypool/<POOL>"
    },
    {
      "Sid": "",
      "Resource": "*",
      "Action": [
```

Reading items from the table (by email)

Getting the Cognito token for Developer Identities

```
          "logs:*"
        ],
        "Effect": "Allow"
      }
    ]
  ]
}
```

A sample screenshot of the `login.html` page is shown in figure 10.7.

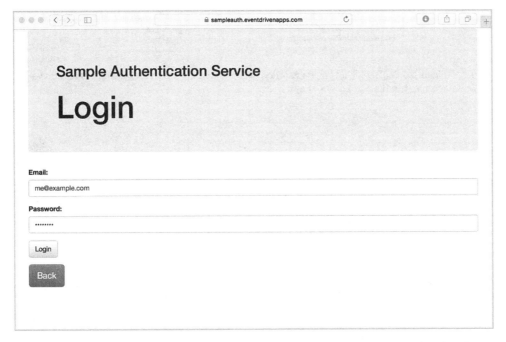

Figure 10.7   The output of the Login page. When a user has logged in correctly, the unique Cognito Identity ID assigned to the authenticated user is shown as confirmation.

10.4   *Getting AWS credentials for authenticated users*

If the user credentials (email and password) are valid, the `login` Lambda function asks Amazon Cognito for a `token` for a developer authenticated identity (figure 10.8). Together with the `token`, Amazon Cognito also returns a unique `identity ID` for the user.

The `token` is returned to the `login.js` script, which can use it to ask for new AWS credentials for the authenticated IAM role of the Cognito identity pool (figure 10.9).

With the new AWS credentials, the client application can use all the resources and actions allowed by the authenticated IAM role of the Cognito identity pool. For example, you can use this approach to allow only authenticated users to change passwords.

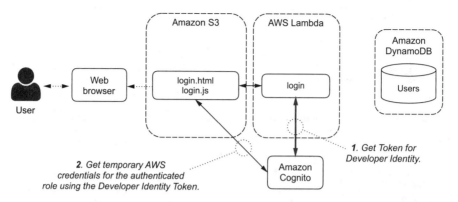

Figure 10.8 **The login Lambda function gets the Cognito token for Developer Identities and returns it to the** `login.js` **script.**

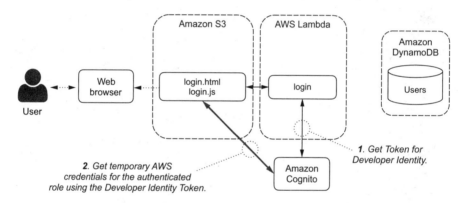

Figure 10.9 **The** `login.js` **script can use the Cognito token to get AWS credentials for the authenticated role of the Cognito identity pool.**

10.5 *Changing passwords*

To change passwords, you need to know the old password; otherwise, you can use the lost/reset password process introduced before. Instead of passing the old password to the changePassword Lambda function, you can use the login functionality to get AWS credentials for the authenticated IAM role, and give access to the changePassword Lambda function only to authenticated users.

The IAM role for the authenticated users of the Cognito identity pool is shown in the following listing. As you can see, access to the changePassword Lambda function has been added (in **bold**), compared with the role for unauthenticated users.

Listing 10.13 Policy_Cognito_Authenticated_Role

```
{
  "Version": "2012-10-17",
  "Statement": [
    {
      "Effect": "Allow",
      "Action": [
        "mobileanalytics:PutEvents",
        "cognito-sync:*"
      ],
      "Resource": [
        "*"
      ]
    },
    {
      "Effect": "Allow",
      "Action": [
        "lambda:InvokeFunction"
      ],
      "Resource": [
        "arn:aws:lambda:<REGION>:<ACCOUNT>:function:createUser",
        "arn:aws:lambda:<REGION>:<ACCOUNT>:function:verifyUser",
        "arn:aws:lambda:<REGION>:<ACCOUNT>:function:changePassword",
        "arn:aws:lambda:<REGION>:<ACCOUNT>:function:lostPassword",
        "arn:aws:lambda:<REGION>:<ACCOUNT>:function:resetPassword",
        "arn:aws:lambda:<REGION>:<ACCOUNT>:function:sampleAuthLogin"
      ]
    }
  ]
}
```

Only authenticated users can access the changePassword Lambda function from the client application.

In this way, the changePassword.html page is the only page in our application that uses two back-end Lambda functions (figure 10.10):

- The login function, to authenticate the user
- The changePassword function, to change the password on the database

The changePassword.html content is shown in the following listing. This page uses the changePassword.js script (listing 10.15) and the changePassword Lambda function (listing 10.16). The IAM role used by the function is shown in listing 10.17.

Listing 10.14 changePassword.html (Change Password page)

```
<html>
<head>
  <title>Change Password - Sample Authentication Service</title>
  <script src="https://sdk.amazonaws.com/js/aws-sdk-2.3.16.min.js"></script>
</head>
<body>
  <h2>Sample Authentication Service</h2>
    <h1>Change Password</h1>
```

```html
<form role="form" id="change-password-form">
  <div>
    <label for="email">Email:</label>
    <input type="email" class="form-control" id="email">
  </div>
    <div>
    <label for="password">Old Password:</label>
    <input type="password" class="form-control" id="old-password">
  </div>
  <div>
    <label for="password">New Password:</label>
    <input type="password" class="form-control" id="new-password">
  </div>
  <div>
    <label for="password">Verify New Password:</label>
    <input type="password" class="form-control" id="verify-new-password">
  </div>
  <button type="submit" id="change-button">Change Password</button>
</form>
<div id="result">
<a href="index.html">Back</a>
<script src="js/changePassword.js"></script>
</body>
</html>
```

All the client logic is in the changePassword.js JavaScript file.

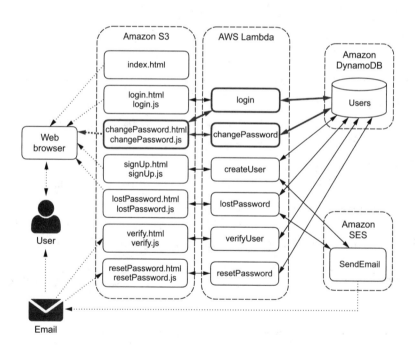

Figure 10.10 The change password page is using the login Lambda function to authenticate the user and give access to the `changePassword` Lambda function.

Listing 10.15   changePassword.js (JavaScript in the browser)

```javascript
AWS.config.region = '<REGION>';
AWS.config.credentials = new AWS.CognitoIdentityCredentials({
  IdentityPoolId: '<IDENTITY_POOL_ID>'
});

var lambda = new AWS.Lambda();

function changePassword() {

  var result = document.getElementById('result');
  var email = document.getElementById('email');
  var oldPassword = document.getElementById('old-password');
  var newPassword = document.getElementById('new-password');
  var verifyNewPassword = document.getElementById('verify-new-password');

  result.innerHTML = 'Change Password...';

  if (email.value == null || email.value == '') {
    result.innerHTML = 'Please specify your email address.';
  } else if (oldPassword.value == null || oldPassword.value == '') {
    result.innerHTML = 'Please specify your current password.';
  } else if (newPassword.value == null || newPassword.value == '') {
    result.innerHTML = 'Please specify a new password.';
  } else if (newPassword.value != verifyNewPassword.value) {
    result.innerHTML = 'The new passwords are <b>different</b>'
      + ', please check.';
  } else {

    var input = {
      email: email.value,
      password: oldPassword.value
    };

    lambda.invoke({
      FunctionName: 'sampleAuthLogin',
      Payload: JSON.stringify(input)
    }, function(err, data) {
      if (err) console.log(err, err.stack);
      else {
        var output = JSON.parse(data.Payload);
        console.log('identityId: ' + output.identityId);
        console.log('token: ' + output.token);
        if (!output.login) {
          result.innerHTML = '<b>Not</b> logged in';
        } else {
          result.innerHTML = 'Logged in with identityId: '
            + output.identityId + '<br>';

          var creds = AWS.config.credentials;
          creds.params.IdentityId = output.identityId;
          creds.params.Logins = {
            'cognito-identity.amazonaws.com': output.token
          };
          creds.expired = true;
```

> The login Lambda function needs only the email and the old password in input.

> The login Lambda function is invoked.

> In case of a correct login, the AWS credentials are renewed as an authenticated user.

```
            var input = {
              email: email.value,
              oldPassword: oldPassword.value,
              newPassword: newPassword.value
            };

            lambda.invoke({
              FunctionName: 'sampleAuthChangePassword',
              Payload: JSON.stringify(input)
            }, function(err, data) {
              if (err) console.log(err, err.stack);
              else {
                var output = JSON.parse(data.Payload);
                if (!output.changed) {
                  result.innerHTML = 'Password <b>not</b> changed.';
                } else {
                  result.innerHTML = 'Password changed.';
                }
              }
            });

          }
        }
      });

    }
  }


var form = document.getElementById('change-password-form');
form.addEventListener('submit', function(evt) {
  evt.preventDefault();
  changePassword();
});
```

The changePassword Lambda function requires both the old and the new password in input.

The changePassword Lambda function is invoked.

Check if the password was changed (or not) by the changePassword Lambda function.

Listing 10.16   `changePassword` Lambda function (Node.js)

```
console.log('Loading function');

var AWS = require('aws-sdk');
var cryptoUtils = require('./lib/cryptoUtils');
var config = require('./config');

var dynamodb = new AWS.DynamoDB();

function getUser(email, fn) {
  dynamodb.getItem({
    TableName: config.DDB_TABLE,
    Key: {
      email: {
        S: email
      }
    }
  }, function(err, data) {
    if (err) return fn(err);
```

The getUser() function reads the user data from the database; in this case it's used only to check if the user exists.

```
    else {
      if ('Item' in data) {
        var hash = data.Item.passwordHash.S;
        var salt = data.Item.passwordSalt.S;
        fn(null, hash, salt);
      } else {
        fn(null, null); // User not found
      }
    }
  });
}

function updateUser(email, password, salt, fn) {
  dynamodb.updateItem({
      TableName: config.DDB_TABLE,
      Key: {
        email: {
          S: email
        }
      },
      AttributeUpdates: {
        passwordHash: {
          Action: 'PUT',
          Value: {
            S: password
          }
        },
        passwordSalt: {
          Action: 'PUT',
          Value: {
            S: salt
          }
        }
      }
    },
    fn);
}

exports.handler = (event, context, callback) => {

  var email = event.email;
    var oldPassword = event.oldPassword;
  var newPassword = event.newPassword;

  getUser(email, function(err, correctHash, salt) {
    if (err) {
      callback('Error in getUser: ' + err);
    } else {
      if (correctHash == null) {
        console.log('User not found: ' + email);
        context.succeed({
          changed: false
        });
      } else {
        computeHash(oldPassword, salt, function(err, salt, hash) {
```

The updateUser() function updates the user password (hash and salt) in the database.

The function exported to AWS Lambda for invocation

Read the user data from the database.

Check if the user exists.

```
      if (err) {
        context.fail('Error in hash: ' + err);
      } else {
        if (hash == correctHash) {                          ◁─┘ Check if the old
          console.log('User logged in: ' + email);              password is correct.
          computeHash(newPassword, function(err, newSalt, newHash) {
            if (err) {
              context.fail('Error in computeHash: ' + err);
            } else {
              updateUser(email, newHash, newSalt,     │ Update the database
                  function(err, data) {                │ with the new password.
                if (err) {
                  context.fail('Error in updateUser: ' + err);
                } else {
                  console.log('User password changed: ' + email);
                  context.succeed({
                    changed: true
                  });
                }
              });
            }
          });
        } else {                                              │ Otherwise the
          console.log('User login failed: ' + email);         │ password
          context.succeed({                              ◁─┘   isn't changed.
            changed: false
          });
        }
      }
    });
  }
}
});
}
```

Listing 10.17   Policy_Lambda_changePassword

```
{
  "Version": "2012-10-17",
  "Statement": [
    {
      "Action": [
        "dynamodb:GetItem",          │ Reading and updating
        "dynamodb:UpdateItem"        │ items on the database
      ],
      "Effect": "Allow",
      "Resource":
        "arn:aws:dynamodb:<REGION>:<AWS_ACCOUNT_ID>:table/<DYNAMODB_TABLE>"
    },
    {
      "Sid": "",
      "Resource": "*",
      "Action": [
        "logs:*"
      ],
```

```
            "Effect": "Allow"
        }
    ]
}
```

A screenshot of the Change Password page is shown in figure 10.11.

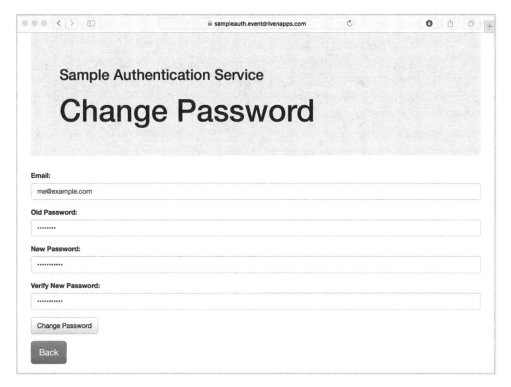

Figure 10.11   The Change Password page asks for the current user credentials (email and old password) and the new password two times to be sure it was written correctly.

Summary

In this chapter you added more features to the sample authentication service. In particular, you learned about the following:

- Implementing a reset password process using an email to validate the email address
- Using the login of the authentication service together with Amazon Cognito to provide authenticated access to AWS resources
- Differentiating the IAM roles used by Amazon Cognito between authenticated and unauthenticated users, to provide authenticated-only access to functions or resources

In the next chapter, you'll use the authentication service and build a sample media-sharing app, a more complex example of event-driven serverless applications.

EXERCISE _____

1   If you create a new `readUserProfile` Lambda function that, as the name suggests, can read all user data from the database, and you want to give access to this function only to *authenticated* users, what would you need to change in the IAM roles used by Amazon Cognito?

2   You want to send back more information to the client in case the login Lambda function is not returning { `login: true` } in the callback. How would you implement that?

Solution

1   You need to add `readUserProfile` to the list of allowed Lambda function in the Policy_Cognito_Authenticated_Role; for example, see the next listing. No changes are required in the Policy_Cognito_Unauthenticated_Role because the new function isn't there, and no access is given to unauthenticated users by default.

Policy_Cognito_Authenticated_Role (with readUserProfile)

```
{
  "Version": "2012-10-17",
  "Statement": [
    {
      "Effect": "Allow",
      "Action": [
        "mobileanalytics:PutEvents",
        "cognito-sync:*"
      ],
      "Resource": [
        "*"
      ]
    },
    {
      "Effect": "Allow",
      "Action": [
        "lambda:InvokeFunction"
      ],
      "Resource": [
        "arn:aws:lambda:<REGION>:<ACCOUNT>:function:createUser",
        "arn:aws:lambda:<REGION>:<ACCOUNT>:function:verifyUser",
        "arn:aws:lambda:<REGION>:<ACCOUNT>:function:changePassword",
        "arn:aws:lambda:<REGION>:<ACCOUNT>:function:lostPassword",
        "arn:aws:lambda:<REGION>:<ACCOUNT>:function:resetPassword",
        "arn:aws:lambda:<REGION>:<ACCOUNT>:function:sampleAuthLogin",
        "arn:aws:lambda:<REGION>:<ACCOUNT>:function:readUserProfile"
      ]
```

```
      }
    ]
}
```

2 A possible solution is to add `info` in the JSON payload given to the callback that
   terminated the Lambda function, which you'd read on the client only if `login`
   is `false`. For example:

```
callback(null, { login: false , info: "User not found"});
```

or

```
callback(null, { login: false , info: "Wrong password"});
```

Building a media-sharing application

This chapter covers

- Mapping the architecture to a technical implementation using AWS Lambda
- Best practices for simplifying, consolidating, and evolving the architecture
- Designing the data model on Amazon S3 and Amazon DynamoDB
- Securely implementing the client application
- Reacting to events in the back end

In the previous chapter, you completed the sample authentication service, adding more features, such as changing and resetting the password, and integrating the login process with Amazon Cognito to get temporary AWS credentials.

Now you'll use the authentication service to manage your users and build a more complex example of event-driven serverless applications: a media-sharing app, where users can upload pictures privately or publicly share the content with other users.

11.1 *The event-driven architecture*

The overall architecture for the media-sharing app (figure 11.1) was the first example of this book, in chapter 1. It's time to use all the things you learned to implement it.

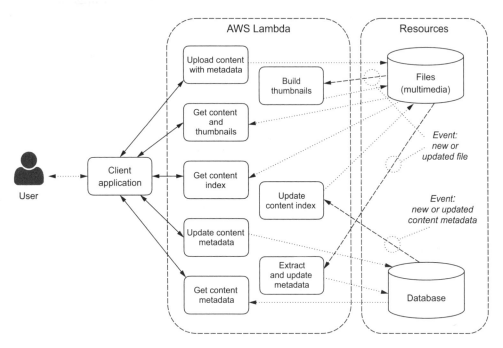

Figure 11.1   Overall event-driven architecture of a media-sharing app, as proposed at the beginning of this book

The app should upload pictures privately or publicly, for all other users to see. Users should see thumbnails of the pictures they're allowed to see, together with metadata, such as a title and a description.

Communication between the client application and the back-end functionality is based on APIs. You'll use JavaScript to build the client application so that it can run in a web page on a desktop or a mobile device. If you're a mobile developer, it will be easy to implement the same client for different devices; for example, using AWS Mobile Hub to kick-start a native app, as described in chapter 7.

> **NOTE**   This example uses both client-side (running in the browser) and server-side (running in Lambda functions) code. Because the code running in the browser is JavaScript, the Lambda function examples are also provided in JavaScript. The implementation of those functions in Python is left as an exercise for you to do on your own, because it doesn't change the architecture or the logic of the application.

For this type of application, you expect uploads of new content to be far less frequent than the number of times that content is accessed by users. For efficiency, you can create a static index of the public and private pictures users can see, so that you can use this index to display the pictures, instead of running queries on a database. For example, the index can be a file containing all the information you need to display the pictures in the client application. You can use any structured format for that, such as XML or YAML. I use JSON because it's natively supported in JavaScript.

> **TIP** Caching is an important optimization that can improve the scalability of your applications and reduce the latency that users experience. Caching is a common architectural pattern in software and hardware implementations: multiple caches exist inside the CPUs we normally use, caches are in the databases (for example, for common retrieved data), caches are in the network stacks (for example, for DNS results), and so on. You should always consider what data you can safely cache, and for how long, when building your applications.

11.1.1 Simplifying the implementation

When implementing a new application, you should look at any service or feature that you can use so that you can reduce the development footprint and the time to market of your solution.

This is even more important if you take a "lean" approach, as suggested, for example, in the book *The Lean Startup* by Eric Ries (Crown Business, 2011). According to this practice, you want to quickly release a *Minimum Viable Product* (MVP) to your users, an early implementation with enough features to validate (or learn and change) your product and business model, and then rapidly iterate with new features on top of that.

Let's use a lean approach here and replace functionalities you need with services that can provide them, making a few implementation decisions that will simplify the architecture to build:

- For the repository of pictures, thumbnails, and index files, you can use Amazon S3. That way, you can directly upload or download pictures or index files using the S3 API, and you don't need to implement that yourself.
- For metadata, such as the title or description or to store the links to the pictures and their thumbnails, you can use Amazon DynamoDB, a NoSQL database service. Again, you can use the DynamoDB API to read or update content metadata without implementing those APIs from scratch.
- To react to changes in the files repository (Amazon S3) or the database (Amazon DynamoDB), you can use Lambda functions triggered by events.

Following these decisions, the architecture in figure 11.1 can be mapped to a technical implementation to become what you see in figure 11.2. Of the eight Lambda functions that we needed to implement in our initial assessment, only three are left in this simplified architecture. The other five functions are replaced by direct usage of S3 and DynamoDB APIs.

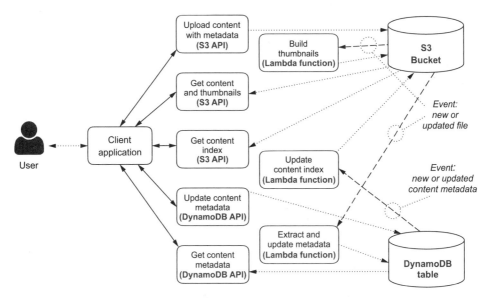

Figure 11.2 Mapping the media-sharing app to a technical implementation using Amazon S3, Amazon DynamoDB, and AWS Lambda. The development is much simpler than the implementation in figure 11.1 because most functions are directly implemented by the AWS services themselves, such as picture upload and download (using the S3 API) and metadata read and update (using the DynamoDB API).

One question that should be on your mind is whether you're sure you can replace all those functions by natively using Amazon S3 or Amazon DynamoDB. To answer that, you need to check whether the functions and the security features satisfy the requirements of your implementation. You'll see that as we build the app.

To authenticate and authorize the client application to use AWS APIs, you can use Amazon Cognito (figure 11.3). As you learned in chapter 6, AWS IAM roles allow a fine-grained control of access to AWS resources; for example, using policy variables to limit client access to the S3 bucket and the DynamoDB table. You'll use those features again in this implementation.

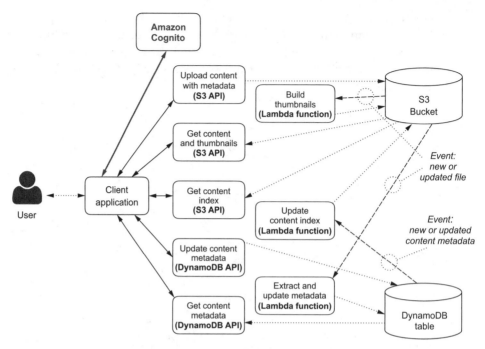

Figure 11.3 Using Amazon Cognito, you can give secure and finely controlled access to AWS resources, such as the S3 bucket and the DynamoDB table, allowing the client application to directly use S3 and DynamoDB APIs.

You can now map the building blocks shown in figure 11.3 to the new, ready-to-use implementation domains that they're part of, such as Amazon S3, Amazon DynamoDB, or AWS Lambda (figure 11.4). Let's see the new simplified architecture in more detail.

The front end to the client application is now all based on the S3 API (for manipulating pictures and files) and DynamoDB API (for the metadata). In particular, you're using the S3 PUT Object to upload or updated content and the GET Object to download it. With Amazon DynamoDB, you're using GetItem, to retrieve an item by primary key, and UpdateItem to update it.

The client doesn't need direct access to DynamoDB PutItem to create a new item in the database, because when a new piece of content is uploaded on the S3 bucket, the extractAndUpdateMetadata Lambda function in the back end will read the custom metadata from the S3 object and insert the new item with that information in the DynamoDB table. The buildThumbnails Lambda function will react to the same event (new or updated file) to create a small thumbnail of the picture that you can use to visualize the content in the client. The thumbnail is stored in the same S3 bucket, with a different prefix.

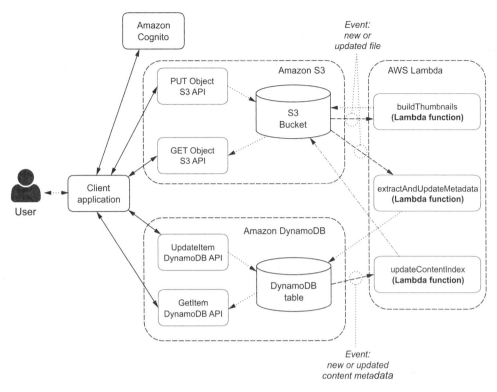

Figure 11.4   Using the new mapping, the building blocks of the architecture are mapped to the implementation domains they're part of, such as Amazon S3, Amazon DynamoDB, or AWS Lambda.

Finally, the `updateContentIndex` Lambda function is triggered by a change in the metadata table on DynamoDB to keep static index files on the S3 bucket updated with all changes.

> **NOTE**   The Lambda functions are triggered in the back end by events and don't need to be directly accessible by clients. Security-wise, this is good because you're exposing well-proven AWS APIs to the clients and not your own custom implementations.

11.1.2   Consolidating functions

When you start designing the architecture of your application, you create different modules for different functionalities. But when you move into the implementation phase, you may find that several of those modules (functions, in the case of AWS Lambda) are tied together by the data they use or by the way they're used by the application.

The `extractAndUpdateMetadata` and `buildThumbnails` Lambda functions are triggered by the same event (new or updated content in the S3 bucket) and can be tied together directly. For example, the first function can asynchronously invoke the second before terminating, as shown in figure 11.5.

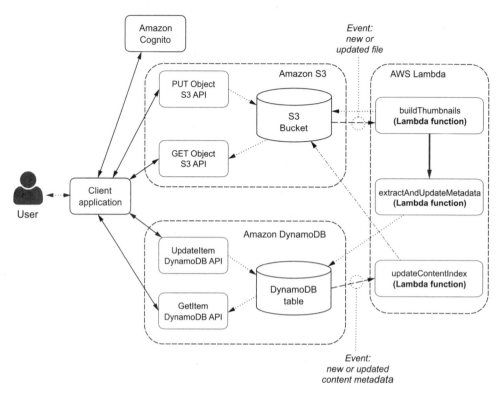

Figure 11.5   When two functions are triggered by the same event, you can decide to group them together. For example, one function can asynchronously invoke the other before terminating, as in the case of `extractAndUpdateMetadata` and `buildThumbnails` here.

Continuing with the implementation of those two functions, both need the same data in input:

- `buildThumbnails` needs the picture file to create the thumbnail.
- `extractAndUpdateMetadata` needs the object metadata to put that information in the database.

But Amazon S3 has two operations that you can use:

- `GET` object, to read the whole object, file, and metadata.
- `HEAD` object, to retrieve only the metadata without the file.

The two functions would need to read the same S3 object twice, once with the `GET` and once with the `HEAD`, but this approach is not optimal at scale, where you can have thousands or even millions of objects.

In this case, my suggestion is to create a single function that will use the same input to create the thumbnail and process the metadata (figure 11.6).

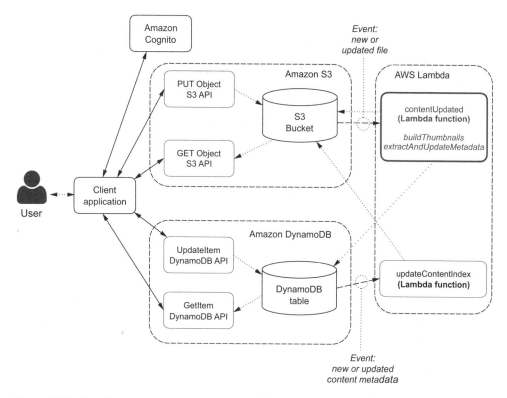

Figure 11.6 Grouping `extractAndUpdateMetadata` and `buildThumbnails` Lambda functions in a single `contentUpdated` function to optimize storage access and read the S3 object only once

---

How small should your function be?

Grouping more functions together is an architectural decision that you should evaluate when you create an event-driven application. You probably have two opposite effects to balance with your decisions:

- Having *more* and *smaller* functions can improve the modularity of your application. Smaller functions also have a quicker startup time on AWS Lambda for the first invocation when the container running the functions is deployed under the hood.
- Having *fewer* and *bigger* functions can simplify code reuse and optimize (as in our case) the flow of data to avoid reading or writing again to the same database or file.

11.1.3 Evolving an event-driven architecture

One of the advantages of event-driven applications, and reactive architectures in general, is that you link the logic (in the functions) to the data flow instead of building a centralized workflow. For example, you may want to add the option for users to delete content from the media-sharing app.

To add this functionality, you need to have a new delete API for your clients. But Amazon S3 already has an implementation for that! It's the DELETE Object API. You only need to manage the deleted file event from the S3 bucket in the contentUpdated Lambda function and keep the content index updated in case of deletion in the updateContentIndex function (figure 11.7).

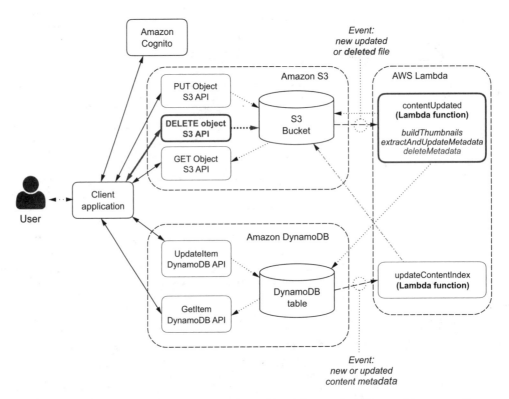

Figure 11.7   Clients can use the S3 DELETE Object API to delete content. You need to manage the deletion event in the Lambda functions to keep the metadata updated in the database and in the content index.

Adding a new feature to an event-driven application is much easier than in a procedural approach because you can focus on the relations between resources. When you use a similar approach in your projects, you'll often find that adding certain features will be easier—as you experienced with deleting content—because of how data is modeled and how you can react to changes. Sometimes this won't be the case, and adding a feature will be complex. In that case, my suggestion is to look again at the data you have and see if a different approach to how data is stored (files, relational, or NoSQL databases) can simplify the overall flow and the implementation of the new feature.

You now have a better idea of how to map functions into software modules and of the services you can use to make your implementation quick but effective. Next, let's see how we structure our data to support the event-driven approach we're undertaking.

11.2 Defining an object namespace for Amazon S3

In the S3 bucket, you have the content (the pictures), the thumbnails, and the static indexes that your Lambda functions keep updated. You need to have a public index for all public content (that is the same for all users) and a private index for each user for their own private content.

Amazon S3 isn't a hierarchical repository, but in defining the keys you want to use for those objects, you can choose a hierarchical syntax that can allow you to do the following:

- Trigger the `contentUpdated` Lambda function only when needed
- Give access to public and private content to only the right users via Amazon Cognito and IAM roles

WARNING You should carefully avoid the possibility of having endless loops of events, such as events triggering functions that can change something on another resource; for example, an S3 bucket or a DynamoDB table that could trigger the same function again.

My proposed hierarchical syntax for S3 keys is depicted in figure 11.8. In the bucket, you have two main prefixes, `public/` and `private/`, to maintain a strong separation between public and private content, which can be mapped into IAM roles.

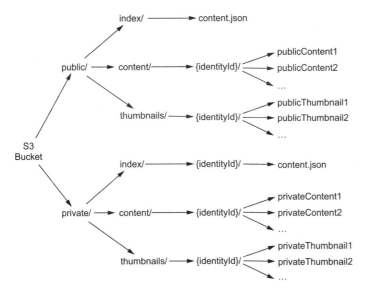

Figure 11.8   A hierarchical syntax for the S3 keys used in the S3 bucket, to protect access via IAM roles and allow events with predefined prefixes to trigger the correct Lambda functions

Each of those two prefixes has a space for content/, as uploaded by the clients, thumbnails/ that are created by the contentUpdated Lambda function, and space for the static index/ files.

The main difference between the private/ and public/ spaces is a single public index file and specific private index file for each user. The {identityId} part of the keys is to be replaced by the actual ID given by Amazon Cognito to the users upon their first login.

For each path in S3, different users (authenticated or not by Amazon Cognito) and Lambda functions can read or write, as described in table 11.1.

Table 11.1 Who can read or write in the different S3 paths

S3 Path	Who can read	Who can write
public/index/content.json	All users (authenticated or not)	The updateContentIndex Lambda function
public/content/{identityId}/*	All users (authenticated or not) and the contentUpdated Lambda function	Authenticated users with the same identityId
public/thumbnails/{identityId}/*	All users (authenticated or not)	The contentUpdated Lambda function
private/index/{identityId}/content.json	Authenticated users with the same identityId	The contentUpdated Lambda function
private/content/{identityId}/*	Authenticated users with the same identityId and the contentUpdated Lambda function	Authenticated users with the same identityId function
private/thumbnails/{identityId}/*	Authenticated users with the same identityId	The contentUpdated Lambda function

Table 11.2 lists the S3 prefixes that will trigger a Lambda function and the corresponding function name.

Table 11.2 Prefixes in the event sources for the Lambda functions

Prefix on S3	Lambda function
public/content/	contentUpdated
private/content/	contentUpdated

11.3 *Designing the data model for Amazon DynamoDB*

DynamoDB tables don't have a fixed schema; when you create a table, you need to define the primary key, which can be a single Partition Key or a composite key with a

Partition Key and a Sort Key. In this case, you can use a `content` table with a composite key, with `identityId` as Partition Key and the `objectKey` as Sort Key (table 11.3). Both attributes are strings.

Table 11.3 DynamoDB content table

Attribute	Type	Description
identityId	Partition Key (String)	Part of the Primary Key. The identityId of the user, as provided by Amazon Cognito. Only authenticated users with the same identityId can read and write an item in the table.
objectKey	Sort Key (String)	Part of the Primary Key. The key of the object on Amazon S3.
thumbnailKey	Attribute (String)	The key of the thumbnail on Amazon S3.
isPublic	Attribute (Boolean)	The content is publicly shared ("true") or not ("false").
title	Attribute (String)	A title for the content.
description	Attribute (String)	A description for the content.
uploadDate	Attribute (String)	The full date of the upload, including time, as taken from S3 metadata.
uploadDay	Attribute (String)	The day (without time) of the upload, taken from S3 metadata, used by a global secondary index to quickly query for recent uploads.

To query for public content, you need to create a Global Secondary Index (GSI) that's composed of a Partition Key (which you can query only by value) and a Sort Key (which you can query by range and use to sort the results).

For the public content, you may want to keep the most recent uploads in the public index, and eventually query the database only if users start to look for old content (for example, browsing by range). In this case, you can use a subset of the `uploadDate` (for example, the `uploadDay` without the time) as Partition Key of the index, and then the full `uploadDate` as Sort Key, as in table 11.4. In this way, you can get the most recent *N* uploads today, and if that isn't enough, you can query for yesterday's uploads, and so on.

Table 11.4 DynamoDB Global Secondary Index (GSI) for public content lookups

Attribute	Type	Description
uploadDay	Attribute (String)	Partition Key for the index. The day (without time) of the upload, taken from S3 metadata.
uploadDate	Attribute (String)	Sort Key for the index. The full date of the upload, including time, as taken from S3 metadata.

If your user base grows and you start to have many uploads, you may want to be more specific in the Partition Key of the index. For example, you can add the hour of the upload and get the most recent uploads in the current hour, and optionally the previous one. As your uploads grow in number, you can add more information. In fact, a better and more flexible name for the `uploadDay` attribute would be `partialUploadDay`, so that you can extend its length as soon as you have more uploads and while each Partition Key doesn't have too many items and wouldn't slow down the index.

> **NOTE** I explicitly used "many" in the previous paragraph, because there isn't a fixed value for deciding whether a Partition Key has too many values. Depending on the access pattern to your data (and indexes), you may reach a volume that can increase the latency of the index. In that case, being more specific with the Partition Key helps. As a rule of thumb, having a Partition Key that can have many different values (such as the `identityId` for the table) is always a good choice.

In this case, I recommend that the GSI project all attributes in the index, so that a single DynamoDB `Query` can return all the information you need to build the content index for the application, without round trips to the table. For example, if you project only the table keys (`identityId` and `objectKey`) in the index, you'd need to run a `GetItem` for each item returned by the query to retrieve the additional attributes you need.

You now have all the information to move forward in the actual implementation of the app. You can start in the front end with the client.

11.4 *The client application*

> **NOTE** I already covered how to implement similar configurations in detail in the previous chapters. Now I'll describe only what you need to build, and you can use what you previously learned to apply the necessary steps using the AWS web console or the AWS CLI.

To build the client application in JavaScript, you need an HTML page that acts as a container (see the following listing).

Listing 11.1 `index.html` **(Home Page)**

```
<html lang="en">
  <head>
    <title>Sample Media Sharing - AWS Lambda in Action</title>
    <meta charset="utf-8">
    <meta name="viewport" content="width=device-width, initial-scale=1">
    <!-- JQuery - required by Bootstrap -->
    <script src="https://code.jquery.com/jquery-1.12.0.min.js">
    </script>
    <!-- Bootstrap -->
    <link rel="stylesheet" href="https://maxcdn.bootstrapcdn.com/bootstrap/
     3.3.6/css/bootstrap.min.css" integrity="sha384-
```

◁ JQuery is required by Bootstrap.

```
                1q8mTJOASx8j1Au+a5WDVnPi2lkFfwwEAa8hDDdjZlpLegxhjVME1fgjWPGmkzs7"
                crossorigin="anonymous">
               <link rel="stylesheet" href="https://maxcdn.bootstrapcdn.com/bootstrap/
                3.3.6/css/bootstrap-theme.min.css" integrity="sha384-fLW2N01lMqjakBkx3l/
                M9EahuwpSfeNvV63J5ezn3uZzapT0u7EYsXMjQV+0En5r" crossorigin="anonymous">
               <script src="https://maxcdn.bootstrapcdn.com/bootstrap/3.3.6/js/
                bootstrap.min.js" integrity="sha384-
                0mSbJDEHialfmuBBQP6A4Qrprq5OVfW37PRR3j5ELqxss1yVqOtnepnHVP9aJ7xS"
                crossorigin="anonymous"></script>
               <script src="https://sdk.amazonaws.com/js/aws-sdk-2.4.6.min.js"></script>
               <style>
                 .public { background-color: LightCyan; }
                 .private { background-color: LightYellow; }
               </style>
             </head>
             <body>
               <div class="container">
                 <div class="jumbotron">
                   <h2>AWS Lambda in Action</h2>
                   <h1>Sample Media Sharing</h1>
                   <p>This is an example of a serverless event-driven
                     media-sharing app.</p>
                 </div>
                 <div class="row" id="result">
                 </div>
                 <div id="actions">
                 </div>
                 <div id="content">
                 </div>
                 <div id="myModalDetail" class="modal fade" role="dialog">
                   <div class="modal-dialog">
                     <div id="detail">
                     </div>
                   </div>
                 </div>
               </div>
               <!-- This is where AWS Lambda is invoked -->
               <script src="mediaSharing.js"></script>
             </body>
           </html>
```

Load Bootstrap JavaScript and CSS stylesheets.

Load the AWS JavaScript SDK.

Stylesheet classes to be used to change the background of public and private content

Make the detail section a modal dialog managed by JavaScript via Bootstrap.

The actual logic of the JavaScript app

NOTE I use Bootstrap to enhance the visual result and make this example responsive on mobile platforms. Bootstrap is a popular HTML, CSS, and JS framework for developing responsive and mobile-ready web projects that was originally created by a designer and a developer at Twitter. For more information on Bootstrap, see http://getbootstrap.com.

The logic of the client application is in the mediaSharing.js JavaScript file (listing 11.2). This is a long file and it's better to have a brief description of how it works:

- To manage users, the client is using Amazon Cognito and the authentication service you built in the previous chapters. You need the sample authentication service running in your AWS account in the same region to use the media-sharing app.

- The login function is similar to the code used by the login page of the authentication service; the main difference is in a custom function added to refresh the content displayed when a user is logged in or not.
- I use S3 custom metadata to return more information, such as title and description, during object upload.
- To periodically check for updates, I use a client pull request to Amazon S3 with the `If-Modified-Since` header as part of the HTTP specification to download new content only if it has been updated since the last download.

TIP   You may want to add to the index page of the media-sharing app a link to the authentication service index page, so that users can easily create and manage their identity for the app.

TIP   To have the server push updates instead of client pull requests, you may use the AWS IoT platform. You don't need a physical device to do that, but you can use the bidirectional MQTT[1] gateway provided as part of the AWS IoT service. Using AWS IoT you can use secure WebSockets in the browser to listen to an MQTT topic for each `identityId`; for example /users/{identityId}. You can then use Lambda functions in the back end to publish updates on those topics. If you're interested in this approach, or for more information on AWS IoT, see https://aws.amazon.com/iot. For an in-depth description about the MQTT protocol, a lightweight publish/subscribe messaging transport, see http://mqtt.org.

Listing 11.2   mediaSharing.js (JavaScript in the browser)

> **The S3 bucket to store pictures, thumbnails, and static content indexes (as JSON files)**

> **The DynamoDB table to store content metadata**

```
var S3_BUCKET = '<BUCKET>';
var ITEMS_TABLE = '<DYNAMODB_TABLE>';
var IDENTITY_POOL_ID = '<IDENTITY_POOL_ID>';
```

> **The Cognito Identity Pool must be the same as in the authentication service to log in.**

```
AWS.config.region = '<REGION>';
AWS.config.credentials = new AWS.CognitoIdentityCredentials({
  IdentityPoolId: IDENTITY_POOL_ID
});
```

> **Getting the AWS temporary credentials from Amazon Cognito for the unauthenticated role**

```
var identityId = null;
var publicContent = emptyContent();
var privateContent = emptyContent();
var index = {};
```

> **At the beginning no public content exists...**

> **...and no private content either...**

> **At the beginning you're not authenticated.**

> **...and the content index is empty.**

---

[1]   MQTT is a publish/subscribe messaging protocol designed to be lightweight and commonly used by machine-to-machine (M2M) and Internet of Things (IoT) projects. For more information, see http://mqtt.org.

```
var result = document.getElementById('result');
var actions = document.getElementById('actions');
var detail = document.getElementById('detail');
var content = document.getElementById('content');

var lambda = new AWS.Lambda();
var s3 = new AWS.S3();
var dynamodb = new AWS.DynamoDB();

function emptyContent() {
  return { lastUpdate: null, index: null };
}

function login() {

  var email = document.getElementById('email');
  var password = document.getElementById('password');

  result.innerHTML = getAlert('info', 'Login...');

  if (email.value == null || email.value == '') {
    result.innerHTML = getAlert('warning',
      'Please specify your email address.');
  } else if (password.value == null || password.value == '') {
    result.innerHTML = getAlert('warning',
      'Please specify a password.');
  } else {

    var input = {
      email: email.value,
      password: password.value
    };

    lambda.invoke({
      FunctionName: 'sampleAuthLogin',
      Payload: JSON.stringify(input)
    }, function(err, data) {
      if (err) {
        console.log(err, err.stack);
        result.innerHTML = getAlert('danger', err);
      } else {
        var output = JSON.parse(data.Payload);
        if (!output.login) {
          result.innerHTML = getAlert('warning', '<b>Not</b> logged in');
        } else {
          result.innerHTML = getAlert('success',
            'Logged in with IdentityId: ' + output.identityId + '<br>');
          identityId = output.identityId;
          var creds = AWS.config.credentials;
          creds.params.IdentityId = output.identityId;
          creds.params.Logins = {
            'cognito-identity.amazonaws.com': output.token
          };
          creds.expired = true;
          updateActions();
          updateContent();
        }
      }
```

Getting the main components to edit from the page DOM

Getting the AWS service objects

The login() function is similar to the one in the authentication service.

```
    });
  }
}
```

The logout() function is clearing out private content when you log out.

```
function logout() {
  identityId = null;
  result.innerHTML = getAlert('info', 'Logged out.');
  privateContent = emptyContent();

  var creds = AWS.config.credentials;
  creds.params.Logins = {};
  creds.refresh(function() {
    renderContent();
    updateActions();
  });
}
```

Updating the possible actions depending on if you are logged in (and can upload) or not

```
function updateActions() {

  if (identityId == null) {
    result.innerHTML = getAlert('info',
      '<p>Please login to upload and see your private content.</p>');
    actions.innerHTML =
      '<form class="form-inline" role="form" id="login-form">' +
        '<div class="form-group">' +
          '<label for="email">Email </label>' +
            '<input type="text" class="form-control" id="email">' +
          '</div> ' +
        '<div class="form-group">' +
          '<label for="password">Password </label>' +
            '<input type="password" class="form-control" id="password">' +
          '</div>' +
          '<button type="submit" class="btn btn-default">Login</button>' +
        '</form>';
    var form = document.getElementById('login-form');
    form.addEventListener('submit', function(evt) {
      evt.preventDefault();
      login();
    });
  } else {
    actions.innerHTML =
      '<form class="form-horizontal" role="form" id="add-picture-form">' +
        '<div class="form-group">' +
          '<label class="control-label col-sm-2" for="mediaFile">' +
            'Photo to Upload</label>' +
          '<div class="col-sm-10">' +
            '<input type="file" name="mediaFile" id="mediaFile">' +
          '</div>' +
        '</div>' +
        '<div class="form-group">' +
          '<label class="control-label col-sm-2" for="is-public">Public</' +
    label>' +
            '<div class="col-sm-10">' +
              '<input type="checkbox" value="" name="is-public" id="is-' +
    public" placeholder="is-public">' +
            '</div>' +
          '</div>' +
```

```
       '</div>' +
       '<div class="form-group">' +
         '<label class="control-label col-sm-2" for="title">Title</label>' +
         '<div class="col-sm-10">' +
           '<input type="text" class="form-control" name="title" id="title"
   placeholder="title">' +
         '</div>' +
       '</div>' +
       '<div class="form-group">' +
         '<label class="control-label col-sm-2"
   for="description">Description</label>' +
         '<div class="col-sm-10">' +
           '<input type="text" class="form-control" name="description"
   id="description" placeholder="description">' +
         '</div>' +
       '</div>' +
       '<div class="form-group">' +
         '<div class="col-sm-offset-2 col-sm-10">' +
           '<button type="submit" class="btn btn-default"> Add Picture</
   button>' +
           '<button type="button" id="logout-button" class="btn btn-
   default"> Logout</button>' +
         '</div>' +
       '</div>' +
     '</form>';
   var form = document.getElementById('add-picture-form');
   form.addEventListener('submit', function(evt) {
     evt.preventDefault();
     addPicture();
   });
   var logoutButton = document.getElementById('logout-button');
   logoutButton.addEventListener('click', logout);
  }
}
function addPicture() {

  var mediaFile = document.getElementById('mediaFile');
  var isPublic = document.getElementById('is-public');
  var title = document.getElementById('title');
  var description = document.getElementById('description');
  var file = mediaFile.files[0];

  if (!file) {
    result.innerHTML = getAlert('warning', 'Nothing to upload.');
    return;
  }
  if (description.value == '') {
    result.innerHTML = getAlert('warning', 'Please provide a description.');
    return;
  }

  result.innerHTML = '';
  var key = (isPublic.checked ? 'public' : 'private') +
      '/content/' + identityId + '/' + file.name;
  console.log(key);
  console.log(isPublic.checked);
```

Uploading a new picture to the S3 bucket

```
    var params = {
      Bucket: S3_BUCKET,
      Key: key,
      ContentType: file.type,
      Body: file,
      Metadata: {
        data: JSON.stringify({
          isPublic: isPublic.checked,
          title: title.value,
          description: description.value
        })
      }};
    uploadToS3(params);
}

function uploadToS3(params) {

    if (identityId == null) {
      result.innerHTML = getAlert('warning', 'Please login to upload.');
    } else {
      result.innerHTML = getAlert('info', 'Uploading...');
      var s3 = new AWS.S3();
      s3.putObject(params, function(err, data) {
        result.innerHTML =
          err ? getAlert('danger', 'Error!' + err + err.stack)
              : getAlert('success', 'Uploaded.');
      });
    }

}

function updateContent() {

    var publicContentIndexKey = 'public/index/content.json';
    checkContent(publicContentIndexKey, publicContent);
    if (identityId != null) {
      var privateContentIndexKey = 'private/index/' + identityId + '/
      content.json';
      checkContent(privateContentIndexKey, privateContent);
    }

}

function checkContent(key, content) {

    var params = {
      Bucket: S3_BUCKET,
      Key: key
    };
    if (content.lastUpdate != null) {
      params.IfModifiedSince = content.lastUpdate;
    }
    s3.getObject(params, function(err, data) {
      if (err) {
        if (err.code == 'NotModified') {
          console.log('Not Modified');
        } else {
          console.log(err, err.stack);
        }
```

The actual function managing the upload to Amazon S3

Checking if there is new public or private content in the content indexes prepared by the updateContentIndex Lambda function

A more generic function to check for updated content indexes, using the IfModifiedSince HTTP header to download content only in case of an update

```
    } else {
      console.log(key);
      console.log(data);
      currentUpdate = new Date(data.LastModified);
      console.log('currentUpdate: ' + currentUpdate);
      console.log('lastUpdate: ' + content.lastUpdate);
      if (content.lastUpdate == null ||
        currentUpdate > content.lastUpdate) {
          content.lastUpdate = currentUpdate;
          content.index = JSON.parse(data.Body);
          renderContent();
          console.log("Updated");
      }
    }
  });
}

function getSignedUrlFromKey(key) {
```

A utility function to sign an Amazon S3 URL using AWS credentials

```
  var params = {Bucket: S3_BUCKET, Key: key, Expires: 60};
  var url = s3.getSignedUrl('getObject', params);
  console.log('The URL is', url); // expires in 60 seconds
  return url;
}

function renderContent() {
```

Rendering content thumbnails and metadata, as downloaded from the indexes

```
    index = {};
    console.log(publicContent.index);
    if (publicContent.index != null) {
      publicContent.index.forEach(function(element) {
        element.isPublic = true;
        element.isOwner = (identityId != null && element.identityId ==
      identityId);
        index[element.objectKey] = element;
      });
    }
    console.log(privateContent.index);
    if (privateContent.index != null) {
      privateContent.index.forEach(function(element) {
        element.isPublic = false;
        element.isOwner = (identityId != null && element.identityId ==
      identityId);
        index[element.objectKey] = element;
      });
    }
    var html = '';
    for(var objectKey in index) {
      var element = index[objectKey];
      console.log(element);

      html += '<div class="col-sm-3 thumbnail alert ' +
         (element.isPublic ? 'alert-success' : 'alert-warning') + '"">' +
         (element.isOwner ? '<button type="button" class="close"
      onclick=deleteContent("' +
         objectKey + '")>&times;</button>' : '') +
```

```
                '<h4 class="text-center">' + element.title + '</h4>' +
                '<a data-toggle="modal" data-target="#myModalDetail" ' +
                'onclick=showContent("' + objectKey + '")>' +
                '<img class="img-rounded" ' +
                'src="' + getSignedUrlFromKey(element.thumbnailKey) + '" ' +
                'alt="' + element.title + '" ' + '>' +
                '</a>' +
                '<p class="text-center">' + element.description + '</p>' +
                '</div>';
        }
        content.innerHTML = html;
    }
    function showContent(objectKey) {
```

> Rendering content
> details (the full picture
> and metadata)

```
        var element = index[objectKey];
        detail.innerHTML =
            '<div class="modal-content">' +
              '<div class="modal-header">' +
                '<button type="button" class="close" data-dismiss="modal">&times;</
        button>' +
                    '<h4 class="modal-title">' + element.title + ' (' +
                    (element.isPublic ? "Public" : "Private") +')</h4>' +
                '</div>' +
                '<div class="modal-body">' +
                  '<p>' + element.description + '</p>' +
                  '<div class="thumbnail">' +
                    '<img class="img-responsive" src="' +
        getSignedUrlFromKey(objectKey) + '">' +
                  '</div>' +
                '</div>' +
                '<div class="modal-footer">' +
                  '<button type="button" class="btn btn-default" data-
        dismiss="modal">Close</button>' +
                  '</div>' +
                '</div>' +
              '</div>';
    }
    function deleteContent(objectKey) {
```

> Deleting a piece of content
> owned by the same user
> (with the same identityId)

```
        console.log(objectKey);
        var params = {
            Bucket: S3_BUCKET,
            Key: objectKey
        }
        deleteFromS3(params);
    }
    function deleteFromS3(params) {
```

> The actual function
> managing the delete
> from Amazon S3

```
        result.innerHTML = getAlert('info', 'Deleting...');
        s3.deleteObject(params, function(err, data) {
            result.innerHTML =
                err ? getAlert('danger', 'Error!' + err + err.stack)
                    : getAlert('success', 'Deleted.');
        });
    }
```

```
function getAlert(type, message) {
  return '<div class="alert alert-' + type + '"  >' +
    '<a href="#" class="close" data-dismiss="alert" aria-
    label="close">&times;</a>' +
    message + '</div>';
}
```
A utility function to generate HTML with Boostrap Alerts

```
function init() {
  updateActions();
  updateContent();
  setInterval(updateContent, 3000);
}
```
An initialization function to prepare content and actions and schedule a recurrent background check for content updates (client polling)

```
window.onload = init();
```
The initialization function is run when the browser window is loaded.

TIP It would be more efficient to introduce a content delivery network (CDN, such as Amazon CloudFront) in front of the S3 bucket, especially to speed up polling for new content. In that case, signed URLs, currently used to access Amazon S3, should be replaced by other techniques used by the CDN providers for private content, such as cookies.

The IAM roles used by the Cognito identity pool are an extension of what you used for the authentication service you built in chapters 8 and 9. With IAM roles, you can attach multiple policies to the same roles. In this case, add the policies in listings 11.3 and 11.4 to the authenticated and unauthenticated roles already in place.

WARNING If you remove or overwrite the previous policies used by the Cognito identity pool of the sample authentication service, your login won't work anymore and the Lambda functions you created to create users, change or reset passwords, and so on can possibly lose the capacity to write to Amazon CloudWatch Logs.

Listing 11.3 Policy_Cognito_mediaSharing_Unauth_Role

```
{
    "Version": "2012-10-17",
    "Statement": [
        {
            "Effect": "Allow",
            "Action": [
                "s3:GetObject"
            ],
            "Resource": [
                "arn:aws:s3:::<BUCKET>/public/*"
            ]
        }
    ]
}
```
You can only see public content in the S3 bucket if you're not authenticated.

Listing 11.4   Policy_Cognito_mediaSharing_Auth_Role

```
{
    "Version": "2012-10-17",
    "Statement": [
        {
            "Effect": "Allow",
            "Action": [
                "s3:GetObject"
            ],
            "Resource": [
                "arn:aws:s3:::<BUCKET>/public/*",
"arn:aws:s3:::<BUCKET>/private/index/${cognito-identity.amazonaws.com:sub}/*",
"arn:aws:s3:::<BUCKET>/private/content/${cognito-identity.amazonaws.com:sub}/
    *",
"arn:aws:s3:::<BUCKET>/private/thumbnail/${cognito-
    identity.amazonaws.com:sub}/*"
            ]
        },
        {
            "Effect": "Allow",
            "Action": [
                "s3:PutObject",
                "s3:DeleteObject"
            ],
            "Resource": [
"arn:aws:s3:::<BUCKET>/public/content/${cognito-identity.amazonaws.com:sub}/*",
"arn:aws:s3:::<BUCKET>/private/content/${cognito-identity.amazonaws.com:sub}/*"
            ]
        },
        {
            "Effect": "Allow",
            "Action": [
                "dynamodb:UpdateItem"
            ],
            "Resource": "arn:aws:dynamodb:<REGION>:<AWS_ACCOUNT_ID>:table/
    <DYNAMODB_TABLE>",
            "Condition": {
                "ForAllValues:StringEquals": {
                    "dynamodb:LeadingKeys": [
                        "${cognito-identity.amazonaws.com:sub}"
                    ],
                    "dynamodb:Attributes": [
                        "title",
                        "description"
                    ]
                },
                "StringEqualsIfExists": {
                    "dynamodb:Select": "SPECIFIC_ATTRIBUTES",
                    "dynamodb:ReturnValues": [
                        "NONE",
                        "UPDATED_OLD",
                        "UPDATED_NEW"
                    ]
                }
            }
```

Annotations:

You can read private content in the S3 bucket only if the prefix includes the user identityId, using policy variables.

You can read all public content in the S3 bucket.

You can upload and delete public or private content in the S3 bucket only if the prefix includes the user identityId, using policy variables.

You can update items in the DynamoDB table only if the user identityId is in the Partition Key.

You can only update title and description in the DynamoDB table.

Limit the visibility of DynamoDB attributes (not important for this implementation, but useful to know).

```
            }
        }
    ]
}
```

TIP Adding multiple policies to the same role can be useful in keeping different duties segregated. In this case, you have for each role a policy that's required by the authentication service, and another policy that extends the role for application-specific requirements.

The client application is uploading the new content (pictures) to Amazon S3 and expecting the public and private indexes to be updated by the Lambda functions in the back end. Let's see how that works.

11.5 Reacting to content updates

The first step to react to a content update is to have the `contentUpdated` function triggered when public or private content is added or deleted in the S3 bucket. Specifically, the two prefixes for the trigger are

- `public/content/`
- `private/content/`

WARNING If you add a different or broader prefix in the trigger, such as `public/` or `private/`, you can have errors or (much worse) endless loops. Because the `contentUpdated` Lambda function is uploading thumbnails on the S3 bucket, that action could trigger the execution of the same function again and again.

The code of the function to react to updated content is shown in the following listing.

> **Listing 11.5 `contentUpdated` Lambda Function (Node.js)**

```javascript
var async = require('async');
var gm = require('gm').subClass({ imageMagick: true });
var util = require('util');
var AWS = require('aws-sdk');

var DDB_TABLE = '<DYNAMODB_TABLE>';
var MAX_WIDTH  = 200;
var MAX_HEIGHT = 200;

var s3 = new AWS.S3();
var dynamodb = new AWS.DynamoDB();

function startsWith(text, prefix) {
  return (text.lastIndexOf(prefix, 0) === 0)
}

exports.handler = (event, context, callback) => {
  console.log('Reading options from event:\n',
    util.inspect(event, {depth: 5}));
```

The async module to simplify asynchronous calls in JavaScript.

Enable ImageMagick integration.

The DynamoDB table in which to store content metadata

The maximum height and width for thumbnails

AWS clients for Amazon S3 and Amazon DynamoDB

Utility function to see if the beginning of a string is equal to another string

```
var srcBucket = event.Records[0].s3.bucket.name;
var srcKey = unescape(event.Records[0].s3.object.key);
var eventName = event.Records[0].eventName;
var eventTime = event.Records[0].eventTime;
var dstBucket = srcBucket;
var dstKey = srcKey.replace(/content/, 'thumbnail');
var identityId = srcKey.match(/.*\/content\/([^\/]*)/)[1];

console.log('eventName = ' + eventName);
console.log('dstKey = ' + dstKey);
console.log('identityId = ' + identityId);

if (startsWith(eventName, 'ObjectRemoved')) {
  s3.deleteObject({
    Bucket: dstBucket,
    Key: dstKey
  }, function(err, data) {
    if (err) console.log(err);
    else console.log(data);
  });
  dynamodb.deleteItem({
    TableName: DDB_TABLE,
    Key: {
      identityId: { S: identityId },
      objectKey: { S: srcKey }
    }
  }, function(err, data) {
    if (err) console.log(err);
    else console.log(data);
  });

} else {

var typeMatch = srcKey.match(/\.([^.]*)$/);
if (!typeMatch) {
  callback('Unable to infer image type for key ' + srcKey);
}
var imageType = typeMatch[1];
if (imageType != 'jpg' && imageType != 'png' && imageType != 'gif') {
  callback('Skipping non-image ' + srcKey);
}
async.waterfall([
  function download(next) {
    // Download the image from S3 into a buffer.
    s3.getObject({
        Bucket: srcBucket,
        Key: srcKey
      },
      next);
    },
  function tranform(response, next) {
    gm(response.Body).size(function(err, size) {
      var scalingFactor = Math.min(
        MAX_WIDTH / size.width,
```

If the event received from Amazon S3 is for the deletion of an object

Delete the corresponding thumbnail from the S3 bucket.

Delete the object metadata from the DynamoDB table.

If the event received from Amazon S3 is for a new object

Infer the image type.

Start a waterfall list of functions using the "async" module; the functions are executed in sequence.

Download the picture from the S3 bucket (including the custom metadata).

Create the thumbnail.

```
      MAX_HEIGHT / size.height
    );
    var width  = scalingFactor * size.width;
    var height = scalingFactor * size.height;          Transform the
                                                       image buffer
    this.resize(width, height)                         in memory.
      .toBuffer(imageType, function(err, buffer) {
        if (err) {
          next(err);
        } else {
          next(null, response.ContentType,
            response.Metadata.data, buffer);
        }
      });
  });
},                                                     Upload the
                                                       thumbnail to
function upload(contentType, metadata, data, next) {   the S3 bucket.
  s3.putObject({
      Bucket: dstBucket,
      Key: dstKey,
      Body: data,
      ContentType: contentType
  }, function(err, buffer) {
    if (err) {
      next(err);
    } else {
      next(null, metadata);
    }
  });                                                  Store the content
},                                                     metadata in the
function index(metadata, next) {                       DynamoDB table.
  var json_metadata = JSON.parse(metadata);
  var params = {
    TableName: DDB_TABLE,
    Item: {
      identityId: { S: identityId },
      objectKey: { S: srcKey },
      thumbnailKey: { S: dstKey },
      isPublic: { BOOL: json_metadata.isPublic },
      uploadDate: { S: eventTime },
      uploadDay: { S: eventTime.substr(0, 10) },
      title: { S: json_metadata.title },
      description: { S: json_metadata.description }
    }
  };
  dynamodb.putItem(params, next);
}], function (err) {                                   Triggered if any error
  if (err) console.log(err, err.stack);               happens in the async
  else console.log('Ok');                             waterfall list of functions
  }
);
  }
}
```

WARNING The contentUpdated function needs the async and gm external modules to be installed locally before zipping the code to upload to AWS Lambda, as you learned in chapter 5. For example, you can use the command npm install async gm.

The policy required by the function, to be added to the AWSLambdaBasicExecution-Role managed policy, is shown in the following listing.

Listing 11.6   Policy_Lambda_contentUpdated

```
{
    "Version": "2012-10-17",
    "Statement": [
        {
            "Effect": "Allow",
            "Action": [
                "s3:GetObject"
            ],
            "Resource": [
                "arn:aws:s3:::<BUCKET>/public/content/*",      Read public and
                "arn:aws:s3:::<BUCKET>/private/content/*"       private content in
            ]                                                   the S3 bucket.
        },
        {
            "Effect": "Allow",
            "Action": [
                "s3:PutObject",
                "s3:DeleteObject"
            ],
            "Resource": [                                       Write public
                "arn:aws:s3:::<BUCKET>/public/thumbnail/*",     and private
                "arn:aws:s3:::<BUCKET>/private/thumbnail/*"     thumbnails in
            ]                                                   the S3 bucket.
        },
        {
            "Effect": "Allow",
            "Action": [
Add or          "dynamodb:PutItem",
delete items    "dynamodb:DeleteItem"
from the    ],
DynamoDB    "Resource":
table.      "arn:aws:dynamodb:<REGION>:<AWS_ACCOUNT_ID>:table/<DYNAMODB_TABLE>"
        }
    ]
}
```

Now content metadata is written in the DynamoDB table. But querying the table for all user visualizations isn't efficient, so let's look at how you can cache those results writing content indexes that you can reuse.

11.6 Updating content indexes

The metadata on the DynamoDB content table is kept in sync by the contentUpdated function described in detail in the previous section. The two main actions provided by the function are

- If a new object is uploaded in the S3 bucket, the custom metadata is extracted and written in a new item in the DynamoDB table.
- If an object is deleted in the S3 bucket, the relative item is deleted in the DynamoDB table.

Using DynamoDB Streams, it's possible to trigger a Lambda function every time the DynamoDB content table is updated. This updateContentIndex function can update static indexes kept as JSON files in the S3 bucket. Those static index files are then read by the JavaScript client application to update the content shown in the device. The code of the updateContentIndex function is in the following listing.

Listing 11.7 updateContentIndex **Lambda Function (Node.js)**

```
console.log('Loading function');

var AWS = require('aws-sdk');
var dynamodb = new AWS.DynamoDB();
var s3 = new AWS.S3();

var S3_BUCKET = '<BUCKET>';
var ITEMS_TABLE = '<DYNAMODB_TABLE>';

function uploadToS3(params) {
  s3.putObject(params, function(err, data) {
    if (err) console.log(err);
    else console.log(data);
  });
}

function indexContent(dynamodb_params, s3_params) {
    var content = [];
    dynamodb.query(dynamodb_params, function(err, data) {
        if (err) {
          console.log(err, err.stack);
        } else {
          data.Items.forEach((item) => {
            console.log(item);
            content.push({
                identityId: item.identityId.S,
                objectKey: item.objectKey.S,
                thumbnailKey: item.thumbnailKey.S,
                uploadDate: item.uploadDate.S,
                title: item.title.S,
                description: item.description.S
            });
          });
          s3_params.Body = JSON.stringify(content);
          uploadToS3(s3_params);
```

The S3 bucket with pictures, thumbnails, and content indexes

The DynamoDB table with content metadata

Utility function to upload to Amazon S3

Generic function that queries the DynamoDB table and uploads the formatted results to the S3 bucket. The parameters to use for the DynamoDB query and to upload to the S3 bucket are given in input to use the same function for both private and public content.

This is where the results from the DynamoDB query are added in JSON format to the S3 object to upload.

```
        }
      });
    }

    function indexPublicContent(day) {
      console.log('Getting public content for ' + day);
      var dynamodb_params = {
        TableName: ITEMS_TABLE,
        IndexName: 'uploadDay-uploadDate-index',
        Limit: 100,
        ScanIndexForward: false,
        KeyConditionExpression: 'uploadDay = :uploadDayVal',
        FilterExpression: 'isPublic = :isPublicVal',
        ExpressionAttributeValues: {
          ':uploadDayVal' : { S: day },
          ':isPublicVal' : { BOOL: true }
        }
      };
      var s3_params = {
        Bucket: S3_BUCKET,
        Key: 'public/index/content.json',
        ContentType: 'application/json'
      };
      indexContent(dynamodb_params, s3_params);
    }

    function indexPrivateContent(identityId) {
      console.log('Getting private content for ' + identityId);
      var dynamodb_params = {
        TableName: ITEMS_TABLE,
        KeyConditionExpression: 'identityId = :identityIdVal',
        FilterExpression: 'isPublic = :isPublicVal',
        ExpressionAttributeValues: {
          ':identityIdVal' : { S: identityId },
          ':isPublicVal' : { BOOL: false }
        }
      };
      var s3_params = {
        Bucket: S3_BUCKET,
        Key: 'private/index/' + identityId + '/content.json',
        ContentType: 'application/json'
      };
      indexContent(dynamodb_params, s3_params);
    }

    exports.handler = (event, context, callback) => {
      var uploadDays = {};
      var identityIds = {};
      event.Records.forEach((record) => {
        console.log(record.eventID);
        console.log(record.eventName);
        console.log('DynamoDB Record: %j', record.dynamodb);
        var image;
        if ('NewImage' in record.dynamodb) {
          image = record.dynamodb.NewImage;
```

Getting the latest public content uploaded in a specific day

The DynamoDB parameters to run the query for public content

The Global Secondary Index (GSI) to use for the query

Limiting results to 100 items

To have results from the newest to the oldest, in reverse order in respect to the Sort Key of the index (the Sort Key is the full uploadDate, including time)

Choosing the Partition Key of the index (the uploadDay)

Filtering for public content only

The actual values used in the expressions

The S3 parameters for the upload of the public content index

Passing the DynamoDB and S3 parameters to the indexContent() function to execute the query and upload results

Getting the private content of a specific user (by identityId)

The DynamoDB parameters to run the query for private content

Choosing the identityId of the user (the Partition Key of the table)

Filtering for private content only

The actual values used in the expressions

The S3 parameters for the upload of the private content index. The prefix contains the identityId.

Passing the DynamoDB and S3 parameters to the indexContent() function to execute the query and upload results

To loop on the DynamoDB Stream records received in input by the Lambda function

```
      } else if ('OldImage' in record.dynamodb) {
        image = record.dynamodb.OldImage;
      } else {
        console.log('Unknown event format: ' + record);
      }
      if ('isPublic' in image &&
          image.isPublic.BOOL &&
          'uploadDay' in image) {
        var uploadDay = image.uploadDay.S;
        uploadDays[uploadDay] = true;
        console.log('Public content found for ' + uploadDay);
      } else {
        var identityId = record.dynamodb.Keys.identityId.S;
        identityIds[identityId] = true;
        console.log('Private content found for ' + identityId);
      }
  });
  var latestUploadDay = Object.keys(uploadDays).sort().pop();
  if (latestUploadDay) {
    indexPublicContent(latestUploadDay);
  }
  Object.keys(identityIds).forEach((identityId) => {
    indexPrivateContent(identityId);
  });
};
```

For public content flag the days to update (in an associative array).

For private content flag the identity IDs to update (in an associative array).

Update content only for the most recent uploadDay.

In addition to the `AWSLambdaBasicExecutionRole` managed policy, the `updateContentIndex` function requires the policy in the following listing to access the S3 bucket and the DynamoDB table (including the index).

Listing 11.8 Policy_Lambda_updateContentIndex

```
{
    "Version": "2012-10-17",
    "Statement": [
        {
            "Effect": "Allow",
            "Action": [
                "s3:PutObject"
            ],
            "Resource": [
                "arn:aws:s3:::<BUCKET>/public/index/*",
                "arn:aws:s3:::<BUCKET>/private/index/*"
            ]
        },
        {
            "Effect": "Allow",
            "Action": [
                "dynamodb:Query",
                "dynamodb:GetRecords",
                "dynamodb:GetShardIterator",
                "dynamodb:DescribeStream",
                "dynamodb:ListStreams"
            ],
```

Write public and private content indexes in the S3 bucket.

Queries the DynamoDB table

Manipulates the DynamoDB Stream of events

```
                    "Resource": [
                        "arn:aws:dynamodb:<REGION>:<AWS_ACCOUNT_ID>:table/
Give access  ┌─▷    <DYNAMODB_TABLE>",
    to the               "arn:aws:dynamodb: <REGION>:<AWS_ACCOUNT_ID>:table/
DynamoDB          <DYNAMODB_TABLE>/*"              ◁─┐
   table              ]                             Give access to the
resource.  │        }                              DynamoDB indexes
           │    ]                                   and streams.
        }
```

Now the application is complete and you can start using it to share pictures publicly or keep them private for your own use. Figures 11.9, 11.10, and 11.11 are a few sample screenshots of the media-sharing application. The photos in these examples are courtesy of NASA and the Wikimedia Foundation.

Figure 11.9   In the media-sharing application, at first you're not logged in and you can see only public pictures, as allowed by the unauthenticated IAM role used by Amazon Cognito.

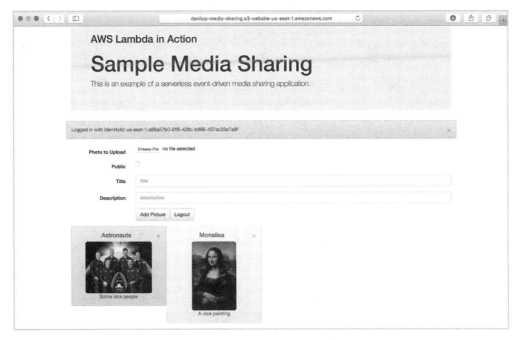

Figure 11.10 After you log in, you can see your own private pictures, as allowed by the authenticated IAM role used by Amazon Cognito.

Figure 11.11 If you select one of the thumbnails, you can see the detail of the full picture and the metadata, such as title and description.

Summary

In this chapter, you finally implemented a media-sharing application using a serverless and event-driven architecture. In particular, you learned about the following:

- Designing the technical implementation of an event-driven architecture
- Using AWS Lambda to react to coordinated events in the back end
- Choosing the right service in the AWS platform to simplify the implementation
- Mapping data with a hierarchical key structure on Amazon S3
- Defining table and index structure on DynamoDB, based on access to data
- Enforcing security using AWS IAM roles and policies for the client and the back end

Congratulations! You now have the skills to design and implement an event-driven application. In the next chapter, you'll learn in more depth what event-driven means and the effects of a distributed architecture on your app.

EXERCISE

1 Add the option to update title or description of public or private content you own. For example, when you select content form the same identityId as your logged in user, the title and description field should be editable. How would you do that? To enable this feature, do you need to change the back-end Lambda function?

2 The Authenticated role used by Amazon Cognito restricts editing of DynamoDB attributes to title and description only. What you would need to manage if you added the possibility to edit the isPublic Boolean attribute?

Solution

1 In the client application, when the identityId of the content is the same as the logged in user, the medisSharing.js showContent() function should change the title and description HTML tags to be <input type="text> and give them a unique ID; for example, "new-title" and "new-description." You should also save the original values before displaying the editable fields. When closing the detail, if the values of the title and the description are different from the original values, you should use the DynamoDB UpdateItem API with the corresponding primary key (identityId and objectKey) to select the item to update. Because the back end is event-driven, you don't need to change it: the update-ContentIndex Lambda function will process the update from the DynamoDB stream and update the public or private index, depending on the configuration of the content.

2 Changing the isPublic attribute is more complex because you need to change the S3 key of the picture and the corresponding thumbnail. Amazon S3 doesn't

allow you to do that, so you need to insert the new objects and delete the old ones, triggering the `contentUpdated` function. The best way to do that is to delete the original content form the S3 bucket and then insert it again with a different value for `isPublic`, and let the back end functions propagate the update. You can encapsulate the delete and re-insert in a Lambda function that you expose to the client, or manage that in the `updateContentIndex` function, monitoring the update of the `isPublic` attribute from the DynamoDB stream.

Why event-driven?

This chapter covers

- Using event-driven architectures in the front end and back end systems
- Relating event-driven architectures to reactive programming
- Using an event-driven approach to implement microservices
- Managing scalability, availability, and resilience
- Estimating costs and using that information to design a business model

In the previous chapter, you completed building a media-sharing application integrated with an authentication service to recognize users. In this chapter, we'll dive more deeply into the implications of what event-driven means and how to use multiple functions together to build an application.

Different architectural styles are also covered in this chapter. We'll compare the solution we're building using AWS Lambda with patterns that have evolved over the years to improve the scalability, security, and manageability of distributed applications, such as reactive programming and microservices.

Before the internet caused us to think about what scalability really means, it was common practice to recommend avoiding distributed systems: management was complex and expensive servers were the best answer to any scalability issue. But nowadays, running applications concurrently on thousands of servers is relatively common for internet-facing companies and designing your application for scalability should be among your main tenets.

No code examples are provided in this chapter, but the tools to design an application to be event-driven are described. You'll get more theory and less practice than in the previous chapters, but you'll put all this theory into practice soon after.

> **TIP** Even though the things you'll learn are focused on AWS Lambda, most of them can be applied to distributed systems in general and will be useful whenever you're going to design a scalable and reliable application that's independent from the technology stack you'll use.

The functions that make up an application interact in different ways. Certain functions are called directly by end users from a browser or a mobile application. Other functions subscribe to receive events from resources used by the application, such as a file store or a database. They're activated by changes in those resources; for example, when a file has been uploaded or a database has been updated. If you look at the overall flow of the application, however, all the logic is driven by events.

12.1 Overview of event-driven architectures

Event-driven applications react to internal and external events, without a centralized workflow to coordinate processing of the resources. Those events are signals that can come from any source: human input, sensors, other applications, timers, or any activity on a resource used by the application. Those signals can bring data with them; for example, a selection made by a user or a change to a resource.

An important aspect of being event-driven is that the application doesn't control or enforce the sequence of events that are processed. Instead, the overall execution flow follows the events that are received and triggers activities, eventually generating other events that can trigger other activities. This is in contrast to normal procedural programming, where a main plan schedules different activities to fulfill a final goal; for example, via a *centralized workflow*.

The event-driven approach gives certain design advantages that you can see immediately:

- It decouples the sender of the event from the receiver.
- You can have multiple receivers for a single event, and you can add or remove a receiver without affecting the others.
- The flow of the application can be changed by modifying how activities react to events—for example, enabling or disabling a specific subscription, without touching the code *inside* the activities (functions, in the case of AWS Lambda).

- Data is shared among activities via events or external repositories (such as databases) and doesn't have a requirement for multiple activities sharing the same execution environment. This allows you to distribute the execution of those activities, and hence the application, in multiple physical servers for resilience and scalability.

Think of an application that solves a large-scale problem. It may be an e-commerce website, an online game, or an application that analyzes genetic data; it doesn't matter. With an event-driven architecture, you implement an application whose software components have a simple, local visibility into

- What they need to know (the events they can receive)
- What they need to do (for example, work on resources, update files, or write to a database)
- What new events they need to publish

This approach forces you to decompose a large-scale application into smaller components, each of which works on a smaller problem. Event-driven architectural patterns have been used for years by the telecom industry to build highly available and possibly self-healing systems to power communications networks. You can find the legacy of those patterns in programming languages like Erlang, originally developed by Ericsson, and toolkits and runtimes like Akka, via the actor model.

The actor model

The actor model, first discussed in computer science in 1973, uses *actors* as the main entities of computation: everything is an actor, and in response to a message that it receives, an actor can (concurrently) take local decisions, create other actors, send messages to other actors, and decide how to deal with future messages. For more information, see the following resources:

"A Universal Modular ACTOR Formalism for Artificial Intelligence," by Carl Hewitt, Peter Bishop, and Richard Steiger (1973), http://dl.acm.org/citation.cfm?id=1624775.1624804.

"Foundations of Actor Semantics," Mathematics Doctoral Dissertation by William Clinger (1981), http://hdl.handle.net/1721.1/6935.

12.2 *Starting from the front end*

When I think of event-driven programming, the first thing that comes to mind is usually a user interface (UI) where you click a button and something happens. To do that using the programming language of your choice, you link a function (or method) to the event you want to catch; for example, "Do this sequence of actions when the user clicks the button."

This makes sense because you don't know when a user will interact with a UI or what the user will do. You need a way to react and do something when that interaction occurs.

Let's imagine you want to track the different people interacting with your website, giving them the ability to create new users within your application. A basic UI to create a new user would be similar to figure 12.1.

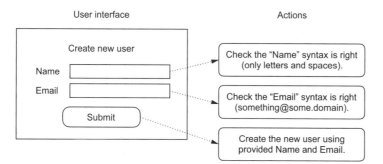

Figure 12.1   Sample UI to create new users: when users interact with UI components, they trigger actions. For example, the syntax used to write "Name" and "Email" is checked every time a character is written or changed in the text boxes, disabling the "Submit" button if the syntax is not valid, and a new user is created when the "Submit" button is enabled and pressed.

To implement the UI, you link actions to possible interactions with the elements that build up the UI. For example,

- Whenever a character is written or changed in the Name text box, you check if the syntax is a valid name according to your syntax (only letters and spaces, no other characters). Additionally, you may capitalize the names as they're written.
- Whenever a character is written or changed in the Email text box, you check if the syntax is a valid email address ("something@some.domain"). Furthermore, you can check whether the domain used in the email address is a valid one.
- If one of the previous checks fails, the Submit button is disabled and a warning is displayed to help the user fix what is not right; for example, "Names can contain only letters and spaces."

In object-oriented languages such as C++ or Java, a UI is usually implemented using the *observer pattern*. The observer is an object where you register the target object to observe and the action (a method) to execute when something happens, such as a user clicking a button or selecting an option from a drop-down menu (figure 12.2).

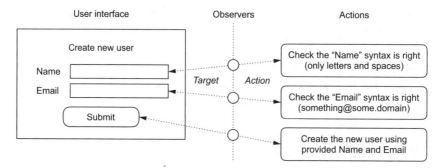

Figure 12.2 In object-oriented languages, the observer pattern is commonly used in a user interface to decouple target UI elements from actions triggered by specific interactions (for example, the characters inside of a text box have changed or a button is pressed).

NOTE In a practical implementation of the observer pattern, an *event loop* is used to process observer events. The event loop is typically single-threaded and should only be used to trigger actions running in other threads, because if the event loop is too busy, newer events need to be queued, slowing down the speed of user interactions with the UI. That should always be avoided. The good news is that with AWS Lambda, events are managed by the platform itself in a scalable way, so you don't need to think about the event loop, as you'll see in the next section.

12.3 *What about the back end?*

In the back end of an application, you put all the logic that can't be safely implemented on the client, either because part of the data must be shared with other clients or for security reasons (because the client can't be trusted to make certain decisions).

Keep in mind these important considerations when developing a back end. First, if you design an application with a procedural approach, when a request from a client arrives in the back end you have to implement a detailed workflow of activities that should be executed to follow the required logic, doing all the necessary data manipulations and checks. This workflow grows in complexity every time the application must be updated to add features, or sometimes even to solve a bug.

Second, as the number of users or interactions grows, you'll need to scale the back end of the application, and you can't assume that it will always run on a single server; eventually you'll need to distribute it on multiple systems.

And third, it's common in a back end to have transactions involving multiple data sources that should be changed synchronously (commit) or not changed at all (roll back). If data isn't locally centralized, but distributed in different repositories, things get far more complex: distributed transactions are slow and complex to manage.

Distributed systems should be designed in a way that doesn't require synchronous access to data but uses eventual consistency: we shouldn't expect data to always be in the same state if it's stored in different repositories. Assuming that your application has synchronous access to data or strong consistency seems safe and practical at first, when you need to design a solution. But such a solution is difficult to implement, manage, and scale in practice.

The CAP theorem

To better understand the complexity of architecting distributed systems, I suggest that you have a look at the *CAP theorem*, also known as *Brewer's theorem*. According to this computer science theorem, it's impossible for a distributed computer system to simultaneously provide all three of the following guarantees (the acronym of which gives name to the theorem):

1 *Consistency* of data across different nodes.
2 *Availability* to requests coming to the distributed system, which should always get a response.
3 *Partition tolerance* (if nodes get disconnected from each other—for example, because of network issues—the system should continue to work).

More information on the CAP theorem and its implications can be found in "Brewer's Conjecture and the Feasibility of Consistent Available Partition-Tolerant Web Services," by Seth Gilbert and Nancy Lynch (2002), http://citeseerx.ist.psu.edu/viewdoc/summary?doi=10.1.1.20.1495.

An ideal approach is to have an application distributed in both space (in different environments) and time (data is sent and updated asynchronously and converges only at a point in time, with eventual consistency).[1] That means that all elements of the architecture should communicate only asynchronously with a predefined interface (a "contract").

It's easy to see that the event-driven architecture I previously introduced takes that approach:

- The execution of each action is independent from other actions, and actions can be executed on different systems.
- Data is exchanged via events, and if multiple actions are accessing the same data, it's the resource containing the data that triggers (via events) all relevant actions when that data is changed.
- Each action knows (only) its input events, the resources it can change, and which events it should eventually trigger. (I'm not considering events triggered by resources manipulated by the action here.)

---

[1] See the talk by Jonas Bonér, creator of the Akka toolkit and runtime, titled "Without Resilience, Nothing Else Matters," for more on this idea.

Let's see in more detail about how to implement such an architecture using AWS Lambda and the possible interactions that you can use.

One way of getting events is from a UI, or in a more general case, from a client application. Let's call those *custom events* to distinguish them from events coming from subscriptions to other resources. Those direct invocations may expect a response (bringing a value back) and are synchronous calls (figure 12.3).

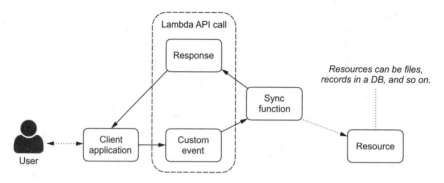

Figure 12.3   Interaction model for a synchronous call from a client application. The function can read or write in some resources (files, databases) and returns a response. This model will be extended further in this chapter to cover other interactions.

You may also have custom events that trigger asynchronous calls that don't return a value but change something in the state of the system; for example, in the resources (files, databases) used by the application. The main difference here is that the client application doesn't need to know when the actions implied by the call are completed; it only needs to know that the request to initiate those actions has been received correctly and the back end will do whatever it can to respect that (figure 12.4).

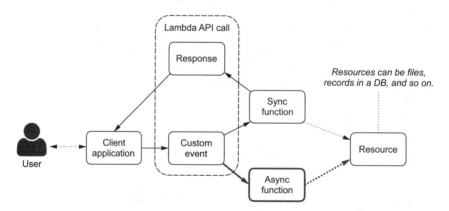

Figure 12.4   Adding asynchronous calls to the previous interaction model. Asynchronous calls don't return a response and the client doesn't need to wait for the function to end.

The resources themselves, when changed, can trigger their own events. If a new picture has been uploaded, you may want to build a thumbnail to render the picture in an index page, or index the picture metadata in a database. If a new user has been created in a database, you may want to send an email to verify that the provided email address is correct and the user can receive emails at that address (figure 12.5).

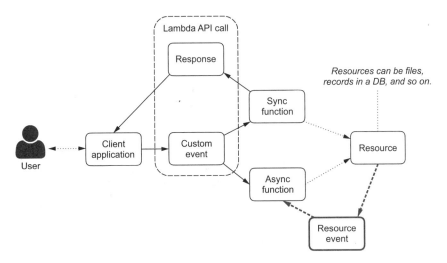

Figure 12.5 Adding events generated by resources to the previous interaction model. If a function created a new file or updated a database, you can subscribe other functions to that event. Those functions will be called asynchronously with an event describing what happened to the resource as input.

Inside the back end, functions can also call other functions, but with AWS Lambda you'd probably avoid calling functions synchronously from another function, because you'd pay for the elapsed time twice: once for the function doing the synchronous call (which is blocked, waiting until the call returns) and once for the function that has been called. With few exceptions, functions are called asynchronously by other functions (figure 12.6).

> **TIP**   A common pattern is to use a first function as a router to call multiple functions asynchronously and have them work in parallel to fulfill a task. If your workload can be split into *chunks*, you can then have multiple functions running concurrently, each function focusing on a single *chunk* and writing the output to a centralized repository where results can be collected.

For certain resources, it's possible to have direct interactions from the client (figure 12.7). For example, a file repository such as Amazon S3, a NoSQL database such as Amazon DynamoDB, or a streaming service such as Amazon Kinesis[2] can be securely

---

[2]   I don't cover Amazon Kinesis in this book, but if you're interested in real-time analytics, or a platform to load and analyze streaming data, using it can save you time. For more information, see https://aws.amazon.com/kinesis.

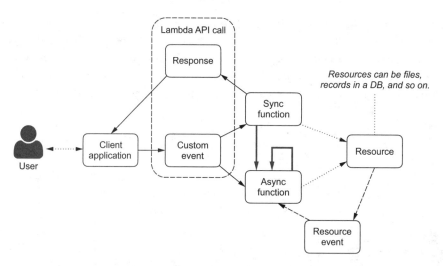

Figure 12.6 Adding functions called asynchronously by other functions to the previous interaction model. In this way you can reuse a function multiple times and for different purposes. The same function can be called directly by a client or by another function.

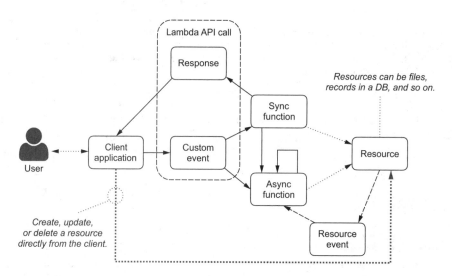

Figure 12.7 Clients can directly access a resource, completing the previous interaction model. For example, a client can upload a file (such as a picture) or write something in a database. This event can trigger functions that can analyze what has happened and do something with the new or updated content; for example, render a thumbnail when a high-resolution picture is uploaded or update a file based on the new content of a database.

used by a client similarly to an AWS Lambda invocation: they're all using the same security framework implemented by AWS Identity and Access Management (IAM) and can be protected by temporary credentials distributed by Amazon Cognito.

The interaction diagram in figure 12.7 shows how an event-driven application can receive events from different sources and how those interactions relate to each other.

Using those interactions, you can follow best practices for architecting and developing distributed systems, such as reactive programming and microservices. For example, you can design a media-sharing application using an event-driven architecture with AWS Lambda, as described in figure 12.8. Remember that the client application can run on any device, such as a smartphone or a web browser.

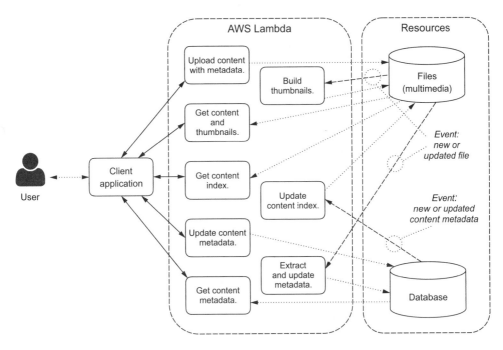

Figure 12.8 Sample media-sharing application with an event-driven design built using AWS Lambda. Certain functions are directly called by the client; other functions are subscribed to events from back-end resources, such as file shares or databases.

12.4 Reactive programming

If you don't want to put a hard limit on the number of users or interactions your application will be capable of handling in production, you have to design your application to be distributed in multiple environments. Distributed applications are inevitable if you need scalability, but they're still difficult to design, manage, and scale.

Sometimes, to speed up development, small teams and startups create a quick prototype of an application that's not designed for scaling but is still shared with users across the internet. Even if that seems to be the right approach when the prototype is under heavy development and many updates need to be implemented rapidly, the paradox is that if the idea they're testing with the prototype is working, then many users could come all at once to try the new application. Those users may be following a review by an important website or a positive comment shared virally on a social network. When users try a new application, it's a unique chance to be appreciated and gain their trust. If the application can't scale to support so many users and slows down or stops working, you'll probably lose those users for good. Wouldn't it be better if a prototype were already capable of scaling?

> **TIP** My advice is to always consider scalability when you develop an application, even if at the beginning it seems out of context. There can be exceptions, such as management applications that are designed to have a few users, but often your user base can be difficult to estimate or can change often due to daily/weekly/monthly cycles.

You can follow different architectural approaches to design an application that can be scaled easily. One of the more interesting approaches is *reactive programming*. With reactive programming, you program your system in a way similar to a spreadsheet: logic is built around data and the propagation of changes in the data flow.

If you think it through carefully, the same syntax has different meanings, depending on whether you interpret it procedurally or in a reactive (event-driven) context. Consider, for example, the formula for the area of a rectangle:

```
area = length x width
```

In procedural programming (including functional nonreactive programming), this syntax represents a function that takes inputs (length, width) and returns a value (the area) synchronously. In reactive programming, this syntax represents a rule that binds data values together: if one of the input values changes (length or width), then the dependent data (the area, in this case) is automatically updated without an explicit request for a new area. Can you see the difference between the procedural and reactive approaches, even if the syntax seems to be the same?

The reactive approach is similar to event-driven programming, where you use subscriptions to events to trigger actions that force the update of dependent data—for example, computing the new area of a rectangle if the length or width is updated in a repository. The main difference is that with reactive programming you bind values together, usually through functions, while with event-driven programming you focus on the messages that are exchanged (events) and the actions that those messages trigger (subscriptions).

> **TIP** To simplify the analysis required to design an event-driven application, I suggest you start with a reactive approach (in a manner similar to data binding for a UI) and then map the result into events and actions.

You have different ways to implement a similar approach and build software that's robust, resilient, flexible, and ready to handle an "unpredictable" workload. I found a good formalization in the Reactive Manifesto, which you can find online at http://www.reactivemanifesto.org.

According to the Reactive Manifesto, a reactive system is a distributed, loosely coupled, and scalable solution that is tolerant of internal failures (figure 12.9). That is, a reactive system meets the following criteria:

- *Responsive*—Providing a response within an acceptable and consistent time makes the system more usable and maintainable.
- *Resilient*—In case of a failure, the system can still provide a response.
- *Elastic*—The system can grow or shrink the resources used depending on the actual workload, avoiding any bottlenecks that could compromise this capacity.
- *Message-driven*—Components of the system should interact via asynchronous nonblocking communications.

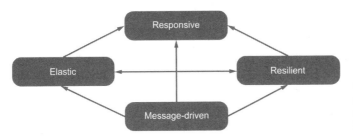

Figure 12.9   The four main characteristics of reactive systems, courtesy of the Reactive Manifesto

Let's look again at the CAP theorem. According to the CAP theorem, it's impossible for a distributed computer system to simultaneously provide all three of the following guarantees:

1 Consistency of data across different nodes.
2 Availability to requests coming to the distributed system, which should always get a response.
3 Partition tolerance (if nodes get disconnected from each other—for example, because of network issues—the system should continue to work).

How do you think the four characteristics in the Reactive Manifesto affect the components of a distributed architecture following the CAP theorem? What would you need to change in a traditional server-based implementation?

I think the most important takeaway from the Reactive Manifesto is the message-driven approach in communication, which implicitly removes the need for data consistency (the "C" in the CAP theorem): if interactions are asynchronous, then multiple interactions don't happen at the same time, and the data doesn't have to be consistent at a point in time. The right way to look at this is that you're sharing *immutable data*, avoiding the risk of contention among different interactions.

NOTE   I suggest that you read the whole Reactive Manifesto online (http://www.reactivemanifesto.org) and try to evaluate how those characteristics can be applied to your application and the concepts you're learning in this book.

12.5   *The path to microservices*

Microservices have no official definition, but the general consensus is that they follow an architectural style where applications are decomposed into small, independently deployable services, with several common characteristics:

- Each service should be built around a business domain and not a technical one; this ensures, among other things, that the boundary around services will last if technologies evolve or are changed.
- Services should be loosely coupled, so that changes within one service shouldn't affect others.
- A service should work within a "bounded context" as part of the entire business domain to simplify modeling of communications among services.

NOTE   Introducing and using the concept of a "bounded context" is part of domain-driven design and goes beyond the scope of this book. I suggest you start with Martin Fowler's description and suggested readings, which can be found at http://martinfowler.com/bliki/BoundedContext.html.

DevOps and microservices

I find it interesting that the core characteristic for microservices of being *independently deployable* is an *operational* requirement. This is clear feedback provided by operations to development, thanks to the adoption of a DevOps culture within companies that pioneered microservice architectures.

Similar to microservices, DevOps has no official definition, but generally speaking, the goal of DevOps is to foster communication and collaboration between development, operations, and other IT-related roles within a company.

How small is "small" for microservices? No specific metric exists, but a good starting point is that you can build or rebuild a service in less than two weeks. In general, I'd say that it should be small enough that you can easily manage to completely rewrite a microservice within your deployment schedule.

You have important consequences of this capacity of rebuilding a service: if a new requirement arises, and it's too hard to add to the current implementation of a service, you can create a new service that will implement the new requirement and all the old ones. In creating this new service, you can decide to use a different technology; for example, migrating from Java to Scala or from Ruby to Python.

TIP   Other than helping developers to always use the best technology for a specific purpose, the possibility to use a new or different technology stack also improves morale and hiring, because developers know that they have the freedom to choose a new programming environment if that makes sense and they won't be forced to work on the same old stack for the rest of their (working) lives.

A possible downside of this freedom is that developers may be tempted to follow trends and choose technologies only because they're "cool." A service can have a long life span, and using a stable technology helps. If the technology used for a service loses traction and support, you can still rebuild the service using another technology in less than two weeks (according to our definition of microservices), but if you've used that technology in more than one service, you'll have to spend more time rebuilding multiple services, which doesn't add value for the end users of your application.

> **NOTE** For a broader description of what microservices are and how to use them for your particular use case, I suggest you start with Martin Fowler's resource guide at http://martinfowler.com/microservices/.

If you recall how to design an event-driven application, and how AWS Lambda works by decomposing your application into small functions that can interact only via events, you'll see that the approach described in this book puts you on the right path to implement microservices—but you still have great responsibility in the implementation.

AWS Lambda provides a framework to build small, mostly asynchronous services with a clean interface and covers some of the main complexities of managing microservice architectures in production, such as

- Centralized logging, via Amazon CloudWatch Logs
- Service discovery, via the AWS Lambda API

It's your responsibility to use those features to your advantage while you build the overall application. For example:

- To simplify debugging microservices, centralized logging needs a traceable "identification" that follows a single request among all the interacting services. That isn't part of what AWS Lambda and Amazon CloudWatch Logs provide, and you need to think about that.
- To automate service discovery, you should use a standard syntax in the function descriptions that you get via the AWS Lambda API.

Another main point that I think is relevant in understanding how AWS Lambda supports a microservice architecture—and one that has been a source of endless discussion in distributed architectures—is whether it's better to favor *choreography* or *orchestration* of services.

To better clarify that, let's continue the parallel with the artistic scenario that the two terms involve, using definitions from the Merriam-Webster English dictionary.

Definitions from the Merriam-Webster dictionary

Choreography: The art or job of deciding how dancers will move in a performance; *also*, the movements that are done by dancers in a performance.

Orchestration: The arrangement of a musical composition for performance by an orchestra.

Let's try to adapt those definitions to IT architectures. With orchestration, you have an automated execution of a workflow, and an *orchestration engine* to execute that workflow and manage all interactions. With choreography, you describe the coordinated interactions between a small subset (usually two) of the elements that are interacting.

If you're familiar with the enterprise deployment of a service-oriented architecture (SOA), it's easy to see the similarity between the orchestration engine and the extended role that's given to the enterprise message bus, for example in routing, filtering, or translating messages depending on a centralized logic. With microservices, messaging platforms shouldn't have an active role and the logic should be kept within the services' boundary.

With an event-driven architecture you're describing the choreography among services, without a centralized workflow that needs to be aware of all aspects of the interactions and that scales in complexity as the number of services (and interactions) increases. As each service probably has more than one interaction with other services, the growth in complexity of a centralized workflow is far more than linear and is difficult to manage in a large-scale deployment.

12.6   *Scalability of the platform*

Scalability is one of the core aspects of IT architectures. Let's start with a definition of scalability in the context of IT systems.

> **DEFINITION**   *Scalability* is the capability of a system, network, or process to handle a growing amount of work, or its potential to be enlarged to accommodate that growth. From "Characteristics of Scalability and Their Impact on Performance," by André Benjamin Bondi (2000), http://dl.acm.org/citation .cfm?doid=350391.350432.

In an event-driven application, scalability is driven by the total concurrent executions across all functions. The number of concurrent executions depends on the number of events coming in and the duration of the functions triggered by those events, according to the following formula:

```
concurrent executions = (number of events per second) x (average duration of
the triggered functions)
```

For example, let's consider this scenario with multiple interactions with AWS Lambda, several directly from users (custom events), and several coming from subscriptions to resources:

- One thousand users are interacting every second via a client application to check if there's a relevant picture close to where they are, using a Lambda function that on average takes 0.2 seconds to execute; this brings 1,000 events x 0.2s = 200 concurrent executions.

- Ten users per second upload a picture on Amazon S3. An AWS Lambda function subscribed to that event that's triggered on upload; it builds a thumbnail of the picture and extracts the metadata, inserting the metadata into an Amazon DynamoDB table. This function takes on average 2 seconds to complete (let's imagine those are high-resolution pictures); this brings 10 events x 2s = 20 concurrent executions.

- Another Lambda function is subscribed to the DynamoDB table; it receives all those events and updates an index of the user pictures. This function takes on average 3 seconds to complete (maybe you can tune it, but for the sake of simplicity let's use this duration as an average); this brings 10 events x 3s = 30 concurrent executions.

- In total for this scenario, 200 + 20 + 30 = 250 concurrent executions.

With AWS Lambda you don't need to manage scalability and concurrency because the service is designed to run many instances of your functions in parallel. Of course, you have to take care of the scalability of the resources used by Lambda functions; for example, if you have multiple concurrent executions of a function reading or writing to a database, you need to be sure that the database is capable of sustaining the workload.

However, a default safety throttle of 100 concurrent executions per account per region limits the impact of errors or recursive functions. If you realize this is a scalability limit for your application, you can request to increase the number of concurrent executions to throttle, opening a case for a service limit increase in the AWS Support Center at no cost.

> **NOTE** The number of concurrent executions to throttle is a cumulative limit for all AWS Lambda functions you have within an account and region.

When an account goes beyond the safety throttle, the function execution is throttled. You can monitor this behavior in the corresponding Amazon CloudWatch metric, available in the AWS Lambda web console in the Monitoring tab.

When throttled, Lambda functions that are invoked synchronously return an HTTP error code 429, for "Too Many Requests." Error code 429 is automatically managed by AWS SDKs, which will retry multiple times with an exponential back-off.

Lambda functions that are invoked asynchronously, when throttled, are automatically retried for 15–30 minutes. If you had a spike of traffic coming to your back end, that period should be enough to absorb the burst and execute the functions. After 15–30 minutes this retry period ends and all incoming events are rejected as throttled.

If the Lambda function is subscribed to events generated by other AWS events, those are retained and retried. The retry period is usually 24 hours, but you should check the documentation of AWS Lambda and the relevant AWS service for further details.

12.7 *Availability and resilience*

Together with scalability, availability defines how and when an IT system can be used in production. A definition of availability will help you to understand what will be discussed in this section.

> **DEFINITION** *Availability* is the proportion of time a system is in a functioning condition.

Finding a definition of resilience to use in an IT context is not as easy because it's usually discussed in the context of biology or psychology, but a general agreement can be made on the following.

> **DEFINITION** *Resilience* is the capacity of adapting to adversity.

According to those definitions, availability is the metric to measure the probability of finding a specific system available and responding. Resilience is the capacity of such a system to automatically recover (self-heal) from issues that could compromise its ability to respond. In large-scale deployments, where hardware and software components are put into place, failures will happen. We want systems that are resilient to improve availability.

AWS Lambda is designed to use multiple features, such as replication and redundancy at the hardware and software level, to provide high availability for both the service itself and the functions it manages. AWS Lambda has no maintenance windows or scheduled downtimes.

Still, a Lambda function can fail because the internal logic terminates with an error; for example, using `context.fail()` on the Node.js runtime, or raising an exception on the Python runtime.

On failure, synchronous functions respond with an exception. Asynchronous functions are retried at least three times, after which the event may be rejected. Events from AWS services, such as Amazon Kinesis streams and Amazon DynamoDB streams, are retried until the Lambda function succeeds or the data expires, usually after 24 hours.

As discussed in section 12.4, asynchronous message passing is a better way to communicate among different components of your back end (functions, in the case of AWS Lambda) and should be your preferred choice whenever possible. Sometimes you have to change part of the internal logic of your application to accommodate asynchronous communications.

12.8 *Estimating costs*

Costs are an important part of cloud computing services. Costs, together with the technical specification of the service, define when and how a service can be used, and what the possible use cases are. A lower cost enables new use cases that wouldn't make sense if they were more expensive to build.

With AWS Lambda you pay monthly for

- Requests across all functions, including test invocations from the web console
- Duration, with each function execution rounded up to the nearest 100 ms, depending on how much memory you configured for the function

The duration costs depend linearly on the memory configured for the function. If you double (or halve) the memory you configure, but keep the same duration, you also double (or halve) the duration costs.

When you give more (or less) memory to a function, you also allocate proportional CPU power and other resources that the function can use during the execution. Hence, giving more memory can also (depending on the function's CPU and I/O usage) speed up the execution of a function.

> **NOTE** Cost information provided hereafter in this section is up to date at the time of writing of this book. Even if certain numbers have now changed, understanding the cost model and how that applies to your application will be useful when you plan to use AWS Lambda. For updated information on AWS Lambda pricing and the AWS Free Tier, see https://aws.amazon.com/lambda/pricing/ and http://aws.amazon.com/free/.

You start paying only after you exceed the AWS Free Tier, available for all AWS accounts. The Lambda free tier doesn't expire after 12 months, unlike for other AWS services, and is available to all AWS customers indefinitely.

The Lambda free tier allows you to learn, test, and scale a prototype at no charge for

- The first 1 million requests per month
- The first 400,000 GB-seconds of compute time per month

In the AWS Lambda free tier, 400,000 GB-seconds is to be interpreted as the sum of the duration (up to the nearest 100 ms) of all function executions within an account, if the functions are configured with 1 GB of memory. If you give less memory, you get more execution time at no charge. For example, if you configure 128 MB of memory (that is, 1/8 of 1 GB), you get 8 x 400,000 seconds = 3.2 million seconds of execution time.

Because every execution time is rounded up to the nearest 100 ms, functions that execute quickly (for example, in about 20 ms) could have a greater impact than expected on costs than functions that are closer to the 100 ms execution time (for example, close to 90 ms).

TIP   For cost optimization, it can sometimes be useful to group more functions into one if the duration of those functions is far less than the minimum of 100 ms. Conversely, having smaller functions can make development and updates easier. You should find your own balance between costs in production (including AWS Lambda) and in development (where time to market can be critical).

When you invoke a Lambda function from another function, there can be two use cases:

1   The second function is invoked asynchronously, so the first function can end while the second is still executing, and the two costs are completely independent.

2   The second function is invoked synchronously, so that the first function will be blocked and wait for the second function to terminate before continuing its own execution. In this case you pay double time for the execution of the second synchronous function, so this isn't always a good practice and it's better to avoid invoking synchronous functions from other functions.

To estimate the costs of an application, you have to estimate all events—both custom events due to direct invocations and those coming from subscription to some resources—and the duration of the functions triggered by those events. You can use (multiple) test events to estimate the duration in the web console. Or you can look at the duration metric recorded by Amazon CloudWatch in the monitoring tab of web console.

Estimating cost (and consumption) per user is the best way to understand your cost model, how many users you need to exceed the free tier, and how your costs are growing with your user base.

For example, consider the media-sharing application I mentioned in chapter 1. You're going to build a similar application in the following chapters of this book. Suppose that after analyzing your first trial users, you measure that each user, on average, is doing 100 function invocations (requests) per month, directly from a mobile app or via subscriptions to the picture store and the database tables. On average, half of those functions are quick and take 30 ms with 128 MB of memory. The other half are slower (for example, when you need to build a thumbnail of a high-resolution picture) and last on average 1 second with 512 MB of memory.

Let's compute how many GB-seconds each user is contributing:

- For the "quick" functions, 50 x 100 ms (because you need to round up from 30 ms) x 128 MB = 5 / 8 GB-seconds (you need to divide by 8 to get GB) = 0.625 GB-seconds.

- For the "slow" functions, 50 x 1s x 512 MB = 50 / 2 GB-seconds (you need to divide by 2 to get GB) = 25 GB-seconds.

The overall contribution to duration costs for each user is 25.625 GB-seconds; as you'd expect, the "quick" functions are contributing far less than the "slow" ones.

You can now build a simple cost model that tells you

- When you're going to exceed the free tier
- How much you'd pay for AWS Lambda for 10, 100, 1,000, and so on, users

WARNING I'm not considering storage and database costs for now, but they're easier to estimate, and Amazon S3 and Amazon DynamoDB both have a free tier.

You can see an example of that in table 12.1, based on current costs at the time of writing of the book.

Table 12.1 AWS Lambda cost model for an application. Thanks to the free tier, you start incurring costs only when approaching 100,000 users. With this table, you can also estimate the average cost per user, a useful metric in defining and validating your business model.

Users	Requests	Duration	Requests to pay	Duration to pay	Request costs	Duration costs	Total costs
1	100	25.63	0	0	0	0	0
10	1,000	256.25	0	0	0	0	0
100	10,000	2,562.50	0	0	0	0	0
1,000	100,000	25,625	0	0	0	0	0
10,000	1,000,000	256,250	0	0	0	0	0
100,000	10,000,000	2,562,500	9,000,000	2,162,500	1.8	36.05	37.85
1,000,000	100,000,000	25,625,000	99,000,000	25,225,000	19.8	420.50	440.30

As you can see from the table, the free tier has no charges unless you approach 100,000 users, and then costs start to grow almost linearly with the user base.

From table 12.1 you can also estimate the average cost per user for your application. If different kinds of users (basic or advanced, for example) interact in different ways, bringing different costs to the platform, you may need to estimate their costs separately. This can be useful in designing your own business model and validating if (or when) it's sustainable. Knowing the cost per user, you can find out, for example,

- If a "freemium" pricing strategy, a popular approach for startups, would work for your application
- If you should have different tiers for your users, with different pricing, depending on what they can do
- If and when advertisements could pay for a significant part of your bill

DEFINITION   *Freemium* is a business model in which a core product or service is provided free of charge to a large group of users, but money (premium) is charged to a smaller fraction of the user base for advanced features or virtual goods. For more information, see *Freemium Economics* by Eric Benjamin Seufert (Savvy Manager's Guides, 2013).

Summary

In this chapter you learned the following:

- How event-driven architectures work
- How they are commonly used in the front end
- The advantages of using the same approach in the back end of your application
- How that relates to architectural best practices for distributed systems, such as reactive programming and microservices
- What the advantages are for two fundamental characteristics of IT architectures, scalability, and availability
- How to estimate AWS Lambda costs for an event-driven application and use that information to design your business model

In the next chapter you'll move into the third part of this book, focusing on the tools and best practices that support the use of AWS Lambda from development to production.

EXERCISE

To test what you've learned in this chapter, try to answer these multiple-choice questions:

1 According to the Reactive Manifesto, it's better for components of the system to interact

 a Via synchronous communications, because that guarantees you get strong consistency in the answer

 b Via asynchronous communication, so that components are loosely coupled and interactions are nonblocking

 c Communication used by interactions isn't important as long as the system remains responsive

2 Implementing an event-driven architecture, you're favoring

 a Choreography vs. orchestration, because you describe the relationship among resources

 b Orchestration vs. choreography, because you have the automated execution of a workflow

 c It depends on how you design the centralized workflow

3 To manage the scalability of functions executed by AWS Lambda

    a You need to keep the number of events per second below the safety throttle of your account

    b You need to keep the number of concurrent executions below the safety throttle for your account

    c You need to keep the number of invocations per second below the safety throttle of your account

4 To estimate the AWS Lambda costs for your application

    a You need to know how many functions you're using and if they're called synchronously or asynchronously

    b You need to understand how many requests are made and the overall duration of function executions. The free tier can be neglected because it has no noticeable impact on the bill

    c You need to understand how many requests are made and the overall duration of function executions, taking into consideration the free tier

Solution

    1 b

    2 a

    3 b

    4 c

Part 3

From development to production

This part of the book focuses on how to enhance development, testing, and deployment to production for your event-driven apps. You'll learn how to use versioning and aliases with AWS Lambda, how frameworks can enhance your development experience, and how to use other services, such as Amazon S3 and AWS CloudFormation, to automate deployment on a single or multiregion architecture. A specific focus is given to monitoring, logging, and managing alarms from your infrastructure.

Improving development and testing

This chapter covers

- Weighing the pros and cons of local development of Lambda functions
- Logging and debugging your code
- Using Lambda function versions and aliases
- Presenting an overview of the most popular tools and framework for building serverless apps
- Implementing a serverless testing framework for Lambda functions

In the previous chapter, you focused on the advantages and pitfalls of event-driven applications and distributed architectures, with a more theoretic approach than the previous chapters.

Now you return to hands-on experience to see how development and testing can be improved using more advanced AWS Lambda features, such as versioning and aliases, and specific tools and frameworks designed to support serverless development and testing.

13.1 *Developing locally*

A common question people ask when I introduce AWS Lambda is how to develop with a local environment. It's easy to wrap a Lambda function with a few lines of code to allow local execution. If you use other AWS services in those functions, you may find tools that can emulate them locally. For example:

- AWS provides a downloadable version of DynamoDB that you can run locally. For more information on running DynamoDB on your computer, see https://docs.aws.amazon.com/amazondynamodb/latest/developerguide/DynamoDB-Local.html.

- A few projects have been developed by the AWS community which you could use to emulate Amazon S3. For example, FakeS3 is a lightweight server that responds to the same calls that Amazon S3 responds to. Another option is Minio, an Amazon S3–compatible object-storage server. For more information on how to use FakeS3 and Minio, see https://github.com/jubos/fake-s3 and https://github.com/minio/minio.

Because the AWS free tier and pricing allows you to run your development with almost no costs, the opportunity to develop on exactly the same platform and underlying infrastructure (such as servers and network connectivity) that you'll use in production is a great advantage. That's not easy to do using traditional architectures, where it's common to have older or even different products in dev and test than are in production. For example, you may have a slightly older server model or a network load balancer from another vendor. Even if the hardware is the same, it's quite complex to have all firmware and software in sync across different environments that may be managed by different teams. This is why technologies such as Docker are helpful—because they allow you to move whole containers (including all user-space dependencies) across different environments.

> **TIP** With AWS, you can use for development, test, and production exactly the same resources, such as Lambda functions or DynamoDB tables, and they're available in different locations across the world (what AWS calls *regions*). I think that using the same platform for development, test, and production can greatly reduce pitfalls and issues during the lifecycle of an application. For this reason, I'm not a big fan of "developing locally." If you find compelling cases where a local development environment makes sense, please contact me and tell me your story. I'm interested in learning about it.

The only downside I can see in using a live AWS environment for development is that you need a (decent) internet connection, but is that a limitation? If you're temporarily without an internet connection, you can still use the time given to improve the architectural design of the application, as you did in chapter 8; design an authentication service; and as demonstrated in the first part of chapter 11, finalize the event-driven architecture and the data model of a media-sharing application. In my experience, as you move up in the technology stack, optimization of the overall architecture becomes easier to think about and implement, and should take a larger percentage of the overall development time.

You may decide to implement your development environment locally; however, let's do a quick test to execute locally the greetingOnDemand function that you built in chapter 2, both for the Node.js and the Python implementations.

13.1.1 Developing locally in Node.js

For your convenience, the Node.js version of the greetingOnDemand function is provided in the following listing.

Listing 13.1 Function greetingOnDemand (Node.js)

```
console.log('Loading function');

exports.handler = (event, context, callback) => {        ◁── The Lambda
    console.log('Received event:',                            function is exported
        JSON.stringify(event, null, 2));                      as "handler."
    console.log('name =', event.name);
    var name = '';
    if ('name' in event) {
        name = event['name'];
    } else {
        name = "World";
    }
    var greetings = 'Hello ' + name + '!';
    console.log(greetings);
    callback(null, greetings);
};
```

In the following listing, a basic wrapper is used to execute the function locally, implemented as a separate file (runLocal.js) to be placed in the same directory as the one in listing 13.1.

Listing 13.2 runLocal (Node.js)

```
var lambdaFunction = require('./greetingsOnDemand');      The name of the function
var functionHandler = 'handler';                     ◁── exported by the module

var event = {}; // { name: 'Danilo'};                ◁── A test event to pass
var context = {};                                         to the function

function callback(error, data) {                     A callback function
    console.log(error);                              to process the data
    console.log(data);                               or error returned
}                                                    by the function

lambdaFunction[functionHandler](event, context, callback);   ◁── The actual function
                                                                  invocation
```

Imports the Lambda function as a module.

A fake context to pass to the function

TIP If your Lambda function is using the context, you need to mock the results instead of passing an empty object as I did. For a description of available information in the context in Node.js, see https://docs.aws.amazon.com/lambda/latest/dg/nodejs-prog-model-context.html.

13.1.2 Developing locally in Python

For your convenience, the Python version of the greetingOnDemand function from chapter 2 is provided in the following listing.

Listing 13.3 Function greetingOnDemand (Python)

```python
import json

print('Loading function')

def lambda_handler(event, context):              ◁⎯⎯  The Lambda
    print("Received event: " +                          function is
        json.dumps(event, indent=2))                    declared here.
    if 'name' in event:
        name = event['name']
    else:
        name = 'World'
    greetings = 'Hello ' + name + '!'
    print(greetings)
    return greetings
```

In the following listing, a basic wrapper (runLocal.py) is used to execute the function locally, to be placed in the same directory as the file in listing 13.3.

Listing 13.4 runLocal (Python)

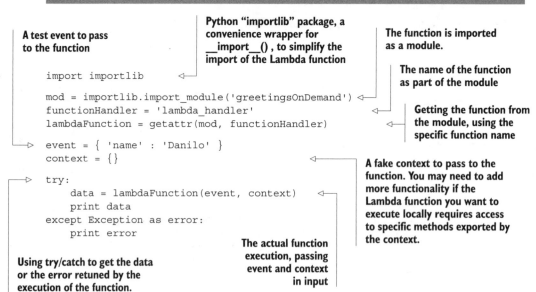

A test event to pass to the function

Python "importlib" package, a convenience wrapper for __import__() , to simplify the import of the Lambda function

The function is imported as a module.

The name of the function as part of the module

```python
import importlib              ◁⎯

mod = importlib.import_module('greetingsOnDemand')  ◁⎯
functionHandler = 'lambda_handler'
lambdaFunction = getattr(mod, functionHandler)      ◁⎯

event = { 'name' : 'Danilo' }
context = {}                                         ◁⎯

try:
    data = lambdaFunction(event, context)           ◁⎯
    print data
except Exception as error:
    print error
```

Getting the function from the module, using the specific function name

A fake context to pass to the function. You may need to add more functionality if the Lambda function you want to execute locally requires access to specific methods exported by the context.

Using try/catch to get the data or the error retuned by the execution of the function.

The actual function execution, passing event and context in input

TIP If your Lambda function accesses the `context`, you need to mock the results instead of passing an empty object as I did. For a description of available information in the context in Python, see https://docs.aws.amazon.com/lambda/latest/dg/python-context-object.html.

13.1.3 Community tools

Now that you understand how to wrap a Lambda function to execute it locally, you can optionally see projects developed by the community that can simplify the process. For example:

- `lambda-local`, for Node.js functions, is easy to use and set up. You can find it at https://github.com/ashiina/lambda-local.
- `aws-lambda-python-local`, for Python functions, is slightly more complex and powerful, but it also covers Amazon API Gateway and Amazon Cognito. You can find it at https://github.com/sportarchive/aws-lambda-python-local.

13.2 Logging and debugging

The output you produce with Lambda functions, using `console.log()` in JavaScript (Node.js) or `print` in Python, is automatically collected by Amazon CloudWatch Logs. By using AWS Lambda, you get a centralized logging framework as a feature. You pay for only the storage of the logs and retention is configurable.

As you saw before, you can quickly see the logs of a Lambda function you test in the web console. For normal executions, after you select a function in the Lambda console, you can find a link to the logs of that function in the Monitoring tab in the CloudWatch console.

Each function has a CloudWatch log group with a name starting with `/aws/lambda/`, followed by the function name. For example:

```
/aws/lambda/greetingsOnDemand
```

TIP If you select a log group, you can customize log retention via the Expire Events After option. The default is Never Expire, to always store and keep all logs. You can change that setting to a retention of one day, three days, and so on, up to 10 years. After that specific amount of time, all logs in that log group are automatically removed.

Within a log group, you can also add a metric filter that can look for a pattern in the logged data and optionally extract values. JSON and space-delimited log events are supported out of the box. The information you extract from the log can be used to create a custom CloudWatch metric that can be monitored in a dashboard or be used by a CloudWatch Alarm to trigger further events. For example, if you use a metric filter to count the number of wrong login attempts in your app, you can use this metric to fire an alarm if more wrong login attempts than expected occur in a specified unit of time, possibly a signal that someone's trying to attack your application.

TIP Amazon CloudWatch is a broad topic and can be used for monitoring AWS cloud resources and the applications you run on AWS. Among other things, you can use Amazon CloudWatch to collect and track metrics, collect and monitor log files, set alarms, and automatically react to changes in your AWS resources. To get a good overview, I suggest you start with https://aws .amazon.com/cloudwatch/.

Inside a log group, you have multiple log streams corresponding to one or more executions of the Lambda function. The log stream names are composed of the day of execution, the function version (as you'll see later in this chapter), and a unique ID. For example

```
2016/07/12/[$LATEST]7eb5d765b13c4649b7019f4487870efd
```

You can use the AWS CLI to check the logs of your Lambda functions, using the following command example:

```
aws logs get-log-events --log-group-name /aws/lambda/<FUNCTION_NAME>
    --log-stream-name 'YYYY/MM/DD/[$LATEST]…'
```

You can send the output of the previous command to text-manipulating tools (such as "grep" on UNIX/Linux systems) to further process the output and search for relevant patterns in the logs.

TIP In the CloudWatch console, you can automatically stream a log group to an Amazon Elasticsearch Service-managed cluster, and use Kibana to further analyze your logs. Kibana is a visualization tool for Elasticsearch. Amazon Elasticsearch Service is a managed service that makes it easy to deploy, operate, and scale Elasticsearch in the AWS Cloud. For more information, see https://aws.amazon.com/elasticsearch-service/.

You can also stream a log group to a Lambda function that can quickly process that information and react to specific patterns or store the logged data in a persistent storage, such as a database. An overview of how the tools and features mentioned in this section can work together is shown in figure 13.1.

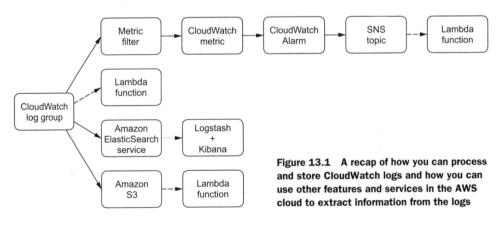

Figure 13.1 A recap of how you can process and store CloudWatch logs and how you can use other features and services in the AWS cloud to extract information from the logs

13.3 *Using function versioning*

AWS Lambda supports the concept of function *versions* natively. By default, there's only the *latest* version of a function, indicated as $LATEST. You can create more versions of a function in three ways:

- When creating a function, you can ask to publish a new version (at function creation, that will be version 1).
- When updating the code of a function, you can ask to also publish a new version that will be incremented from the latest version created—for example, 2, 3, and so on.
- At any time, you can publish a new version, based on the content of the current $LATEST function, which will be incremented sequentially.

As you create more versions, you can browse and access them from the web console or the CLI. In the web console, you can use the Qualifiers button to change the version you're working on. Using the CLI, you can specify a version of a function using the --version argument. For example, you can add the --version argument to invoke an older version of a function rather than the latest.

Previously, when you configured roles and permissions to invoke a Lambda function, you used the function ARN (Amazon Resource Name) to specify which function to use. You have two different ways to specify a function via ARNs:

- *Unqualified ARN*, the one you used so far, without a version suffix at the end, pointing at the current $LATEST version
- *Qualified ARN*, with an explicit version suffix at the end

An example of an Unqualified ARN for the helloWorld function is the following code:

```
arn:aws:lambda:<REGION>:<ACCOUNT_ID>:function:helloWorld
```

If you want to be more specific, you can point at the latest version using this Qualified ARN:

```
arn:aws:lambda:<REGION>:<ACCOUNT_ID>:function:helloWorld:$LATEST
```

For example, to use version 3 of a function, you can use a Qualified ARN ending with ":3":

```
arn:aws:lambda:<REGION>:<ACCOUNT_ID>:function:helloWorld:3
```

You can use a Qualified ARN and explicitly specify which version of a function to use when configuring how Lambda interacts with other AWS services, including integration with the Amazon API Gateway or in subscriptions to trigger the function in response to events.

TIP   To practice with function versions, use the greetingsOnDemand function (you can use either the Node.js or Python implementation) and create multiple versions. For example, you can change "Hello" into "Hi" and "Goodbye," and then invoke the distinct versions to see the different results.

13.4 *Using aliases to manage different environments*

When you have multiple versions of a function, those versions can correspond to different environments. For example, the most recent version is probably the one you're currently working on in the development environment. Before going into production, a function can go through different stages of testing, such as an integration test or a user-acceptance test.

TIP   The Amazon API Gateway has the concept of multiple stages and the option to create stage variables to host values that depend on the stage (such as the database name, which will probably be different between development and production). Don't confuse those stages with the AWS Lambda aliases.

With AWS Lambda, you can assign an alias to a specific version, and those aliases can be used in configurations as part of a Qualified ARN to reference the version of the function you want to use. When you update an alias to use a different version of a function, all references to that alias will automatically use the new version. Let's see an example.

NOTE   You cannot use an Unqualified ARN when creating or updating an alias. Only Qualified ARNs are accepted by AWS Lambda in this case.

Suppose you work on a function and you have multiple versions of it. You're currently working on $LATEST, but versions 1 to 5 come before that. Of those versions, a couple of them are used in test environments, and one of the oldest is in production. You can see a recap of the current situation in figure 13.2.

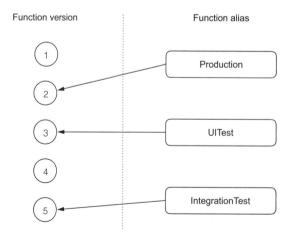

Figure 13.2 **An example of how to use Lambda function versions and aliases. Each alias corresponds to a different environment (production, UI test, integration test) that's using a specific version of an AWS Lambda function.**

Starting from the example in figure 13.2, if UI tests on version 3 complete correctly, you may want to move that version into production and start new UI tests for version 4. You can update the alias UITest to point to version 4 and the alias Production to version 3. You can see how aliases change (before and after) in figure 13.3.

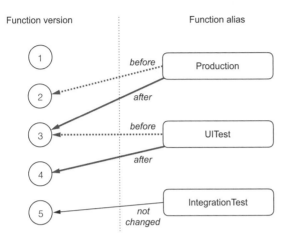

Figure 13.3 An example of how to update Lambda function aliases when moving a new version into Production and a new version for UI test

TIP To familiarize yourself with aliases, use the multiple versions I suggested to modify the `greetingsOnDemand` function to assign them different aliases. For example, the most recent (higher) version can be "Dev," the previous one "Test," and the first one "Production."

13.5 Development tools and frameworks

AWS Lambda and other AWS services you may want to use (such as Amazon S3, Amazon DynamoDB, and Amazon API Gateway) are building blocks that you can use to build complex applications, such as the sample authentication service, or the media-sharing app you built previously while reading this book.

Those services offer advanced functionality to simplify development and common operations such as versioning and aliases, which you've learned. However, in the same way you don't use plain JavaScript to build a web application but use frameworks such as Express, a growing number of tools and frameworks are available for developing serverless apps using AWS Lambda and other Cloud tools.

The purpose of those frameworks is to make the development experience easier, especially when the complexity of the application and the number of Lambda functions or other services you use grows.

NOTE Some of the frameworks you're going to test in this section are designed to run only on UNIX/Linux environments. If you have issues using a Windows system, I suggest creating an Amazon EC2 `t2.micro` instance using a Linux (or Ubuntu) Amazon Machine Image (AMI). As part of the AWS Free

Tier, new AWS accounts can run a Linux EC2 `t2.micro` instance at no costs for the first 12 months. For more (and updated) information on the AWS Free Tier, see https://aws.amazon.com/free.

A number of interesting frameworks exist, but only a small subset of them is showcased in this book. Look at them as examples of what can be done rather than as a list of what you should use. Check other options and choose the tool you're most comfortable with, depending on your development and deployment style. Most of the tools and frameworks are open-source projects, and you can support your favorite and make a difference by contributing your feedback and ideas.

> **NOTE**   At the time of writing this book, AWS is working on Flourish, a runtime app model for serverless applications, which has a similar approach to what SwaggerHub is for APIs. You can find more info on SwaggerHub at https://swaggerhub.com.

13.5.1   *Chalice Python microframework*

One tool I appreciate for its simplicity is Chalice, developed by the AWS Developer Tools team and currently published as a preview project (and not yet recommended for production). The idea of Chalice is to provide a CLI tool for creating, deploying, and managing your app.

> **NOTE**   Chalice works for the Python runtime and resembles the syntax of Flask and Bottle, two popular and interesting web microframeworks for linking your custom logic to HTTP interactions with an endpoint.

Microframeworks can make API development easy and can be extended to cover generic web development as well. In this case, Chalice uses a single app file to generate all the necessary API resources and methods on the Amazon API Gateway, and the Lambda function to be executed by those method calls.

Chalice is also experimenting with automatic IAM policy generation, inspecting the code to find the AWS resources that you need to access, such as S3 buckets, and automatically generating the required IAM policies for the Lambda functions.

To install Chalice, you can use "pip:"

```
pip install chalice
```

The following code shows a quick example of how to re-implement the `greetingsOn-Demand` function and Web API that you built in chapter 3 using Chalice. This app will use the default AWS region and credentials configured in the AWS CLI:

```
chalice new-project greetingsOnDemand
cd greetingsOnDemand
chalice deploy
```

The output of the previous commands shows what's done by Chalice; it creates the Lambda function, the IAM role for the Lambda function, and then wires the API to an HTTPS endpoint using the Amazon API Gateway:

```
Initial creation of lambda function.
Creating role
Creating deployment package.
Lambda deploy done.
Initiating first time deployment...
Deploying to: dev
https://<ENDPOINT>.execute-api.<REGION>.amazonaws.com/dev/
```

You can test the HTTPS endpoint in the final line of the previous output (that will be unique for your deployment) using curl or, because it's answering to a normal HTTPS GET, using any web browser. For example, with curl you get the following (be sure to replace <ENDPOINT> and <REGION> in the next command with the values from your output):

```
curl https://<ENDPOINT>.execute-api.<REGION>.amazonaws.com/dev
{"hello": "world"}
```

The logic and the web interface of the application are in the app.py file. The example app.py automatically generated as a skeleton by Chalice is similar to what you see in the following listing.

Listing 13.5 app.py generated by Chalice (Python)

```
from chalice import Chalice

app = Chalice(app_name='greetingsOnDemand')

@app.route('/')
def index():
    return {'hello': 'world'}
```

> This annotation is linking the logic of the index() function to the "/" resource if the API.

This app returns a JSON-wrapped {'hello': 'world'} when calling the API endpoint root "/". By default, the HTTP GET method is used, but you can specify other methods, such as POST. People familiar with the Flask or Bottle microframeworks in Python will find the syntax familiar. You can make the routing more dynamic using parameters as part of the URL, and return a customized greeting adding a "route" for "/greet/…", noted in bold in the following listing.

Listing 13.6 app.py customized to return a custom greeting by name (Python)

```
from chalice import Chalice

app = Chalice(app_name='greetingsOnDemand')

@app.route('/')
def index():
    return {'hello': 'world'}
```

```
@app.route('/greet/{name}')
def hello_name(name):
    return {'hello': name}
```

> {name} parameter taken
> from the URL and passed
> to hello_name()

Change the `app.py` code to that shown in listing 13.6 and update the API using `chalice deploy` again, getting a new output that confirms the update of the Lambda function and the API Gateway configuration to answer to the new route:

```
Updating IAM policy.
Updating lambda function...
Regen deployment package...
Sending changes to lambda.
Lambda deploy done.
API Gateway rest API already found.
Deleting root resource id
Done deleting existing resources.
Deploying to: dev
https://<ENDPOINT>.execute-api.<REGION>.amazonaws.com/dev/
```

You can now try the new route using `curl` or a web browser, as before. For example, using `curl`

```
curl https://<ENDPOINT>.execute-api.<REGION>.amazonaws.com/dev/greet/John
{"hello": "John"}
```

With Chalice, you also have quick and easy access to the Lambda function logs stored by CloudWatch; for example, you can see the latest logs using this command in a project directory:

```
chalice logs
```

To deploy in a different API Gateway stage than dev, you can add a different stage name at the end of the deploy command, and Chalice will automatically create the new stage for you; for example

```
chalice deploy prod
```

And the result would be

```
Updating IAM policy.
Updating lambda function...
Regen deployment package...
Sending changes to lambda.
Lambda deploy done.
API Gateway rest API already found.
Deleting root resource id
Done deleting existing resources.
Deploying to: prod
https://<ENDPOINT>.execute-api.<REGION>.amazonaws.com/prod/
```

TIP Project-specific configuration is stored in the `.chalice` subdirectory in the project folder (notice the starting "dot" to make the directory hidden in UNIX/Linux environments). There, for example, you can change the default API Gateway stage stored in the config.json file.

To download the Chalice source code, use it with `virtualenv` (a tool to create isolated Python environments). To find more examples and updated information on the current status of the project, go to https://github.com/awslabs/chalice.

13.5.2 *Apex serverless architecture*

Apex is a framework that makes it easy to build, deploy, and manage AWS Lambda functions. It supports all native runtimes (Node.js, Python, and Java) and allows you to use languages that aren't supported natively by AWS Lambda, such as Golang,[1] through the use of a Node.js wrapper function automatically introduced into the build.

The most important features of Apex are how it can improve development and deployment workflows; for example, for testing functions, rolling back deployments, viewing metrics, and tailing logs.

You can start installing Apex on macOS, Linux, or OpenBSD with the following commands (you may need to add "sudo" before the "sh" command if your user can't write on "/usr/local"):

```
curl https://raw.githubusercontent.com/apex/apex/master/install.sh | sh
```

TIP You can find a Windows binary on the Apex website at http://apex.run.

To create your first functions, use the following lines:

```
mkdir test-apex && cd test-apex
apex init
```

With Apex, you have an interactive output to create your project:

Type the name of your project. It should be machine-friendly because it's used to prefix your functions in Lambda:

```
Project name: test
```

---

[1] For more information on the Go Programming Language, please see https://golang.org.

Enter an optional description of your project:

```
Project description: Just a Test

[+] creating IAM test_lambda_function role
[+] creating IAM test_lambda_logs policy
[+] attaching policy to lambda_function role.
[+] creating ./project.json
[+] creating ./functions
```

Setup is complete, so deploy those functions:

```
$ apex deploy
```

You can proceed with deployment as suggested by the interactive script:

```
apex deploy
```

- creating function   function=hello
- created alias current   function=hello version=1
- function created   function=hello name=test_hello version=1

You can now invoke and test your newly created Lambda function:

```
apex invoke hello

{"hello":"world"}
```

You can see all available options (and features) with apex help. You can use the previous options to do the following:

- See the list of functions using apex list, or recent logs using apex logs
- Roll back a deployment to the previous function version, using apex rollback
- Delete the function, with apex delete
- Get the Apex documentation, using apex docs

For more information and examples on the Apex project, visit the following links:

- http://apex.run for the project home page
- https://github.com/apex/apex for the open-source project

13.5.3 *Serverless Framework*

The Serverless Framework, formerly known as JAWS, is an application framework for building web, mobile, and IoT (Internet of Things) apps powered by AWS Lambda, AWS API Gateway, and in the future, tools from other providers.

Since its origin, the Serverless Framework has been designed to scale from a single Lambda function to a complex Web API using multiple Lambda functions and different API Gateway endpoints. It's also designed to be extensible via a plugin system. You can replace or extend every plugin.

> **TIP** Compared with Chalice and Apex, the Serverless Framework is designed to support more complex applications. This makes its initial learning curve steeper, but you can use a broader platform and ecosystem.

To install the Serverless Framework, you can do the following:

```
npm install -g serverless
```

> **TIP** Depending on your Node.js installation, you may need to prefix the `npm` command with `sudo`.

The Serverless Framework supports Node.js, Python, and Java. You can choose which runtime to use for this quick example.

To create the sample service in Node.js, use the `aws-nodejs` template, as in the following command:

```
serverless create --template aws-nodejs –path my-service
```

As an alternative, to create the sample service in Python, use the `aws-python` template:

```
serverless create --template aws-python –path my-service
```

The following output confirms the creation of the service:

```
Serverless: Creating new Serverless service...

 _____                 __
|         |   .-----.----.--.--.-----.----|   .-----.-----.-----.
|   |__|  | -_|   _|  |  |  | -_|   _|   _|   | -_|_   --|_   --|
|_____|   |_____|__|   \__/|____|__|  |_|   |_|____|_____|_____|
|   |     |                  The Serverless Application Framework
|   |     |                        serverless.com, v1.0.0-beta.2
|   -------'

Serverless: Successfully created service in the current directory
Serverless: with template: "aws-<RUNTIME>"
Serverless: NOTE: Please update the "service" property in serverless.yml with
your service name
```

You can now proceed to deploy the service by entering the project path and using the deploy command:

```
serverless deploy
```

The output highlights the steps on AWS to implement the service:

```
Serverless: Creating Stack...
Serverless: Checking stack creation progress...
......
Serverless: Stack successfully created.
Serverless: Zipping service...
Serverless: Uploading .zip file to S3...
```

```
Serverless: Updating Stack...
Serverless: Checking stack update progress...
...............
Serverless: Deployment successful!

Service Information
service: aws-<RUNTIME>
stage: dev
region: <REGION>
endpoints:
  None
functions:
  aws-<RUNTIME>-dev-hello:
arn:aws:lambda:<REGION>:<AWS_ACCOUNT_ID>:function:aws-<RUNTIME>-dev-hello
```

You can now invoke the Lambda function (whether using Node.js or Python) as part of the service:

```
serverless invoke --function hello

{
    "message": "Go Serverless v1.0! Your function executed successfully!",
    "event": {}
}
```

To clean up your account, you can use

```
serverless remove

Serverless: Getting all objects in S3 bucket...
Serverless: Removing objects in S3 bucket...
Serverless: Removing Stack...
Serverless: Checking stack removal progress...
.....
Serverless: Resource removal successful!
```

For more information and examples on the Serverless Framework, see

- http://serverless.com for the project home page
- https://github.com/serverless/serverless for the open-source project

13.6   *Simple serverless testing*

Everything can be automated on AWS, and Lambda functions are no exception. You have multiple ways to automate your tests—for example, building scripts that use the AWS CLI (or any AWS SDK, such as that for Python or Ruby) to automate your tests and compare your results with the expected outcome.

To help you understand how easy that is and to kick start your imagination, consider the following: among the blueprints that are suggested when you create a new Lambda function from the web console, there's a lambda-test-harness template (Node.js only, but you can test Python functions and then easily prepare your own Python equivalent when you understand how it works). You can use this template to run unit or load tests on Lambda functions. Isn't using a Lambda function to test other Lambda functions an interesting idea?

First, create a new Lambda function from the web console and select `lambda-test-harness` from the available blueprints. Give the function a name (for example, `lambdaTest`) and look at the code, which I copied to listing 13.7. The function needs an IAM role that allows it to invoke the Lambda function (`lambda:InvokeFunction` to test) and, in the case of unit tests, to write results to a DynamoDB table that you must create (`dynamodb:PutItem`).

Listing 13.7   `lambdaTest` (Node.js)

```
'use strict';

let AWS = require('aws-sdk');
let doc = require('dynamodb-doc');

let lambda = new AWS.Lambda({ apiVersion: '2015-03-31' });
let dynamo = new doc.DynamoDB();

const asyncAll = (opts) => {                    ◁─┐  Utility function to
    let i = -1;                                    │  asynchronously run a given
    const next = () => {                           │  function mutiple times, used
        i++;                                       │  in case of load test
        if (i === opts.times) {
            opts.done();
            return;
        }
        opts.fn(next, i);
    };
    next();
};
const unit = (event, callback) => {          ◁─┐  Function used in
    const lambdaParams = {                      │  case of unit tests
        FunctionName: event.function,
        Payload: JSON.stringify(event.event)
    };
    lambda.invoke(lambdaParams, (err, data) => {  ◁─┐  Invoke the Lambda
        if (err) {                                   │  function to test.
            return callback(err);
        }
        // Write result to Dynamo
        const dynamoParams = {
            TableName: event.resultsTable,
            Item: {
                testId: event.testId,
                iteration: event.iteration || 0,
                result: data.Payload,
                passed:
    !JSON.parse(data.Payload).hasOwnProperty('errorMessage')
            }
        };
        dynamo.putItem(dynamoParams, callback);   ◁─┐  Store result of the unit
    });                                              │  test on DynamoDB
};
```

```
const load = (event, callback) => {
    const payload = event.event;
    asyncAll({
        times: event.iterations,
        fn: (next, i) => {
            payload.iteration = i;
            const lambdaParams = {
                FunctionName: event.function,
                InvocationType: 'Event',
                Payload: JSON.stringify(payload)
            };
            lambda.invoke(lambdaParams, (err, data) => next());
        },
        done: () => callback(null, 'Load test complete')
    });
};

const ops = {
    unit: unit,
    load: load
};

exports.handler = (event, context, callback) => {
    if (ops.hasOwnProperty(event.operation)) {
        ops[event.operation](event, callback);
    } else {
        callback(`Unrecognized operation "${event.operation}"`);
    }
};
```

> **Function used in case of load tests, using the asyncAll utility function previously defined**

The idea is to pass an event that contains all the information required to run unit, or load, tests on another Lambda function as input to the lambdaTest function.

Suppose you want to run a unit test on the greetingsOnDemand function, providing a name as input. Using the JSON syntax you used before, the greetingsOnDemand is expecting an event containing the following. For example:

```
{ "name": "John" }
```

To run the unit test, you should pass the following event, specifying all necessary information, as input to the lambdaTest function to execute the test. For example:

```
{
  "operation": "unit",
  "function": "greetingsOnDemand",
  "event": { "name": "John" },
  "resultsTable": "myResultTable",
  "testId": "myTest123"
}
```

Results are stored in a DynamoDB table that you create (remember to give permissions to the function to write). You can customize the test in the passed attribute, stored in the DynamoDB table, to match your specific use case. Currently, the lambdaTest function checks for an error message in the payload returned by the function invocation. The optional `testId` can be used to differentiate multiple tests in the same table.

To run a load testing with 50 invocations of the previous functions, you need to change the operation to load and add the number of iterations you need (you don't need the DynamoDB table anymore). For example:

```
{
  "operation": "load",
  "iterations": 50,
  "function": "greetingsOnDemand",
  "event": { "name": "John" }
}
```

In the case of a load test, you can look for performance results in the Lambda or in the CloudWatch console.

> **TIP** To test HTTPS endpoints created with the Amazon API Gateway, you can use any web testing tool supporting HTTPS. Optionally, you can customize the `lambdaTest` function to support HTTPS requests instead of Lambda invocations; for example, using the "https" Node.js module.

Summary

In this chapter, you learned how development and testing of a serverless application can benefit from the advanced features of AWS Lambda or specific frameworks that have been developed to simplify and automate all the necessary steps that those new technologies require.

In particular, you learned how to do the following:

- Use versions and aliases with Lambda functions
- Use function logs to simplify debugging
- Use a few of the most popular serverless frameworks and understand their approach to development and testing
- Use Lambda functions to execute unit and load tests of other Lambda functions

In the next chapter you'll move on to deployments to bring your functions in production. Automation will be an important focus again, especially to support a continuous integration process.

EXERCISE

1 Create a `testMe` Lambda function that always returns a fixed string. For example, "Test Me." You can use Node.js or Python, as you prefer. Create three versions of the `testMe` function, returning a different output for each—for example "Test Me One," "Test Me Two," and "Test Me Three." Invoke all three versions using the AWS CLI.

2   Create three aliases ("dev," "test," and "prod") for the testMe function, pointing to the previous three versions; "dev" should point to the newest, "prod" to the oldest. Invoke all three aliases using the AWS CLI.

3   Run 10 asynchronous executions of the testMe function using the lambdaTest function introduced in this chapter. What is the input event for the lambda-Test function?

4   Use the lambdaTest function to test the default result of the greetings-OnDemand function, when an empty event is given as input, writing the result in a defaultResults DynamoDB table you already created. What is the input event for the lambdaTest function?

Solution

1   The testMe function in Node.js is

```
exports.handler = (event, context, callback) => {
    callback(null, 'Test Me');
};
```

In Python the testMe function is

```
def lambda_handler(event, context):
    return 'Test Me'
```

To create multiple versions, save the new edited code and then publish a new version from the Actions menu of the Lambda console. Every time you want to edit the function, go back to the latest ($LATEST) version.

Using the AWS CLI, you can publish a new version (based on the current content of the $LATEST version) with

```
aws lambda publish-version --function-name testMe --description newVersion
```

To invoke the three versions using the AWS CLI, you can use

```
aws lambda invoke --function-name testMe:1 output1.txt
aws lambda invoke --function-name testMe:2 output2.txt
aws lambda invoke --function-name testMe:3 output3.txt
```

From the Actions menu of the Lambda console, create the three aliases. Using the AWS CLI, you can invoke the version specified by the aliases using

```
aws lambda invoke --function-name testMe:dev output_dev.txt
aws lambda invoke --function-name testMe:test output_test.txt
aws lambda invoke --function-name testMe:prod output_prod.txt
```

2 You can use this event:

```
{
  "operation": "load",
  "iterations": 10,
  "function": "testMe",
  "event": {}
}
```

3 You can use this event:

```
{
  "operation": "unit",
  "function": " greetingsOnDemand ",
  "event": {},
  "resultsTable": " defaultResults "
}
```

Automating deployment

This chapter covers

- Using Amazon S3 to store the code of Lambda functions and trigger an automatic deployment
- Using AWS CloudFormation to manage deployments as code
- Managing deployments for multiregion architectures

In the previous chapter, you learned how to improve development and testing using advanced AWS Lambda features and frameworks that simplify the programming experience.

Now you'll see how to automate deployment of Lambda functions using tools and services such as AWS CloudFormation templates and Amazon S3 buckets to host your code.

14.1 Storing code on Amazon S3

You used Amazon S3 multiple times in the examples in this book to store different kinds of information, such as pictures or HTML files. In the same way, you can store the ZIP file of a Lambda function on an S3 bucket.

To simplify deployment, AWS Lambda supports the deployment of a Lambda function straight from a ZIP file stored on Amazon S3. In this way, you don't need to upload and send the ZIP file when creating or updating the code of a Lambda function. You can use any available tool (such as the S3 console, the AWS CLI, or any third-party tool supporting Amazon S3) to upload the ZIP file to an S3 bucket, and then call the `CreateFunction` or `UpdateFunctionCode` Lambda API to use the S3 object as the source of the function code. See figure 14.1.

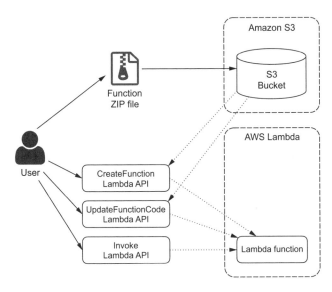

Figure 14.1 After you upload the ZIP file containing the function code to Amazon S3, you can use the web console, the AWS CLI or SDKs, or the Lambda API to create a new function or update an existing function to use the code in the ZIP file. After that, you can invoke the function as usual.

You could use the Lambda web console and point the source code to a file on Amazon S3. But to prepare ourselves for a more automated approach, let's use the AWS CLI to upload the `greeetingsOnDemand` function (which we've used multiple times during this book) and create and then update the function code.

> **NOTE** I use Node.js code here, but what you're doing doesn't depend on the actual runtime, unless you're not in some specific configuration, and applies to Python as well.

First, you need to create a bucket (or reuse one you already have) for hosting the ZIP files that contains the following function code:

```
aws s3 mb s3://<BUCKET>
```

> **TIP** Remember that bucket names are a globally unique resource, and you need to find one that's available; otherwise bucket creation will fail. For example, you can replace "danilop" with a common username you choose.

Create an empty directory and put the code of the greeetingsOnDemand function (as in the following listing) in a single file called index.js.

> **Listing 14.1   index.js (Node.js) for the greeetingsOnDemand function**

```
console.log('Loading function');

exports.handler = (event, context, callback) => {
    console.log('Received event:',
        JSON.stringify(event, null, 2));
    console.log('name =', event.name);
    var name = '';
    if ('name' in event) {
        name = event['name'];
    } else {
        name = "World";
    }
    var greetings = 'Hello ' + name + '!';
    console.log(greetings);
    callback(null, greetings);
};
```

This function doesn't have any dependencies, so you don't need to use npm to install any modules. From within the directory, use any ZIP tool to create a compressed archive of the code (containing a single file in this case). For example:

```
zip -r ../greetingsOnDemand-v1 .
```

> **TIP**   Note that I included a version identifier as part of the ZIP file name. This is a good practice to avoid confusion when you work with multiple versions of the same function. However, linking this versioning to Lambda function versions and aliases is up to you and isn't managed automatically by the platform.

Upload the file to the S3 bucket you created. You can add the code/ prefix to use only that part of the bucket for code and leave the rest of it available for different use cases, as in the following command:

```
aws s3 cp greetingsOnDemand-v1.zip s3://<BUCKET>/code/
```

Now you can create the Lambda function using the web console (you need to specify that the code is on Amazon S3) or using the AWS CLI. For example:

```
aws lambda create-function  \
    --function-name anotherGreetingsOnDemand \
    --code S3Bucket=<BUCKET>,S3Key=code/greetingsOnDemand-v1.zip \
    --runtime nodejs4.3 \
    --role arn:aws:iam::123412341234:role/lambda_basic_execution \
    --handler index.handler
```

WARNING You need to replace the bucket name and the IAM role ARN in the previous command. As for the IAM role ARN, you can use the one for the basic execution role that you created at the beginning of this book for the `greetingsOnDemand` function. Look for the role in the IAM console, or look using the AWS CLI with `aws iam list-roles`

TIP The value of the `--handler` option is `<file name without extension .function name>`, so `index.handler` works if you used index.js as the file name. If you used a different file name, change it accordingly.

Let's see how you can use the same approach to update the function code. Change something in the function code (for example, replace "Hello" with "Goodbye"), and then create a new ZIP file and upload it on S3. For example

```
zip ../greetingsOnDemand-v2 . -r
aws s3 cp greetingsOnDemand-v2.zip s3://<BUCKET>/code/
```

NOTE I used a different name (v2) for the ZIP file to differentiate this version from the first so I don't overwrite the previous version. This practice leaves the first version available in case I need to inspect the code or rollback the code in production.

To update the function code from the Lambda console, select the "Code" panel and type the new coordinates of the ZIP file on Amazon S3. You can use the AWS CLI similarly to how you created the function, this time using the `update-function-code` option, as in the following code:

```
aws lambda update-function-code \
    --function-name anotherGreetingsOnDemand \
    --s3-bucket <BUCKET> --s3-key code/greetingsOnDemand-v2.zip
```

To publish a new version of the Lambda function, you can add `--publish` at the end of the previous command.

TIP If you implement a continuous integration process to produce the ZIP files of your Lambda functions, you can use the synchronization functionality of the AWS CLI (try `aws s3 sync help` for more info) as the final step to copy the output of the build process to Amazon S3.

14.2 *Event-driven serverless continuous deployment*

If you followed all the steps here from the beginning of this chapter, you're probably thinking, "Okay, I can upload to Amazon S3, but where's the automation?"

What's interesting with this approach is that you can use the S3 bucket where you upload the ZIP file with the function code to trigger another Lambda function—a function that can take care of creating or updating the `greetingsOnDemand` function—and building an event-driven, serverless, continuous-deployment process (figure 14.2).

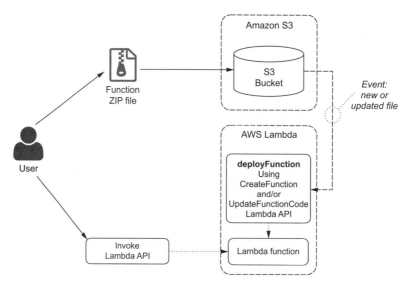

Figure 14.2 A serverless, event-driven, continuous-deployment process using Amazon S3 as the trigger for a deploying Lambda function that can keep another Lambda function automatically updated

In this way, every time a ZIP file with a new version of the code is uploaded to Amazon S3, you can trigger a new deployment. To make it clean, you can use a specific prefix such as code/ for the trigger, and react to uploads only in specific folders. The deployFunction can use the same Lambda API that we used through the AWS CLI (UpdateFunctionCode) and can be written in any supported runtime, such as Node.js and Python.

In Node.js, using the AWS SDK for JavaScript, you can use the updateFunction-Code() method of the Lambda service object, as shown in the following listing.

Listing 14.2 updateFunctionCode (Node.js)

```
var lambda = new AWS.Lambda();
var params = {
  FunctionName: 'anotherGreetingsOnDemand',
  S3Bucket: 'danilop-functions',
  S3Key: 'code/greetingsOnDemand-v2.zip'
  Publish: true,
};
lambda.updateFunctionCode(params, function(err, data) {
  if (err) console.log(err, err.stack);
  else     console.log(data);
});
```

The parameters required to update the code of a Lambda function

Publishing a new version of the function. If you don't want a new version you can use "false."

The actual call to the Lambda API to update the function call

In Python, using Boto version 3, the AWS SDK for Python, you can use the update_function_code() method of the Lambda client, as shown in the next listing.

Listing 14.3 updateFunctionCode **(Python)**

```
awslambda = boto3.client('lambda')                          The call to the Lambda API
                                                            to update the function call
response = awslambda.update_function_code(      ◁─┘
    FunctionName='anotherGreetingsOnDemand',        The parameters required
    S3Bucket='danilop-functions',                   to update the code of a
    S3Key='code/greetingsOnDemand-v2.zip',          Lambda function
    Publish=True                          ◁─┐
)                                           Publishing a new version of the
                                            function; if you don't want a new
                                            version you can use "false."
```

When using these methods in a deploying Lambda function, you can get the S3 bucket and key of the ZIP file from the input event. A single function can be triggered by different S3 buckets and deploy code uploaded in those buckets and with different file names.

Optionally, you can use part of the S3 key (prefix or file name) to bring specific information to the deploying function, such as the stage (dev, test, or prod) to be impacted by the deployment. For example:

- deploy/dev/function.zip to deploy a function, publish a new version, and move the dev alias to this version
- deploy/prod/function.zip to deploy a function, publish a new version, and move the prod alias to this version

In this section I only scratched the surface of the possibilities of using Lambda functions to deploy other Lambda functions, triggered by events such as a ZIP file uploaded to Amazon S3. You can use this or similar deployment patterns to integrate AWS Lambda in your deployment pipeline.

> **TIP** If the size of your function grows beyond a few megabytes, uploading to S3 is a much better option than uploading the code during the Lambda function creation or update. For large functions, or if you're using an unreliable network during uploads, you can also use S3 multipart uploads to recover from transfer errors. In this way, you can upload your function in smaller parts, also in parallel, and retransmit a single part in case you have an error during the upload. For more information on S3 multipart upload, see https://docs.aws.amazon.com/AmazonS3/latest/dev/uploadobjusingmpu.html.

14.3   *Deploying with AWS CloudFormation*

When managing an IT infrastructure, automation is key in simplifying operations and reducing the possibility of human error. Over the years, multiple tools were introduced to describe management and configuration steps and how to apply them to an infrastructure automatically. For example, you can look at Chef,[1] Ansible,[2] or Fabric.[3]

With cloud computing, IT resources can be managed using an API, and implementing automation is much easier. But describing what you want to build and how to update it can still be complex if you have to use a general-purpose programming language.

With AWS CloudFormation, AWS introduced a declarative language based on a YAML[4] (or JSON) syntax that describes the AWS services you want to use and how to configure them up to application deployment. In this way, all the operational steps with the AWS CLI you did in the previous sections can be replaced by a single text file or a collection of text files.

> **TIP**   This is the idea behind managing infrastructure as code and provides advantages; for example, the option to use coding best practices such as versioning and testing with infrastructure management.

You use this language to write a `template`—a text file that provides all the necessary information to implement a set of resources on AWS and prepare the infrastructure for your functions and applications. AWS CloudFormation can use a template to implement a `stack` of actual resources. In a way, a template is like a recipe and a stack is an implementation of that recipe.

> **NOTE**   In this section, I focus on AWS CloudFormation support for AWS Lambda. For more information and a broader coverage of other AWS services, see https://aws.amazon.com/cloudformation.

Let's start with a basic Lambda function that will always return a fixed "Hello World" string. You can call the function `helloWorldFromCF`. Because the function is small, let's put all the source code of the function within the template. You can see an example in listings 14.4 (YAML) and 14.5 (JSON).

---

[1] Chef is an open-source software agent that automates your infrastructure management and configuration. For more information, see https://www.chef.io/chef.

[2] Ansible has a different approach for IT automation, with no agents to install. For more information, see https://www.ansible.com.

[3] Fabric is a Python library and CLI tool for using SSH for application deployment or systems administration tasks. For more information, see http://www.fabfile.org.

[4] YAML is a data serialization standard that is (according to my personal opinion) more human-readable than JSON. For more information, see http://yaml.org.

Listing 14.4 helloWorld_template (YAML) for AWS CloudFormation

The resources to be created by this CloudFormation template: a Lambda function in this case, but you may add more functions, S3 buckets, or DynamoDB tables to have everything your application needs in the same template.

The resource properties

```
Resources:
  HelloWorldFunction:
    Type: AWS::Lambda::Function          The resource type; a Lambda
    Properties:                          function in this case
      Code:
        ZipFile: |                                              The function
          exports.handler = (event, context, callback) => {      code,
            callback(null, 'Hello World from AWS CloudFormation!');  provided
          };                                                       inline in the
      Description:                                                  template in
        A sample Hello World function deployed by AWS CloudFormation  this case
      FunctionName: helloWorldFromCF
      Handler: index.handler
      MemorySize: 256
      Role: arn:aws:iam::123412341234:role/lambda_basic_execution
      Runtime: nodejs4.3
      Timeout: 10
```

All the usual parameters required to create a new Lambda function, similar to what you already saw in the web console or the AWS CLI. Remember to update the IAM role ARN.

Listing 14.5 helloWorld_template (JSON) for AWS CloudFormation

The resources to be created by this CloudFormation template: a Lambda function in this case, but you may add more functions, S3 buckets, or DynamoDB tables to have everything your application needs in the same template.

The resource properties

```
{
  "Resources" : {                        The resource type; a Lambda
    "HelloWorldFunction": {               function in this case
      "Type" : "AWS::Lambda::Function",
      "Properties" : {                    The function code, provided inline
        "Code" : {                        in the template in this case
          "ZipFile" : { "Fn::Join": ["\n", [
            "exports.handler = (event, context, callback) => {",
            "  callback(null, 'Hello World from AWS CloudFormation!');",
            "};"
          ]]}
        },
        "Description" :
        "A sample Hello World function deployed by AWS CloudFormation",
        "FunctionName" : "helloWorldFromCF",
        "Handler" : "index.handler",
        "MemorySize" : 256,
        "Role" : "arn:aws:iam::123412341234:role/lambda_basic_execution",
        "Runtime" : "nodejs4.3",
        "Timeout" : 10
      }
    }
  }
}
```

All the usual parameters required to create a new Lambda function, similar to what you already saw in the web console or the AWS CLI. Remember to update the IAM role ARN.

Using the Fn::Join CloudFormation intrinsic function to put the inline code in multiple strings and make it more human readable

Now go to the AWS CloudFormation web console in the Management Tools section. If you don't have a CloudFormation stack already created, you're presented with a page similar to figure 14.3. From here, you can design a new template graphically. Use a tool called CloudFormer to create a template based on your existing resources (this is useful if you want to replicate with AWS CloudFormation what you already did manually), or create a new stack. Choose the option of creating a new stack.

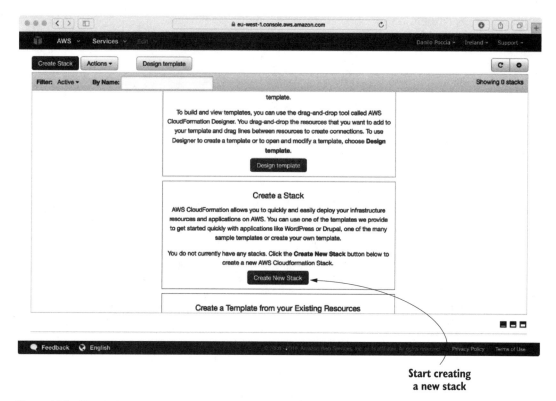

Figure 14.3   The AWS CloudFormation console provides options to create a new stack, design a template graphically, or use the CloudFormer tool to create a template from your existing resources.

You can now choose the template to implement the new stack you're creating (figure 14.4). You can look at sample templates, specify a template uploaded in an S3 bucket, or upload a template that you have on your local disk.

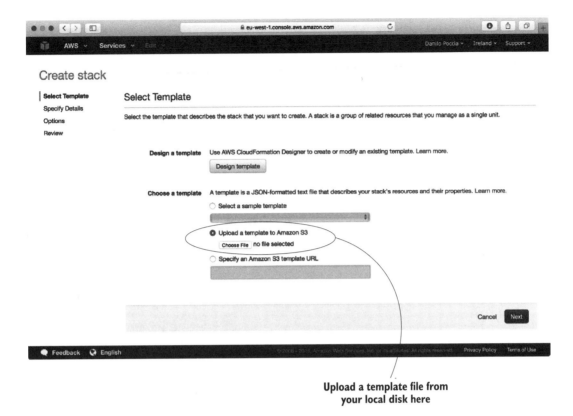

Upload a template file from
your local disk here

Figure 14.4   To start the creation of a new CloudFormation stack, you can choose from sample templates, a local file, or a file already uploaded to Amazon S3.

Choose your favorite syntax, YAML or JSON, and create locally on your computer either the helloWorld_template.yaml file or the helloWorld_template.json file from listings 14.4 and 14.5. Upload the file you created.

Name your new stack (for example, "MyFirstLambdaStack"), and click Next (figure 14.5).

You can skip the step with the option to add tags and configure advance settings for now. You're then presented with a recap of all your choices so far. If everything is okay, proceed to create the stack. You'll see a list of stacks and a list of events, similar

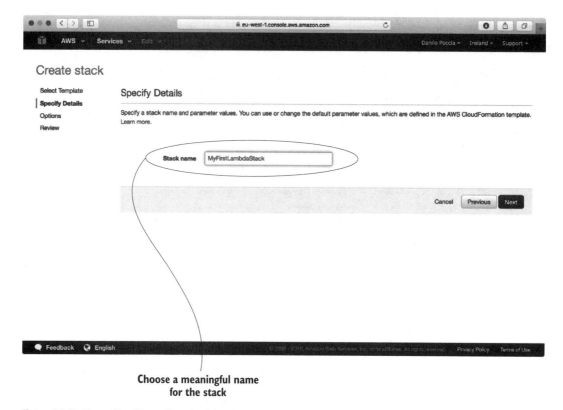

Choose a meaningful name
for the stack

Figure 14.5 Every CloudFormation stack has a name that you can use from the web console or programmatically from the AWS CLI and SDKs to access its information and update or delete it.

to figure 14.6. This is the main CloudFormation console, where you can see all the stacks in the upper section (one in this case), and all the information on the selected stack (such as the events, the template, and the resources that have been created) in the lower section.

After a time, the status of the stack transitions to "CREATE_COMPLETE" and the color changes to green. If errors exist, the default behavior of AWS CloudFormation is to rollback all changes. You can use the information in the Events tab to understand what happened and fix the error. If you get an error such as "Cross-account pass role is not allowed," you probably didn't update the role ARN to use your AWS account ID.

TIP If you need more analysis, you can disable automatic rollback for this stack and leave the resources created before the error occurs available for further diagnosis.

You can now go to the Lambda console and look for the `helloWorldFromCF` function that was created by AWS CloudFormation. You can test the function from the console to see whether you receive the "Hello World" message as output.

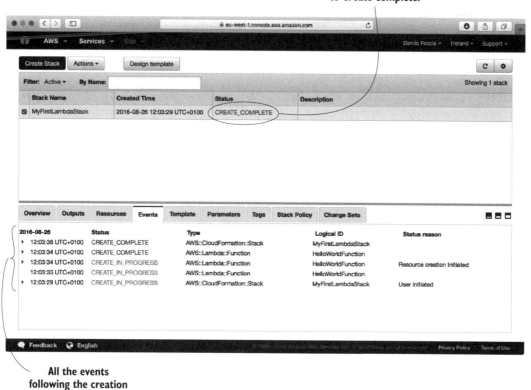

If everything is correct, after some time the status will change to Create Complete.

All the events following the creation of the stack are here.

Figure 14.6 In the top half of the screen you have the list of the CloudFormation stack, the one you created. In the bottom half, you have multiple tabs showing, among other things, the events generated by the creation of the stack and the resources created.

CloudFormation stacks are interesting because you can also update them by providing an updated template (or changing the input parameters, which I don't cover in this tutorial). To test an update, change the code section in the template file to have a different output in the final callback of the function (for example, replace "Hello" with "Goodbye"). Try to avoid nonstandard ASCII characters that could create problems with the JSON syntax of the template.

Now, from the stack list in the CloudFormation console, select the stack you created and, in the Actions menu, choose to update the stack. You have options similar to what was shown in figure 14.4. Choose to upload the updated template file.

When the update completes and the status of the stack is green again, go back to the Lambda function and test the updated function to see that the result of the function is different than before and is the one you wrote in the updated template.

If the Lambda function code is long or you have dependencies that require you to create a ZIP file to include them, using inline code in the CloudFormation template isn't an option because you can't express the function as a plain text file. Another option is to point CloudFormation to a ZIP file already uploaded to Amazon S3.

Let's use the ZIP file of the greetingsOnDemand function that you uploaded to Amazon S3 in chapter 13. You need to update the bucket name, the ARN of the IAM role, and maybe the object key in the template in listing 14.6 (YAML) or 14.7 (JSON).

Listing 14.6   greetingsOnDemand_template (YAML) for AWS CloudFormation

```
Resources:
  GreetingsOnDemandFunction:
    Type: AWS::Lambda::Function
    Properties:
      Code:
        S3Bucket: danilop-functions
        S3Key: code/greetingsOnDemand-v1.zip
      Description: Say your name and you'll be greeted
      FunctionName: greetingsOnDemandFromCF
      Handler: greetingsOnDemand.handler
      MemorySize: 256
      Role: arn:aws:iam::123412341234:role/lambda_basic_execution
      Runtime: nodejs4.3
      Timeout: 10
```

This time you don't put the code in the template, but in the reference (bucket, key) to a ZIP file uploaded to Amazon S3.

Listing 14.7   greetingsOnDemand_template (JSON) for AWS CloudFormation

```
{
  "Resources" : {
    "GreetingsOnDemandFunction": {
      "Type" : "AWS::Lambda::Function",
      "Properties" : {
        "Code" : {
          "S3Bucket" : "danilop-functions",
          "S3Key" : "code/greetingsOnDemand-v1.zip"
        },
        "Description" : "Say your name and you'll be greeted",
        "FunctionName" : "greetingsOnDemandFromCF",
        "Handler" : "greetingsOnDemand.handler",
        "MemorySize" : 256,
        "Role" : "arn:aws:iam::123412341234:role/lambda_basic_execution",
        "Runtime" : "nodejs4.3",
        "Timeout" : 10
      }
    }
  }
}
```

This time you don't put the code in the template, but in the reference (bucket, key) to a ZIP file uploaded to Amazon S3.

Verify that the S3 bucket and key in the template are correct. You can look at the S3 console, or use the AWS CLI. For example:

```
aws s3 ls s3://danilop-functions/code/greetingsOnDemand-v1.zip
```

Now use this template to create a new stack, as you did before. When this new stack is green and the resource creation is completed, you can go on the Lambda console to test the new function.

> **NOTE** I used a different name for the Lambda function than before (`greet-ingsOnDemandFromCF`), because if a function with the same name is already present, the stack creation would fail and return an error.

You can create and update a CloudFormation stack using the AWS CLI. The syntax is straightforward and you need to provide the same information as in the web console. For more information about the syntax, use these two commands:

```
aws cloudformation create-stack help
aws cloudformation update-stack help
```

Now you have an idea of how you can use AWS CloudFormation to automate the creation of a stack with multiple functions: list them one after the other in the JSON template.

Many more features that I don't mention here for the sake of time, such as stack parameters, can be useful for applying the same template in multiple use cases. For example, you can use the same template in development and test, and use different memory sizes (passing this value as a parameter) for your Lambda functions to reduce your development costs. My suggestion is to experiment with those features from the web console or the AWS CLI.

> **TIP** If you host the CloudFormation template on a managed source control system (such as GitHub or AWS CodeCommit), you can receive events from an update (for example, a `git commit`) and use those to trigger a deploying Lambda function to update the stack implemented by the template, building an event-driven, continuous-deployment process for your application, similar to what you did using Amazon S3 in the previous section of this chapter. The `git` branch can be used to decide which stack to update—for example, the production stack in the case of the `master` branch, or the test stack in the case of the `dev` branch.

14.4 *Multiregion deployments*

Large-scale deployments on AWS can use multiple AWS regions to minimize latency or increase availability. Amazon S3 makes it easy to automate multiregion deployments of Lambda functions with a few steps:

- The S3 bucket where you upload function code can use *cross-region replication* to replicate its content to an S3 bucket in another region.
- In each region, you can have a deploying Lambda function triggered by the new file in the S3 bucket, to apply the update locally.

For example, if you have a source bucket in the EU (Ireland) region, you can add the AWS region at the end of the bucket name, such as `danilop-functions-eu-west-1`.

This source bucket can replicate all changes to another S3 bucket in the Tokyo region, named `danilop-functions-ap-northeast-1`.

> **NOTE**   To enable automatic replication from the S3 console, create the two buckets and then select the source bucket. In the bucket properties tab, look for "Cross-Region Replication." You need to enable versioning for source and target buckets because that's a requirement for cross-region replication.

You can now upload the ZIP file containing the code of your function in your source region—for example, EU (Ireland)—and have the function automatically deployed in both regions, EU (Ireland) and Tokyo. See figure 14.7 for a description of the overall flow.

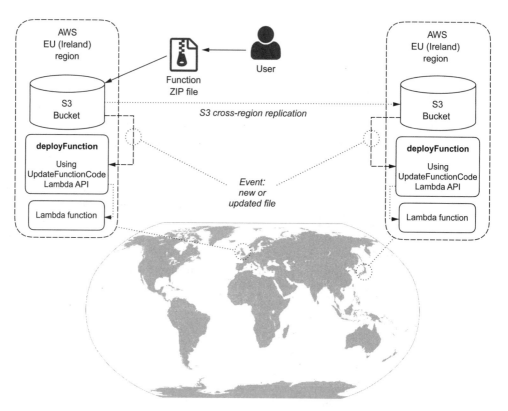

Figure 14.7   Multiregion, event-driven, serverless deployment implemented between the EU (Ireland) and Tokyo AWS regions, using S3 cross-region replication to replicate the ZIP file with the function code, and a local deployment function triggered by the new file on the S3 bucket to manage the update.

You can keep replication manual, for example, if you want to wait a few hours before updating a disaster recovery site in another region to reduce the possibility of replicating an error. In this case, you can schedule the execution of the AWS CLI to synchronize the content of the source bucket with the target bucket with a command such as the following:

```
aws s3 sync s3://source-bucket s3://target-bucket --source-region eu-west-1
--region ap-northeast-1
```

TIP Note that in the previous command synchronizing two buckets, you must add an argument explicitly indicating the source region.

Summary

In this chapter, you learned how to automate deployment, using Amazon S3 as the repository of your function code and AWS CloudFormation to use templates to describe what you want to build. In particular, you learned about

- Creating a Lambda function from code stored in an S3 bucket
- Using a deploying function to automatically update a Lambda function when new code is uploaded on Amazon S3
- Creating CloudFormation templates to describe the functions required by your application, and implementing those functions in a stack
- Using S3 cross-region replication to implement a multiregion, continuous-deployment process

In the next chapter, you'll learn how to use AWS Lambda for not only the business logic of your application, but also to automate the management of your server-based or serverless infrastructure on AWS.

EXERCISE

1 Suppose you have three versions of the code of a `helloWorld` function uploaded on Amazon S3 with the following URLs:

    ```
    s3://mybucket/code/helloWorld-v1.zip
    s3://mybucket/code/helloWorld-v2.zip
    s3://mybucket/code/helloWorld-v3.zip
    ```

    The function has already been created, and you want to use the AWS CLI to update the function three times, using the three ZIP files, each time creating a new version on AWS Lambda. What commands should you use?

2 Write a CloudFormation template that will use the three ZIP files from question 1, and create three different functions called `helloWorldOne`, `helloWorldTwo`, and `helloWorldThree`. Each ZIP file contains a single `hello.py` file. In that file, the function AWS Lambda should call is `say_hi()`. Use 512 MB of memory and 30 seconds timeout for all of them. Basic execution permissions, used in the other examples in this chapter, are enough.

Solution

1   Use the following three commands:

```
aws lambda update-function-code --function-name helloWorld \
    --s3-bucket mybucket --s3-key code/helloWorld-v1.zip --publish
aws lambda update-function-code --function-name helloWorld \
    --s3-bucket mybucket --s3-key code/helloWorld-v2.zip --publish
aws lambda update-function-code --function-name helloWorld \
    --s3-bucket mybucket --s3-key code/helloWorld-v3.zip –publish
```

2   Use the template in the next listing (YAML) or the final listing (JSON). You need to update the Role ARN with yours.

helloWorldThreeTimes_template (YAML) for AWS CloudFormation

```
Resources:
  HelloWorldOneFunction:
    Type: AWS::Lambda::Function
    Properties:
      Code:
        S3Bucket: mybucket
        S3Key: code/helloWorld-v1.zip
      Description: HelloWorld One
      FunctionName: helloWorldOne
      Handler: hello.say_hi
      MemorySize: 512
      Role: arn:aws:iam::123412341234:role/lambda_basic_execution
      Runtime: python
      Timeout: 30
  HelloWorldTwoFunction:
    Type: AWS::Lambda::Function
    Properties:
      Code:
        S3Bucket: mybucket
        S3Key: code/helloWorld-v2.zip
      Description: HelloWorld Two
      FunctionName: helloWorldTwo
      Handler: hello.say_hi
      MemorySize: 512
      Role: arn:aws:iam::123412341234:role/lambda_basic_execution
      Runtime: python
      Timeout: 30
HelloWorldThreeFunction:
  Type: AWS::Lambda::Function
  Properties:
    Code:
      S3Bucket: mybucket
      S3Key: code/helloWorld-v3.zip
    Description: HelloWorld Three
    FunctionName: helloWorldThree
    Handler: hello.say_hi
    MemorySize: 512
    Role: arn:aws:iam::123412341234:role/lambda_basic_execution
    Runtime: python
    Timeout: 30
```

helloWorldThreeTimes_template (JSON) for AWS CloudFormation

```json
{
  "Resources": {
    "HelloWorldOneFunction": {
      "Type": "AWS::Lambda::Function",
      "Properties": {
        "Code": {
          "S3Bucket": "mybucket",
          "S3Key": "code/helloWorld-v1.zip"
        },
        "Description": "HelloWorld One",
        "FunctionName": "helloWorldOne",
        "Handler": "hello.say_hi",
        "MemorySize": 512,
        "Role": "arn:aws:iam::123412341234:role/lambda_basic_execution",
        "Runtime": "python",
        "Timeout": 30
      }
    },
    "HelloWorldTwoFunction": {
      "Type": "AWS::Lambda::Function",
      "Properties": {
        "Code": {
          "S3Bucket": "mybucket",
          "S3Key": "code/helloWorld-v2.zip"
        },
        "Description": "HelloWorld Two",
        "FunctionName": "helloWorldTwo",
        "Handler": "hello.say_hi",
        "MemorySize": 512,
        "Role": "arn:aws:iam::123412341234:role/lambda_basic_execution",
        "Runtime": "python",
        "Timeout": 30
      }
    }
  },
  "HelloWorldThreeFunction": {
    "Type": "AWS::Lambda::Function",
    "Properties": {
      "Code": {
        "S3Bucket": "mybucket",
        "S3Key": "code/helloWorld-v3.zip"
      },
      "Description": "HelloWorld Three",
      "FunctionName": "helloWorldThree",
      "Handler": "hello.say_hi",
      "MemorySize": 512,
      "Role": "arn:aws:iam::123412341234:role/lambda_basic_execution",
      "Runtime": "python",
      "Timeout": 30
    }
  }
}
```

Automating infrastructure management

This chapter covers

- Using CloudWatch alarms to trigger Lambda functions to solve infrastructure issues
- Using Amazon SNS as a trigger for AWS Lambda
- Using CloudWatch events and Lambda functions to synchronize a DNS or a service discovery tool
- Using Lambda functions to process CloudWatch logs
- Using CloudWatch events to schedule management activities
- Designing a multiregion architecture using Amazon API Gateway, Lambda functions, and DynamoDB tables

In the previous chapter, you learned how to implement automatic deployment using Amazon S3 as the trigger of Lambda deploying functions, or using AWS CloudFormation to manage Lambda functions via a text file.

Now you'll apply what you learned in this book to a different area: infrastructure management. With a pure serverless architecture, you don't have much infrastructure to manage. You may still have to configure throughput provisioning to a DynamoDB table or shards for a Kinesis stream. But it's likely you'll have components that use virtual servers or load balancers that need to be managed.

Using AWS Lambda, you can automate how you manage alarms or process logs—steps that normally require human interactions. The idea here is to have a smarter architecture that can recover automatically in case of application or infrastructure errors.

15.1 *Reacting to alarms*

Managing an IT infrastructure has never been an easy task. You can have problems with your servers, the storage, or the network. It can be a software or hardware problem. It can be something related to your application, or a system driver used by the operating system. Cloud computing makes this easier because you can use APIs to monitor your infrastructure.

On AWS, Amazon CloudWatch is a broad service that can simplify and automate monitoring of the cloud resources and the applications you use. You already used CloudWatch Logs to monitor how Lambda functions work and see their logging information. Another important component of CloudWatch is metrics, which yield quantitative information about how you use a resource and which can be provided automatically by other AWS services, such as AWS Lambda or Amazon DynamoDB, or populated with custom values using the CloudWatch API.

For example, you can use CloudWatch metrics to monitor a Lambda function and know whether invocations return errors (and how many) or to understand how much of the provided throughput a DynamoDB table uses.

If you go to the CloudWatch web console, you can navigate multiple features by selecting them on the left. Start by selecting Metrics and look at the metrics that are displayed on the console, grouped by AWS services. You used Amazon DynamoDB in a few examples in the book, and if you select DynamoDB Metrics from the console, you can see much information at the table, index, or stream levels. Metrics are kept for two weeks, so if more time has passed since you used DynamoDB, there's a chance that you don't have any metrics left.

> **TIP** If you want to store metrics for more than two weeks, you can copy the values to a persistent data storage such as Amazon S3, keeping them as files or in a database such as Amazon Redshift, in a relational format.

To understand whether your application is working correctly, use Amazon CloudWatch to set up alarms that are triggered if one of the metrics you specify is outside the range of values you expect. For example, you can set the consumed read or write capacity of a DynamoDB table too close to the provisioned throughput. If you grow more with the usage, you can have DynamoDB calls throttled, slowing the speed of your application. Let's create an alarm that informs you if you approach your DynamoDB throughput limits.

In the CloudWatch console, select Alarms and then the Create Alarm button. In the DynamoDB Metrics, select Table Metrics. (If you don't have DynamoDB Metrics in the CloudWatch console, you can choose any other available metric to understand how creating an alarm works. This can happen if more than two weeks have passed since you last used Amazon DynamoDB. The name of the metric will be different, but the process is the same.) You now have a list of tables and metrics. For a table of your choice, select a row with `ConsumedReadCapacityUnits` by clicking the small box on the left (again, if you don't have that metric, chose another one to follow the flow). You can see a graph of that metric with a time range that you can customize. Click Next and type a name and a description for the alarm. For example, you can name the alarm `Check-Throughput` and add "Checking consumed throughput" as the description.

Suppose your provisioned throughput for the table is 100 capacity units (you probably have a much smaller value to stay in the free tier, but in production that's a reasonable value). Configure the alarm to trigger if the metric is greater than 80 (>=80). You're alerted when the throughput is at 80 out of 100, or 80% of what has been provisioned. In Actions, when the state is `ALARM`, you can send a notification to a list. You can create a new list and put your email address there. It's interesting to know that the list is an Amazon SNS topic.

> **NOTE** Amazon SNS is a notification service that can send notifications to multiple endpoints, including emails, HTTP listeners, or Mobile Push providers such as Apple and Google. For more information on Amazon SNS, see https://aws.amazon.com/sns/.

Amazon SNS is one of the triggers supported by AWS Lambda, so instead of receiving an email if an alarm is triggered (as in the default configuration of a CloudWatch Alarm), you can invoke a Lambda function and take automatic steps to correct or mitigate what's causing the alarm (figure 15.1). This is the core concept of *self-healing* architectures.

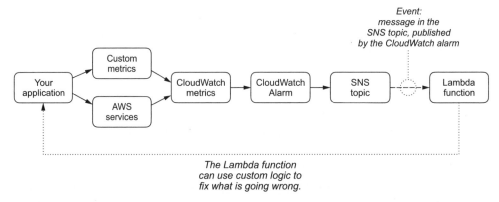

Figure 15.1   Metrics from your application can trigger CloudWatch alarms that will invoke a Lambda function via Amazon SNS. That function can try to understand and solve the issue automatically, implementing a self-healing architecture.

For example, if you approach the provisioned throughput of a DynamoDB table, you can increase it in the Lambda function. If you use little of your provisioned throughput, you can reduce it and save money. You have to set up a low limit alarm to trigger a Lambda function to reduce the provisioned throughput. This is how you implement an auto-scaling functionality for Amazon DynamoDB.

It's a little more complex than that because limits do exist for how often you can do that. Currently, you can increase the throughput as much and as often as you want, and you can decrease it up to four times per table per day. For more information on those limits, see https://docs.aws.amazon.com/amazondynamodb/latest/developer-guide/Limits.html.

> **TIP** You can find a few implementations of auto-scaling for Amazon DynamoDB created by AWS customers (using AWS Lambda or a custom script running on a server). For example, you can see https://github.com/channl/dynamodb-lambda-autoscale.

Another possible use case for managing alarms via Lambda functions is with Amazon RDS, the managed relational database service provided by AWS. You can have an alarm that tells you if the available space for your database goes below a threshold, for example 100MB, and use a Lambda function to automatically extend the space adding 1GB. If your database is bigger and growing quickly, you may want to use larger values for the alarm and the space increase.

Many possible use cases exist for using Lambda functions to react to CloudWatch alarms, and I don't want to write a long list here. Depending on which services you use in your AWS infrastructure and whether you added custom metrics for your application, try to think of what can go wrong and how you can manage that automatically using the AWS API to fix (or mitigate) the issue. For example, you can set up a CloudWatch alarm to automatically recover an EC2 instance if it becomes impaired due to an underlying hardware failure.

> **TIP** Amazon CloudWatch is a powerful tool, covering logs, metrics, alarms, and generic events happening on the AWS cloud. You can also create dashboards to have a centralized overview of how your application is doing. For an overview of all the features, I recommend that you start with https://aws.amazon.com/cloudwatch/.

15.2 Reacting to events

Another interesting feature of CloudWatch is events, which allow you to be informed of state changes in your AWS resources. Multiple sources are available, such as generic AWS API calls, EC2 instance state transitions (for example, from pending to running), or signing in to the AWS console. Similar to what we explored in the previous section for alarms, with CloudWatch events you can create rules that wait for an event to happen and add Lambda functions as targets triggered by those events.

An interesting use case is to listen for EC2 instance state transitions (such as instances that are started or stopped) and register (or deregister) the metadata of those instances in a repository, such as a DNS (you can use Amazon Route 53 for this). You can use this approach to automatically update a DNS with running instances.

Often load balancers are the entry point of an internal or external service. Using CloudWatch events, you can automatically register new load balancers created on AWS and update a service discovery tool (a DNS, or a more advanced tool such as Netflix Eureka or HashiCorp Consul). Having a service discovery in place, a tool where you can look up the endpoint of your services, is well suited for a microservice architecture, where you have by definition "a lot" of services to manage and you don't want to put service endpoints in static configuration files.

TIP If you use Amazon ECS for managing containers and services running on top of them, you can find a complete solution, using the approach I described to register/deregister ECS services, in this blog post at https:// aws.amazon.com/blogs/compute/service-discovery-an-amazon-ecs-reference-architecture/.

15.3 Processing logs in near real-time

When debugging Lambda functions, you learned how to use CloudWatch logs in the console, or via the AWS CLI. You can automate that in multiple ways (figure 15.2), including the following:

- By creating a metric filter that extracts information in the logs and publishes that as a CloudWatch metric. For example, this approach can be used to extract memory usage from all your Lambda function invocations and create a metric that shows how you're using memory over multiple invocations and an extended period of time.
- By streaming a log group to a Lambda function that can process those logs and do whatever you need with them. In this case, CloudWatch logs are the trigger of your Lambda function.

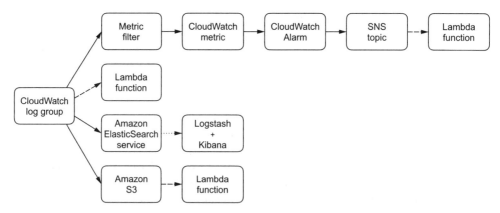

Figure 15.2 Possible ways to process CloudWatch logs automatically. In particular, you can trigger a Lambda function directly, via a metric filter that extracts information from the logs, or by storing the logs as a file on Amazon S3.

- By streaming a log group to the Amazon Elasticsearch Service, where you can use tools, such as Logstash and Kibana, to dive deeper on them. This option is in the Actions menu of the console.

- By exporting the logs to Amazon S3 and then using any tool that can read from an S3 bucket. You can also copy those files locally or in an EC2 instance using the S3 API or the AWS CLI. You can also let Amazon S3 trigger a Lambda function to process those logs when new files are put in the bucket.

All of these options are available in the CloudWatch logs console. If you select to stream a log group to the Amazon Elasticsearch Service (an option in the Actions menu), you use a Lambda function that's automatically provisioned for you to process the logs and write to the Elasticsearch cluster. You can use that function as a template to understand how to process logs and add your own logic to that.

15.4 Scheduling recurring activities

If you have an infrastructure to manage, especially if your application isn't 100% serverless, you may have to periodically execute a few housekeeping activities. For example:

- Take a daily snapshot of all the Elastic Block Store (EBS) volumes used by your EC2 instances. (You could limit that only to instances with a particular tag, such as "Backup=True".)

- Monthly you may want to delete older files from an S3 bucket. You can use S3 Object Lifecycle Management to do that, but sometimes the structure of file names and paths in your application may be more complex than what you can specify in the native S3 feature.

- Rotate security credentials used by your database once every three months.

Considering their low costs, Lambda functions are perfect for scheduling management tasks, but be sure that you can stay within the limits of the timeout of the function. For a few examples of schedulable activities, see figure 15.3.

For example, in chapter 5 in the face-detection example, we used a Lambda function to remove temporary files from the S3 folder where users can upload pictures

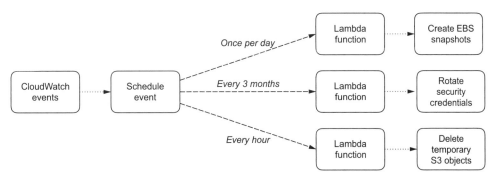

Figure 15.3 An example of activities that can be scheduled using CloudWatch events and executed using Lambda functions

that were immediately processed by the face-detecting function. In that case, you didn't need to wait one day—the minimum elapsed time for S3 Object Lifecycle Management—because Lambda functions could be scheduled more frequently; for example, every hour.

> **NOTE** Scheduled Lambda functions use CloudWatch events as triggers. Because function scheduling was released before CloudWatch events, that wasn't previously apparent from the console.

15.5 *Multiregion architectures and data synchronization*

In the previous chapter, you learned how to automate multiregion deployments with AWS Lambda, using S3 buckets for cross-region replication of the function code, and Lambda functions to automate deployment, as shown in figure 15.4.

Let's look more closely at what a multiregion deployment might look like. We'll discuss a simple scenario using Lambda functions to expose via the Amazon API Gateway data stored on a DynamoDB table.

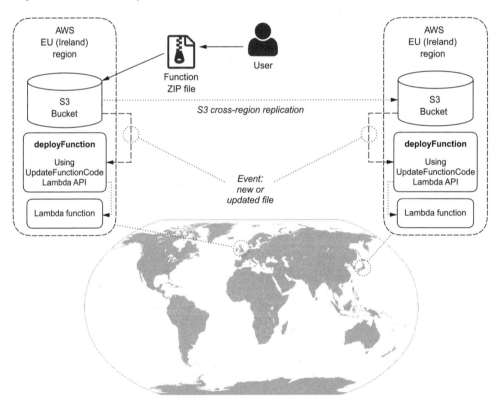

Figure 15.4 Using S3 cross-region replication and deploying Lambda functions in two different regions to automate cross-region deployments. The ZIP file with the function is uploaded in one region, S3 cross-region replication copies the file in the bucket in the other region, and each of the two buckets has a deploying Lambda function triggered by the new ZIP file. The deploying Lambda functions can create or update the Lambda function in their own region.

To work with multiple AWS regions, you can use the following configurations:

- Amazon Route 53, AWS global DNS, to route requests to two identical APIs, managed by the Amazon API Gateway in two different regions. Remember that all APIs are automatically distributed via Amazon CloudFront, AWS global CDN. Having two different APIs here means that the origins of the CloudFront distributions will be in different regions.
- Each API uses Lambda functions in its own region. Those Lambda functions could be automatically deployed as described in the previous chapter. You can have the Amazon API Gateway use Lambda functions in different regions, but the purpose of this example is to distribute the architecture across multiple regions.
- Each region has a DynamoDB table containing the data to be exposed. You can use DynamoDB streams to replicate (and keep in sync) the content of the table to another region.

TIP Currently, the suggested procedure to have cross-region replication for DynamoDB is using an open source CLI tool available from https://github.com/awslabs/dynamodb-cross-region-library. Some time ago, AWS provided a cross-region replication solution based on AWS CloudFormation. This solution has now been deprecated in favor of the open source CLI tool.

The multiregion deployment is described in figure 15.5.

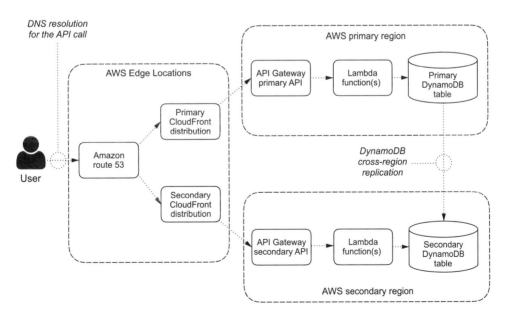

Figure 15.5 The flow of a multiregion deployment using the Amazon API Gateway, Lambda functions, and DynamoDB tables in two different AWS regions. NDS resolution via Amazon Route 53 is used to route traffic towards the primary, or secondary, region.

Let's dive deeper into the flow:

1 The client application of the user performs an HTTPS API call.
2 The client device OS resolves the DNS name used by the API endpoint.
3 The DNS resolution is managed by Amazon Route 53, and sends users to the primary or secondary CloudFront distributions managed by the Amazon API Gateway.
4 Both Amazon Route 53 and Amazon CloudFront are based in AWS Edge Locations, distributed globally, and are often closer (in terms of latency) to the users than the AWS regions.
5 Each CloudFront distribution forwards the API call to its own Amazon API Gateway, in the primary or the secondary AWS region.
6 The API Gateway integration invokes the Lambda functions in the same region.
7 The Lambda function accesses data in the DynamoDB table in the same region.
8 DynamoDB cross-region replication keeps the source table (in the primary region) and the destination table (in the secondary region) in sync.

TIP In case of failover, the primary and secondary region can be swapped. As usual in these fail-over situations, data consistency is critical. Depending on how your application accesses the data, you have to understand whether swapping the primary and secondary DynamoDB table is doable and how.

NOTE Depending on how frequently data is updated in the source DynamoDB table and how much delay in the synchronization is acceptable for your use case, you can use an *active/active* or *active/passive* balancing to the two CloudFront distributions. Normally, I opt for an active/passive solution because it's much easier to manage.

Summary

In this chapter, you saw different scenarios using AWS Lambda—not to implement the logic of your application, but to manage the infrastructure or deploy other Lambda functions. In particular, you learned about the following:

- Processing CloudWatch alarms via Lambda functions
- Triggering Lambda functions via SNS topics
- Synchronizing a configuration tool using CloudWatch events to trigger AWS Lambda
- Processing CloudWatch logs with AWS Lambda
- Scheduling recurring activities on your infrastructure
- Using Lambda functions to deploy other Lambda functions, with an example for a multiregion application

EXERCISE

1 CloudWatch alarms are sent as

   a SQS messages

   b SNS notifications

   c EC2 instances

   d CloudWatch events

2 You can react to the creation of a new EC2 instance or a new Elastic Load Balancer using

   a CloudFormation templates

   b CloudWatch logs

   c CloudWatch events

   d CloudFormation stacks

3 A service discovery tool is recommended in case you adopt

   a A client-server architecture

   b A three-tier architecture

   c A monolithic architecture

   d A microservice architecture

Solution

   1 b

   2 c

   3 d

Part 4

Using external services

This final part opens the doors of your application to eternal services such as Slack, IFTTT, and GitHub, giving you an idea of how to integrate external services with Lambda functions and event-driven applications, and securely manage their credentials using AWS KMS. Both directions will be considered: reaching out to external services or being called by them. A few architectural patterns, such as webhooks and log monitors, are discussed in depth.

Calling external services

In the previous chapter, you learned how to use Lambda functions to automate management activities on your infrastructure, react to alarms, and automatically deploy other functions.

Now you'll extend the reach of your possibilities with common patterns and practical examples of how you can securely call external services, such as IFTTT (If This Then That), Slack, or GitHub from a Lambda function.

16.1 Managing secrets and credentials

Storing secrets such as passwords or API keys inside your code is never a good approach, because during the lifecycle of the application you may accidentally give access to the code (and the secrets) to non-authorized people. With AWS Lambda you can easily use AWS Key Management Service (KMS), a service that makes it easy for you to create and control encryption keys and to encrypt your data. AWS KMS uses hardware security modules (HSMs) to protect the security of your keys.

TIP   HSMs are pieces of hardware that provide cryptographic functions, such as encryption, decryption, key generation, and physical tamper-resistance. For more information on HSMs, visit https://safenet.gemalto.com/data-encryption/hardware-security-modules-hsms/.

NOTE   With AWS KMS you pay 1$/month per key at the time I'm writing this book. The first 20,000 requests per month (including encryption and decryption requests) are in the free tier. To see updated pricing for this service, please check https://aws.amazon.com/kms/pricing/.

The idea is to wrap the whole logic of your Lambda functions in an internal function in your code. For example, you can call this internal function `processEvent` (figure 16.1). When the Lambda function is invoked, it checks whether the secrets have already been decrypted by a previous execution of the function. If yes, the `processEvent` function is called. If no, AWS KMS is (asynchronously) called to decrypt the secrets, and the `processEvent` is returned as a callback to be invoked as soon as the KMS decrypt call returns successfully.

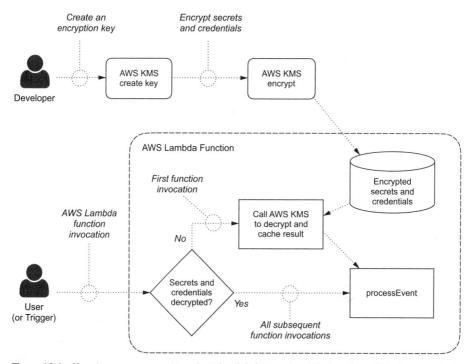

Figure 16.1   How to manage secrets and credentials in your Lambda functions. Data is encrypted using AWS KMS. The first invocation is decrypting the data and caching the result before processing the event. All subsequent invocations use the cached results and go straight to processing the event.

To encrypt your secrets, you can use the AWS CLI or any AWS SDK. First, you have to create an AWS KMS-managed key:

1 In the IAM console, choose Encryption Keys on the left and create a new key.
2 As key alias, use `functionConfig`.
3 Choose users and/or roles with admin privileges for the key.
4 Select users and/or roles that can use the key within applications.
5 Review the policy and then accept to create the key.

If you prefer, you can use the AWS CLI to create the key. Use the following key for more information:

```
aws kms create-key help
```

> **TIP** If you have multiple teams or different levels of security, you can create multiple keys and use IAM policies to give encryption or decryption access to only the keys they need to use.

Now you can encrypt using the new key you created. For example, using the AWS CLI, you can use this command:

```
aws kms encrypt --key-id alias/functionConfig --plaintext \
    '{"user":"me","password":"this"}'
```

The plaintext option is a string. In this case I used JSON syntax to send structured data to the Lambda function that will use this secret.

In output that you get from the encrypt command, you should look for the `CiphertextBlob`, which contains the encrypted result and the reference to the key that was used to encrypt (the order of the properties doesn't matter):

```
{
    "CiphertextBlob": "AbCdF…==",
    "KeyId": "<KEY_ARN>"
}
```

You can see an example Lambda function that uses AWS KMS to manage secrets in listing 16.1. The value of `<ENCRYPED_CONFIG>` in the listing should be replaced by the content of the `CiphertextBlob` in the previous output. The IAM role required by this function to give access to AWS KMS decrypt functionality is shown in listing 16.2.

> **TIP** You can quickly give the Lambda function access to AWS KMS from the console by creating a new role from a template and selecting the KMS policy from the list. You can optionally create a new role from the IAM console, as you learned in chapter 4.

Listing 16.1   Function `encryptedConfig` (Node.js)

Creating the AWS KMS
service object from the SDK

Keeps the
decrypted
configuration
parameters

The Base64 encoded, encrypted
configurations parameters, as in the
CiphertextBlob output of the KMS Encrypt
call. This example uses a JSON syntax to
pass multiple parameters at once.

If the
configuration
parameters
have not
been
decrypted
yet, prepare
the content
for KMS
Decrypt.

Prepare the
CiphertextBlob
property as a
Base64 buffer.

If the configuration
parameters have already been
decrypted, process the event.

In case of error,
log it and exit.

Extract the decrypted payload
from the KMS Decrypt call, parse
it as JSON, and process the event.

Call KMS
Decrypt
asynchronously.

Convert the
encrypted payload to
the Base64 format.

The actual function
processing the event

```javascript
var AWS = require('aws-sdk');

var kms = new AWS.KMS();

var fnEncryptedConfig = '<ENCRYPED_CONFIG>';
var fnConfig;

exports.handler = (event, context, callback) => {
    if (fnConfig) {
        processEvent(event, context, callback);
    } else {
        var encryptedBuf = new Buffer(fnEncryptedConfig, 'base64');
        var cipherText = { CiphertextBlob: encryptedBuf };

        kms.decrypt(cipherText, function (err, data) {
            if (err) {
                console.log("Decrypt error: " + err);
                callback(err);
            } else {
                fnConfig = JSON.parse(data.Plaintext.toString('ascii'));
                processEvent(event, context, callback);
            }
        });
    }
};

var processEvent = function (event, context, callback) {
    console.log('user: ' + functionConfig.user);
    console.log('password: ' + functionConfig.password);
    console.log('event: ' + event);
};
```

Listing 16.2   Policy_encryptedConfig

The Lambda function
needs access to the
KMS Decrypt action.

You must give access
to the KMS Key used
to encrypt.

```json
{
    "Version": "2012-10-17",
    "Statement": [
        {
            "Effect": "Allow",
            "Action": [
                "kms:Decrypt"
            ],
            "Resource": [
                "<your KMS key ARN>"
            ]
        }
    ]
}
```

NOTE This approach was inspired by a few blueprints that are available when creating a new Lambda function from the web console, and external services such as the Slack and Algorithmia. You can look at those in the Lambda console to see more examples.

Now that you have a safe way to store secrets and credentials with your Lambda functions, you can use that to call any public APIs that you can think of. You need to store the credentials safely using AWS KMS and use the public API SDKs in your functions. If the public APIs are easy to implement, you can build the Web requests of the public APIs in your code. I'll show you a few examples with popular services, such as IFTTT, Slack, and GitHub. You can easily add your own here; for example, using Twilio to send SMS to mobile devices.

TIP To rotate your credentials, you can update the Lambda functions to use the new credentials so that the cache will be emptied and the secrets will be decrypted again.

16.2 *Using IFTTT Maker Channel*

IFTTT gives you creative control over multiple products and apps. You can prepare recipes, which are simple connections between products and apps. IFTTT recipes run automatically in the background. You can create powerful connections with one simple statement: "If this (happens) then (do) that".

To extend IFTTT recipes beyond the supported products and services, you can use the Maker Channel, which allows you to connect IFTTT to your personal projects. With the Maker channel, you can connect a recipe to any device or service that can make or receive a web request.

A big advantage of using the IFTTT Maker Channel is that once you create your own integration, you have easy access to all those products and services that are natively supported by IFTTT. For example, using IFTTT as the broker, you can have a Lambda function that can turn the Philips Hue lights on or off, or change the color of the lights to red in case you receive a CloudWatch alarm. Or it can send a notification to a mobile device or to a Skype account, post something on Twitter, or publish a picture on a Facebook or Instagram account. For an overview of the IFTTT available channels, see https://ifttt.com/channels.

After you sign up for IFTTT at https://ifttt.com, you can configure your Maker Channel at https://ifttt.com/maker. There you can write down your secret key. You can now trigger an IFTTT recipe using an `HTTPS GET` or `POST` request similar to the following example:

```
https://maker.ifttt.com/trigger/<EVENT>/with/key/<IFTTT_MAKER_SECRET_KEY>
```

Using an `HTTPS POST`, you can add a body to your HTTPS request and pass a JSON object with values that can be used by the recipe. For example

```
{ "value1" : "One", "value2" : "Two", "value3" : "Three" }
```

Using the same syntax with an HTTPS GET, the JSON object can be included as a query parameter. Let's build a recipe that will send a message from AWS Lambda to your Twitter account (see listing 16.3). Start configuring the IFTTT Twitter Channel to use your Twitter account at https://ifttt.com/twitter.

Now create a new IFTTT recipe that is triggered by the Maker Channel (this) and acts on the Twitter Channel (that):

1 In the Maker Channel (this), choose to receive a web request and give a meaningful event name; for example, "aws_lambda".

2 In the Twitter Channel (that), choose "Send a direct message to yourself" (so that you don't spam your followers with these tests). You can repeat the same configuration posting a "real" tweet in your timeline afterward.

3 Click inside the textbox containing the proposed message to publish, and then click the test tube icon on the top right of the box. Note: the icon doesn't show up until you click inside the box.

4 You can now add another ingredient and you can use "Value1" that will be sent by the Lambda function.

5 Remove everything else and leave only {{Value1}} in the box. In this way, the message that will be sent is only what the Lambda function passes in the value1 parameter.

6 Create a Lambda2IFTTT function using listing 16.3. Replace the <EVENT> with what you used in the Maker Channel; for example "aws_lambda" and <IFTTT_MAKER_SECRET_KEY> with the secret key you wrote down previously. A basic execution role is enough because you only need to do the HTTPS POST to IFTTT.

7 The Lambda function will look for a message property in the event and send that as "value1" to IFTTT, so that the recipe can use it to send the message.

Listing 16.3   `Lambda2IFTTT` (Node.js)

```
console.log('Loading function');

var https = require('https');
var querystring = require("querystring");

var iftttMakerEventName = '<EVENT>'            ◁   The EventName used
var iftttMakerSecretKey = '<IFTTT_MAKER_SECRET_KEY>';   ◁   in configuring the
                                                            IFTTT recipe
var iftttMakerUrl =                            ◁   Your IFTTT Maker
    'https://maker.ifttt.com/trigger/'             Channel Secret Key
    + iftttMakerEventName
    + '/with/key/'                     The full URL to use to call
    + iftttMakerSecretKey;        ◁   the IFTTT Maker Channel

exports.handler = (event, context, callback) => {
    var output;                          ◁   The output message to send;
    if ('message' in event) {                contains the "message"
        output = event.message;      ◁   property of the event
    } else {
```

```
        callback('Error: no message in the event');
    }
    console.log('Output: ', output);
```
The output message is sent as "Value1" to the IFTTT recipe.

```
    var params = querystring.stringify({value1: output});
```

```
    https.get(encodeURI(iftttMakerUrl) + '?' + params, function(res) {
        console.log('Got response: ' + res.statusCode);
        res.setEncoding('utf8');
        res.on('data', function(d) {
            console.log('Body: ' + d);
        });
```
Making the HTTPS GET to the IFTTT Maker Channel URL

```
        callback(null, res.statusCode);
    }).on('error', function(e) {
        console.log("Got error: " + e.message);
        callback(e.message);
    });
};
```
Sending the HTTP response status code back from the function

In case of error, sending it back from the function

You can now test your function by running a test in the Lambda console. Try to send a message using this sample event:

```
{
  "message": "Hello from AWS Lambda!"
}
```

If you're looking for more examples of using IFTTT to integrate AWS services, you can check these two open source projects I shared on GitHub:

- This example sends EC2 Auto Scaling activities to IFTTT; for example, if a new instance is added or removed in the Auto Scaling Group. This project is available at https://github.com/danilop/AutoScaling2IFTTT.
- This is a more generic function to push any Amazon SNS message to IFTTT. This project is available at https://github.com/danilop/SNS2IFTTT.

16.3 Sending messages to a Slack team

Slack is a powerful communication tool for teams. It allows you to create channels where team members can share information on a specific topic. Slack has also opened its platform via APIs that allow you to send and receive messages from an external platform. It's possible to use both the sending and receiving features together to build an automated bot that can manage the integration of a Slack channel with external tools using a simple chat interface.

In this example, we'll use the Slack API to send a message to a Slack team from a Lambda function. In the next chapter, you'll see also how to receive events from Slack. In both cases, you need to configure a *webhook* in your Slack account.

> **DEFINITION** A *webhook* is substantially an HTTP callback: you can use it to notify or be notified that something happened; for example, that new information is available, or that action must be taken.

To try this example, you need a Slack account. Follow these steps to prepare and test your Slack team:

1   Create a new Slack team at https://slack.com.
2   In the main menu (named as the slack team), select apps & integrations.
3   Search for "incoming webhooks" and add a configuration.
4   Choose one of the team channels; for example, #random. If you prefer, you can create a new custom channel.
5   Use any Slack client (on the web, a smartphone, or a tablet) to log in in your team and open the channel you set up at step 2.
6   Write down the full webhook. It will be a URL with a format similar to https://hooks.slack.com/services/<HOOK>.
7   Test that the previous configuration on the webhook is working with the `curl` tool we already used in chapter 3. Be sure to replace your own webhook in the following command:

```
curl --data '{"text":"Hello!"}' https://hooks.slack.com/services/<HOOK>
```

The previous `curl` command is doing an `HTTP POST` to the webhook you configured, passing the JSON payload with some "text" as the body of the message. If the test was successful, anything you put as the value of the "text" property of the JSON payload displays on Slack in the channel you configured for the incoming webhook; for example, #random.

As you can imagine, it's easy to use a Lambda function to do the `HTTP POST` and send text to a Slack channel. A sample implementation is shown in listing 16.4.

WARNING   Note that the webhook path in listing 16.4 must start with a slash character—for example, "/path"—otherwise you get an error because the URL isn't well formed.

TIP   For better security, you can encrypt the webhook using AWS KMS as described at the beginning of this chapter. I don't encrypt the webhook in this code example.

> **Listing 16.4   Function `Lambda2Slack` (Node.js)**

```
const https = require('https');

var webhook_host = '<YOUR_WEBHOOK_HOST>';
var webhook_path = '<YOUR_WEBHOOK_PATH_STARTING_WITH_A_SLASH>';

exports.handler = (event, context, callback) => {
    var post_data;
    if ('text' in event) {
        post_data = '{"text":"' + event['text'] + '"}';
    } else {
        post_data = '{"text":"Hello from AWS Lambda!"}';
    }
```

Look for a "text" property in the event or send a default message.

To simplify the configuration of the HTTPS POST, split the Slack webhook (in the format https://HOST/PATH) between the host and the path. The PATH must start with a slash.

```
var post_options = {                        Preparing the
    hostname: webhook_host,                 options for the
    port: 443,                              HTTPS POST
    path: webhook_path,
    method: 'POST',
    headers: {
        'Content-Type': 'application/json',
        'Content-Length': Buffer.byteLength(post_data)
    }
};

var post_req = https.request(post_options, function(res) {    Preparing
    res.setEncoding('utf8');                                  the HTTPS
    res.on('data', function(chunk) {                          request
        console.log('Response: ' + chunk);
    });
});                                          Posting
                                            the data
post_req.write(post_data);
post_req.end();                             Terminating the
};                                          HTTP request
```

TIP   Among the blueprints that are provided by the AWS Lambda console when creating a new function, you'll find an example of how to send Cloud-Watch alarms to Slack. This can be an interesting approach to keep all your team updated on what's happening in your AWS application and the underlying infrastructure.

16.4   *Automating the management of your GitHub repository*

If the source code of your application is hosted on GitHub, you may want to automate several recurring activities. For example, you can create an automatic response for anybody creating a new issue, with a link to a knowledge base on how you manage issues and what they should expect.

GitHub has an extended API that you can use to do that. To call the GitHub API, you need a token to authenticate yourself. You can create a token for your account by following these steps:

1 Create a new GitHub account (or use your existing account).
2 In the top right, select your small profile picture to open a drop-down menu, and then select settings.
3 Click "Personal access tokens" in the sidebar, as part of the "Developer settings."
4 Click "Generate a personal access token."
5 Add a token description, leaving everything else as is, then click "Generate token."
6 Write down the token for later use.

You can now include the GitHub SDKs in your Lambda function and use the token to authenticate your calls. For additional security, you can protect the token using AWS KMS as described at the beginning of this chapter. For an overview of the

available GitHub SDKs and the supported platforms, see https://developer.github
.com/libraries/.

As an example, the function in listing 16.5 is posting a comment to an issue on
GitHub, based on the parameters passed in the event. To use this example, you need
to install locally the "github" SDK and zip the function with the dependencies before
uploading it to AWS Lambda. To install the "github" module, you can use

```
npm install github
```

Listing 16.5   Lambda2GitHub (Node.js)

```
var GitHubApi = require('github');
var github = new GitHubApi({           ◁── Using the GitHub
    version: '3.0.0'                        Node.js SDK
});

exports.handler = (event, context, callback) => {

    if (!('user' in event) || !('repo' in event) ||        ◁── Validating the
        !('issue' in event) || !('comment' in evet)) {         syntax of the event
        callback('Error: ' +
            'the event must contain user, repo, issue and comment')
    } else {

        var githubUser = event.user;        ◁── Extracting the
        var githubRepo = event.repo;            information
        var githubIssue = event.issue;          from the event
        var comment = event.comment;

        github.authenticate({               ◁── Authenticating
            type: 'oauth',                      with GitHub
            token: '<GITHUB_TOKEN>'         ◁── Remember to use
        });                                     your token here.

        github.issues.createComment({       ◁── Creating a comment
            user: githubUser,                   to a GitHub issue
            repo: githubRepo,
            number: githubIssue,
            body: comment
        }, callback(null, 'Comment posted'));

    }
};
```

TIP   For an extended example of how to create a GitHub bot using AWS
Lambda, I recommend that you look at the blog post at https://aws.amazon
.com/blogs/compute/dynamic-github-actions-with-aws-lambda/.

Summary

In this chapter, you learned how to encrypt credentials for external services and call external APIs from a Lambda function. In particular, you learned about the following:

- Encrypting secret data or credentials required by Lambda functions using AWS KMS
- Decrypting data dynamically and caching the result within a Lambda function
- Using IFTTT as a bridge for a Lambda function to use other services available as IFTTT channels
- Sending messages to a Slack channel from a Lambda function; for example, to notify your team that a CloudWatch alarm has changed status
- Using Lambda functions to manage a GitHub repository; for example, to automatically create an issue

EXERCISE

Modify listing 16.3 to use AWS KMS to store encrypted credentials (your Slack webhook in this case), applying the generic pattern shown in listing 16.1.

Solution

A possible solution is shown in the following listing.

Function `Lambda2SlackKMS` (Node.js)

```
var AWS = require('aws-sdk');

var kms = new AWS.KMS();

const https = require('https');

// Enter the base-64 encoded, encrypted configuration here (CiphertextBlob)
// { "webhook_host": "", "webhook_path": "" }
var functionEncryptedConfig = '<ENCRYPED_CONFIG>';        ◁── The webhook host and
var functionConfig;                                           path are now encrypted
                                                              as a JSON object.
exports.handler = function (event, context) {
    if (functionConfig) {
        // Container reuse, simply process the event with the key in memory
        processEvent(event, context);
    } else {
        var encryptedBuf = new Buffer(functionEncryptedConfig, 'base64');
        var cipherText = { CiphertextBlob: encryptedBuf };

        kms.decrypt(cipherText, function (err, data) {
            if (err) {
                console.log("Decrypt error: " + err);
                context.fail(err);
            } else {
                functionConfig =
                    JSON.parse(data.Plaintext.toString('ascii'));
                processEvent(event, context);
```

After decryption, the JSON payload is parsed.

```
            }
        });
    }
};

var processEvent = function (event, context) {
    var post_data;
    if ('text' in event) {
        post_data = '{"text":"' + event['text'] + '"}';
    } else {
        post_data = '{"text":"Hello from AWS Lambda!"}';
    }

    var post_options = {
        hostname: functionConfig.webhook_host,
        port: 443,
        path: functionConfig.webhook_path,
        method: 'POST',
        headers: {
            'Content-Type': 'application/json',
            'Content-Length': Buffer.byteLength(post_data)
        }
    };

    var post_req = https.request(post_options, function(res) {
        res.setEncoding('utf8');
        res.on('data', function(chunk) {
            console.log('Response: ' + chunk);
        });
    });

    post_req.write(post_data);
    post_req.end();
};
```

The properties containing the webhook host and path are used in building the HTTPS request.

Receiving events from other services

In the previous chapter, you learned how to call external services in Lambda functions, encrypting credentials before including them in your code or in your configuration repositories.

Now you'll see the other side of that: how to have Lambda functions triggered by external services. I'll share specific examples and best practices, and the architectural patterns that are introduced here can be used with many more services than those included in this chapter.

17.1   *Who's calling?*

You can use other AWS services, such as the Amazon API Gateway and Amazon SNS, to receive events from sources outside of AWS. In that case, you can't trust anyone and you should have a process in place to verify that the source of the event is who you expect. Usually, you can verify that by adding a shared secret (between you and the source) to all events, or even better, by adding a digital signature to the request, similar to how the AWS API works.

When you use a shared secret, you have to agree with the sender on a random string—difficult to find if unknown—and always send this shared secret over an encrypted channel, such as HTTPS. If you want to implement a digital signature, I suggest you rely on frameworks that have already been tested, such as the AWS API.

To share a secret safely with a third party, you can use AWS KMS similarly to the way you used it in the previous chapter. In this case, the third party acts as the Lambda function and needs to have permissions (for example, through an IAM user or a cross-account IAM role that they can assume within their AWS account) to use your KMS key to decrypt. A summary of these two options is shown in figure 17.1.

TIP   Cross-account roles are a powerful tool that enable the delegation of AWS activities to another AWS account and can be used in multiple use cases.

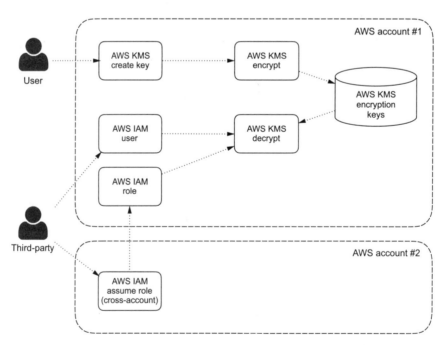

Figure 17.1   You can share an encryption key managed by AWS KMS by giving access to the decrypt action to an IAM user in your AWS account (and then give the credentials for the user to the third party) or by creating a cross-account role (that third-party users can assume in their AWS accounts).

For example, to share data with another AWS account, you can let the other account read a shared "folder" (a prefix) in one of your S3 buckets. For more information on assuming cross-account roles, see https://docs.aws.amazon .com/IAM/latest/UserGuide/tutorial_cross-account-with-roles.html.

17.2 The webhook pattern

When you started using AWS Lambda with external services in the previous chapter, you probably noticed that a common pattern used by several of those services (such as Slack and IFTTT) to receive notifications is to publish a URL where they could listen and be triggered. For clarity, I repeat here the definition of a webhook:

> **DEFINITION** A *webhook* is substantially an HTTP callback: you can use it to notify or be notified that something happened; for example, that new information is available or that some action must be taken.

At the beginning, webhooks were mainly based on POST actions, but GET is used more and more for its simplicity and the possibility of adding information using query parameters.

In the previous chapter, you used webhooks to send information to external services. In this chapter you use them in the opposite direction: to receive events from external sources.

> **TIP** Webhooks are a cool concept and had an active role in the evolution of the web toward the interactive platform that we know. Using webhooks made it easy for developers to integrate multiple web applications together, using HTTP as a common language. You can get an idea of how intriguing and revolutionary they were a few years ago by looking at these two blog posts from 2007 and 2009: http://progrium.com/blog/2007/05/03/web-hooks-to-revolutionize-the-web/ and http://timothyfitz.com/2009/02/09/what-web-hooks-are-and-why-you-should-care/.

Implementing a serverless webhook is simple using the Amazon API Gateway to receive the HTTP GET or POST and AWS Lambda to run the custom logic associated with the event (figure 17.2).

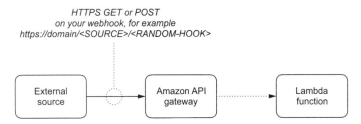

Figure 17.2 A webhook can be easily built using the Amazon API Gateway to trigger a Lambda function. To protect your webhook from unauthorized users, you can use a random URL, configuring a hard-to-find resource in the API.

You probably don't want anybody except an authorized user to use a webhook you create. You can share a secret as a parameter or a header in the HTTP request, but you must authenticate the request in the Amazon API Gateway; for example, using a custom authorizer or in the Lambda function. In both cases you can return an error if the input event doesn't contain authentication, but the request would still reach your serverless architecture.

An additional level of security—based on the fact that the actual path of the URL will be transmitted encrypted by the HTTPS protocol—is to use a difficult-to-find resource in the API implementing the webhook, something that you can create randomly and then share with the other party. This way all calls to different resources of your API will miss an integration and return immediately with an error.

If you want to manage multiple sources in your API, you can build webhooks using the following format

```
https://domain/<SOURCE>/<RANDOM-HOOK>
```

where <SOURCE> can be replaced with the name of the source, and <RANDOM-HOOK> is a random path that only you and the source know. Let's now look at a couple of examples using webhooks to receive events in a Lambda function with services such as Slack and Twilio.

17.3   Handling events from Slack

One of the interesting features of Slack is the possibility to add slash commands, commands starting with the "/" character, to your teams. Slash commands can then use custom apps and even—you probably already thought of that—call a webhook.

To set up your Slack account, follow these steps:

1   Use the Slack web interface to your team (a team you administer); for example, https://<YOUR-TEAM>.slack.com.
2   From the main drop-down menu of the team, at the top left of the window, select Apps & integrations.
3   Search for "slash commands" and select the result.
4   Add a configuration, and choose a command; for example, "/lambda".
5   Now add the command integration.

The Slack console is well documented and you should now see many options. Let's focus on the most important ones for your integration. You still have to create your webhook, and you don't know the final URL. You need to come back to this configuration page to update the URL after you deploy the API with the Amazon API Gateway. But you can already choose whether you want Slack to use a POST or a GET. Leave POST for now; you can experiment with GET later. And most importantly, write down the token that acts as a shared secret to authenticate Slack on your side. You'll check the value of the token in the Lambda function to authenticate your requests.

Because you'll use AWS KMS to decrypt the token in your Lambda function, it's time to encrypt it as you did at the beginning of the previous chapter:

1 Create a new KMS key, if you haven't already. From the AWS IAM console, choose Encryption Keys and use `functionConfig` as the key alias.

2 Use the AWS CLI to encrypt the Slack `token` using the KMS key (be sure to replace `<TOKEN>` with yours):

```
aws kms encrypt --key-id alias/functionConfig --plaintext '<TOKEN>'
```

3 Write down the result in the `CiphertextBlob` property. You need to put that value in the Lambda function that you'll create shortly.

You can now create the Lambda function to receive the event from Slack: it will be easy, because you can start from one of the blueprints in the console. Create a new Lambda function, and search for "Slack" when asked to select a blueprint. Look for the "slack-echo-command" blueprints. You can choose between two implementations, in Node.js or Python.

The console automatically preconfigures the integration with the Amazon API Gateway for you, but you need to change the Security to be "Open." Give a name to the function (for example, "Slack2Lambda") and to the Role (for example, "Slack2Lambda-role"). The role is already configured to give access to AWS KMS.

In the code, look for the parameter where the encrypted `token` that you got from Slack and encrypted using AWS KMS must be replaced. All other defaults are okay.

Deploy the changes, creating a "prod" stage, and go back to the Slack slash command configuration to update the URL with the full path of the resource you configured with the Amazon API Gateway. The easiest way to find the full path is in the Trigger tab for the function, in the Lambda console.

Try the new slash command in your Slack team. The blueprints you used send back ("echo") the information on the slash command, but they can easily be extended to add your custom logic or call other APIs. For example, you can create a slash command such as "/lambda list" to list all the Lambda functions in that region.

NOTE If something doesn't work as expected, look at the Lambda function logs and test the integration in the Amazon API Gateway console. Blueprints are updated frequently, so look for additional information in the code of the functions; for example, in comments.

TIP For an extended example of how to use Slack with AWS Lambda, you can see the GitHub repository of the Zombie Apocalypse Workshop, a lab to set up a serverless chat application at https://github.com/awslabs/aws-lambda-zombie-workshop.

17.4   *Handling events from GitHub*

GitHub is natively integrated with certain AWS services. In particular, Amazon SNS is supported by GitHub and is probably the easiest way to receive SNS notifications that can then trigger Lambda functions. In this case, you have to create an SNS topic and an AWS IAM user with the necessary permissions to publish on the SNS topic. The AWS Access Key ID and AWS Secret Access Key are stored by GitHub to authenticate the sending of notifications.

> **TIP** You can periodically rotate those AWS credentials, creating a new one and updating the configuration on GitHub. AWS users can have two credentials active at the same time to simplify their rotation.

Another approach, not using the native AWS integration that GitHub provides, is to set up a webhook in the settings of a GitHub repository, similar to what you did for Slack.

You can then set up the Amazon API Gateway to receive the event and pass it to a Lambda function. To protect access to the Lambda function, you can add a random string to the payload URL used by GitHub. That random string will be the resource you configure in the API and acts as a shared secret, because it's always transmitted encrypted (over HTTPS) between GitHub and the Amazon API Gateway.

> **TIP** For additional security, you can periodically rotate the shared secret part of the URL by creating a new random method in the API, calling the same Lambda function, and updating the GitHub console. You can then remove the old resource in the API when you're sure it won't be called anymore.

Now you have a way to receive events from GitHub. In the previous chapter, you learned how to change things on GitHub, having access to the GitHub API from within your Lambda functions. Using these two capabilities together, you can implement an automated bot that can react to activities in the repository (for example, a new issue has been created) and automate the management of that event (for example, looking in a knowledge base if part of the information can be automatically returned as a comment to the issue).

17.5   *Handling events from Twilio*

Twilio is a service that exposes a globally available cloud API that developers can interact with to build intelligent and complex communications systems. You can get a developer key for free and start experimenting with their APIs.

The way Twilio sends data is similar to how Slack and GitHub work, using a webhook that you can implement with the Amazon API Gateway calling a Lambda function. Similar to Slack, when you create the Lambda function, you can use a blueprint: search for Twilio and select "twilio-simple-blueprint" (Node.js).

> **TIP** If something doesn't work as expected, look at the Lambda function logs and test the integration in the Amazon API Gateway console. Blueprints are updated frequently, so look for additional information in the code of the functions; for example, in comments.

Zombie Apocalypse Workshop

For an extended example of how to use Twilio with AWS Lambda, you can see this GitHub repository, where the code and a detailed walkthrough have been shared by AWS:

https://github.com/awslabs/asw-lamba-zombie-workshop

The purpose of the workshop is to set up a serverless chat application, and integrate with multiple communication channels to save the world from a fictitious "Zombie Apocalypse."

17.6 Using MongoDB as a trigger

In this section, I want to give you an example of how to integrate a third-party product to trigger a Lambda function. We used Amazon DynamoDB as the source of events in a few examples in the book, but what if you want to use a different database, such as MongoDB?

The idea is to find a place where the third-party product stores information on what it's doing, often in a log file. MongoDB databases, when configured in a *replica set*, write a log of their operations in the *oplog* (operations log), a special *capped collection* that keeps a rolling record of all operations that modify the data stored in the database.

Capped collections in MongoDB have a fixed size and support high throughput operations. They're similar to circular buffers: once a collection fills its allocated space, it makes room for new documents by overwriting the oldest documents in the collection.

You can browse a capped collection using a *tailable cursor*, which remains open after the client exhausts the results in the initial cursor (similar to the "tail -f" Unix command). After clients insert new additional documents into a capped collection, the tailable cursor continues to retrieve documents.

Using the tools provided by MongoDB, it's possible to build an oplog Monitor that can continuously look at the oplog and trigger the invocation of a Lambda function when a specific pattern is found. An example of this flow is depicted in figure 17.3.

Building the actual oplog Monitor is outside the scope of this chapter because you need to go deeper into MongoDB skills that aren't a requirement for this book. But the idea of why to build it and how it works should be clear. For an example of how to use MongoDB drivers to build the oplog Monitor in different programming languages, such as Python or Node.js, see https://docs.mongodb.com/ecosystem/drivers/.

> **TIP** This section is based on MongoDB, but most databases have replication capabilities, and that's the part where you should look to find how to monitor changes and trigger events.

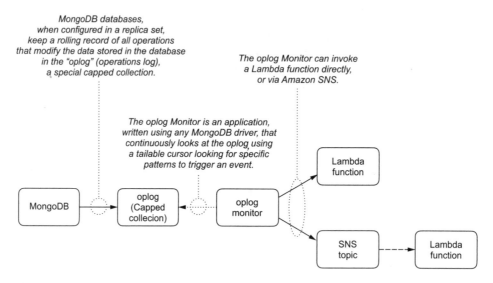

Figure 17.3   Monitoring the MongoDB oplog to look for a specific pattern and trigger a Lambda function

17.7   *The log monitoring pattern*

A more generic approach to integrating third-party products as triggers for AWS Lambda is to check if the information you're looking for to trigger a function is available in a log file written by the third-party product (figure 17.4).

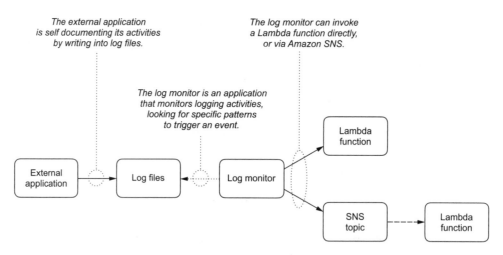

Figure 17.4   Monitoring logs is a common approach to trigger Lambda functions from events happening in an external product. You can invoke Lambda functions directly or by using Amazon SNS.

WARNING Logs can use a lot of disk space (especially if you increased the log level of the app). Implement automatic rotation for log files so that the old ones are automatically deleted or archived after a time. To avoid an impact on storage performance, you can move the logs used by this monitor to a small RAM disk capable of holding the logs for only a few minutes. You can safely store the old logs in a more permanent storage afterward or in parallel (if configurable by the app).

Even if you can trigger a Lambda function directly from a log monitor, my suggestion is to send SNS notifications and then use those notifications to trigger Lambda functions. In this way, you decouple the invocation and can use SNS logging to monitor the communication between the log monitor and AWS Lambda.

With Amazon SNS, the Lambda function receives the message payload as an input parameter and can manipulate the information in the message, publish the message to other SNS topics, or send the message to other AWS services. In addition, Amazon SNS also supports message delivery status attributes for message notifications sent to Lambda endpoints. Decoupling the Lambda invocation from the monitor, you can configure the specific version or alias of the Lambda function to be invoked in the SNS trigger, instead of the configuration of the log monitor.

WARNING You have to manage the reliability of the log monitor in terms of availability (not missing possible triggers) and performance (catching up with the speed at which the logs are written).

Summary

In this chapter you saw how to have triggers external to AWS calling your Lambda functions. In particular, you learned about the following:

- Building webhooks with the Amazon API Gateway and AWS Lambda to receive events from external sources
- Receiving events from an external application, monitoring its logs to trigger Lambda functions using Amazon SNS
- Being triggered by other platforms such as Slack, GitHub, and Twilio, an example of the power of webhooks
- Designing a specific log monitor for an external database, such as MongoDB, to trigger Lambda functions

EXERCISE

1 To authenticate calls to your webhook you can use

   a An IAM role with a custom policy

   b An IAM user with a custom policy

    c A shared secret that must be sent only over encrypted channels, such as HTTPS

    d A shared secret that you can send by email, using Amazon SES

2 What are the best ways a log monitor can use to invoke a Lambda function?

    a Using Amazon SNS as a trigger

    b Using AWS IAM roles

    c Using AWS CloudTrail

    d Using the AWS Lambda Invoke API

Solution

1 c

2 a and d

index

MORE TITLES FROM MANNING

Amazon Web Services in Action
by Michael Wittig and Andreas Wittig

ISBN: 9781617292880
424 pages
$49.99
September 2015

Secrets of the JavaScript Ninja,
Second Edition
by John Resig, Bear Bibeault, and Josip Maras

ISBN: 9781617292859
464 pages
$44.99
August 2009

Serverless Architectures on AWS
With examples using AWS Lambda
by Peter Sbarski with Sam Kroonenburg

ISBN: 9781617293825
425 pages
$44.99
April 2017

For ordering information go to www.manning.com

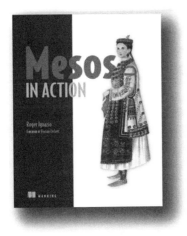

Mesos in Action
by Roger Ignazio

ISBN: 9781617292927
272 pages
$44.99
May 20116

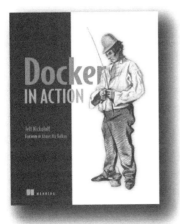

Docker in Action
by Jeff Nickoloff

ISBN: 9781633430235
304 pages
$49.99
March 2016

Docker in Practice
by Ian Miell and Aidan Hobson Sayers

ISBN: 9781617292729
372 pages
$44.99
April 2016

MORE TITLES FROM MANNING

Java 8 in Action
Lambdas, streams, and functional-style programming
by Raoul-Gabriel Urma, Mario Fusco,
    and Alan Mycroft

ISBN: 9781617291999
424 pages
$49.99
August 2014

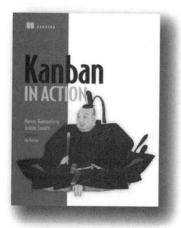

Kanban in Action
by Marcus Hammarberg and Joakim Sundén

ISBN: 9781617291050
360 pages
$44.99
February 2014

Elastic Leadership
Growing self-organizing teams
by Roy Osherove

ISBN: 9781617293085
240 pages
$39.99
October 2016

For ordering information go to www.manning.com